IMAGES
of America

BREWTON AND EAST BREWTON

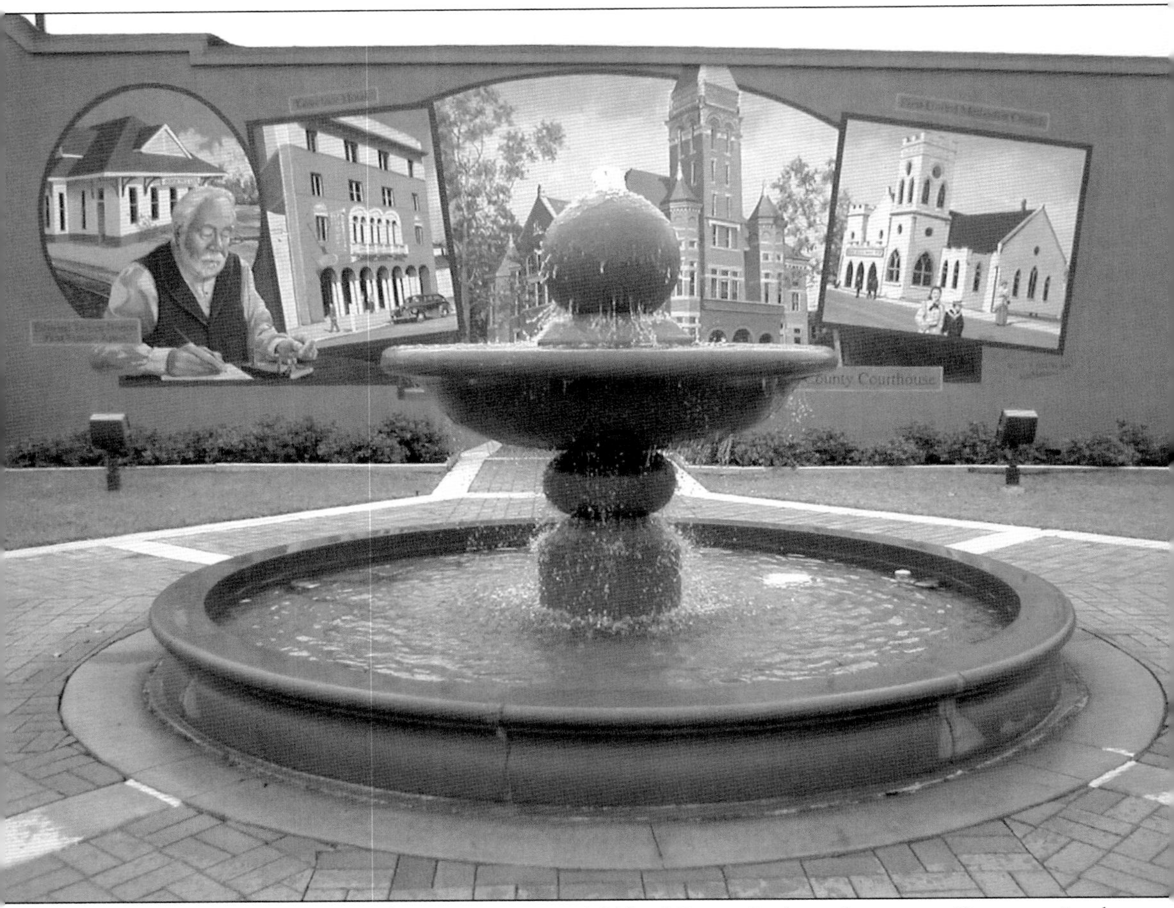

This modern fountain is the centerpiece in Mildred Street Park in downtown Brewton. In the background is a mural painted by Wes Hardin to commemorate the different things that make Brewton and East Brewton the historical towns they are today. It represents, from left to right, the origin of the naming of Brewton, with businesses such as the Lovelace Hotel; government, with the 1902–1960 courthouse; and religion, represented by an area church, the First United Methodist Church. (Courtesy of author.)

On the Cover: The citizens of Brewton decided they needed a fire department after a series of fires had destroyed much of the downtown area. This is what that fire department looked like in 1900. Members are, from left to right, (on wagon) driver John Bell, Howard Rankin, Marion Bell, and Stacy Douglas; (standing) John Purifoy, Walter Smith, Henry Rabb, Dave Bell, Earnest Davis, Aubrey Strong, Tom Jernigan, and Oscar Wigley. (Courtesy of Lawrence Weaver.)

IMAGES
of America

BREWTON AND EAST BREWTON

Lydia Grimes

ARCADIA
PUBLISHING

ISBN 978-0-7385-8751-6

Published by Arcadia Publishing
Charleston, South Carolina

Printed in the United States of America

Library of Congress Control Number: 2010942463

For all general information, please contact Arcadia Publishing:
Telephone 843-853-2070
Fax 843-853-0044
E-mail sales@arcadiapublishing.com
For customer service and orders:
Toll-Free 1-888-313-2665

Visit us on the Internet at www.arcadiapublishing.com

To those residents of Brewton and East Brewton who have kept the rich history of the area, both in words and in photographs.

Contents

ACKNOWLEDGMENTS

People in Brewton and East Brewton were kind enough to share their photographs with me for this project. It is impossible to name them all. My regular job with the local newspaper, the *Brewton Standard*, has given me the opportunity to talk to many different people. Most of them have been kind enough to share what they have, and for that, I am so grateful.

I want to thank a few individuals that have shared the most. First of all, thanks to the McMillan family for allowing me to go through their collection of historical articles and photographs. Through the efforts of Ed Leigh and Iva Lee Miller McMillan and their descendants, many photographs have been saved and cataloged. The collection covers more than 100 years.

The Escambia County Historical Society members have worked really hard to collect and catalog as many photographs as they can. This collection is housed in the Thomas E. McMillan Museum, located in the Fine Arts Center of Jefferson Davis Community College.

Then there are the individuals who have shared their memories, such as Yank Lovelace, who has a very fine collection of photographs and period postcards. Robert Crenshaw, who rummaged through his family photographs to uncover some wonderful personal and public jewels, is another who was kind enough to share. The late James Wilson from East Brewton shared his collection with me, as did Charles Blair, Barbara Carden, and Scott Hillman, to name just a few.

I also wish to thank my editor at Arcadia Publishing, Brinkley Taliaferro. She listened to my complaints, pushed me when I slowed down, and gave me encouragement when I was feeling that this book would never come to life.

For all of these people and those I may have overlooked, please accept my thanks and my apologies.

Unless otherwise noted, the photographs in this publication are from my own collection.

INTRODUCTION

Most people are proud of their hometowns and can tell many stories about them. The area that comprises Brewton and East Brewton has a long and colorful history. Long before East Brewton was incorporated, a fort was built on the bluff overlooking Murder Creek, which flows between the two towns today. Around 1816, Fort Crawford was built as one of many forts associated with Gen. Andrew Jackson. It was a short-lived fort and was deserted by the mid-1820s. The only thing left in the area of the fort is Fort Crawford Cemetery and the modern First Baptist Church of East Brewton. That same area was the site of a girls' school from the early 1900s until the mid-1940s. East Brewton was incorporated in 1918, but there were settlers there many years before. Some of the noted early settlers were the Harolds, the Arrends, and others who immigrated to the area from Germany. They brought their language and religions with them and settled in their own community.

As the late 1850s approached, the industry that would be the driving force from then until now had begun—lumber and timber. There is nothing more plentiful in this area than trees. With the trees coming down, a better way for shipping was needed. Early on, the trees were floated down the rivers to the Gulf Coast, but what the industry really needed were trains to carry the goods to the market. Thus was the beginning of Brewton. A small town a few miles south of Brewton called Pollard was where train tracks met and stretched out in several directions. One track came through what became the town of Brewton. By the time of the Civil War, the railroad was one of the mainstays of the area.

With the coming of the war, Brewton sent its young—and sometimes old—men off to fight. Brewton is about 50 miles north of Pensacola, Florida, and after the Union took over the Gulf city, the only thing standing between it and south Alabama was a Confederate camp established at Pollard. The camp's main purpose was to patrol and watch out for anyone coming out of Pensacola and guard the coast of Alabama. Pollard suffered greatly in the war, and the Union army swept over it. Brewton, so far as is known, avoided any fighting within its immediate area.

Reconstruction was not easy on this area, but a new kind of industry had taken hold, and after the war, there were several men who took the chance to go into the lumber business. By the late 1800s, there were several lumber mills in the immediate area. These included the Cedar Creek Lumber Mill, the Lovelace Lumber Mill, and the one that still remains a large part of the community, the T.R. Miller Mill Company. Many men became rich in the business, and they were often called "lumber barons." On a drive up Belleville Avenue, one can see the results of the money that was being made. The avenue is lined by some of the most beautiful mansions to be seen in the South. People hired famous architects to design their homes, had them built on prime property, and furnished them with the best to be bought.

There are many colorful stories told about the early years in Brewton. The county seat was first located in Pollard, but when Brewton began to expand and grow, its citizens decided the courthouse should be relocated. This did not sit too well with the people who lived in Pollard.

There was so much going on between the two towns that a local newspaper compared it to a cat fight. It is said by some that the citizens of Pollard loaded a train car with stray cats, brought them to Brewton, and turned them loose. Brewton citizens decided to take matters into their own hands and made a night run to Pollard to steal the county books.

When all was said and done, Brewton won the vote to be the county seat. A new courthouse was built on Belleville Avenue in 1886 and was used for county business for the next 14 years. In 1900, the building was condemned, and a new courthouse went up across the street. The old courthouse was not so bad after all, and instead of being torn down, 100 years later, it is still standing. It is called Leigh Place and houses offices of the McMillan family.

The story of Brewton could not be told without the mention of the yellow fever epidemic of 1883. No one knows for sure how the disease got to Brewton in the late summer of 1883, but by the time cooler weather came in the fall, many had come down with the fever, and 23 people had died.

The death of Sheriff Sylvester Edward McMillan in 1895 was not a tale but a true story. A railroad bandit called "Railroad Bill" had been tormenting the local residents for several months, but on July 3, 1895, Railroad Bill made a big mistake. He shot and killed the sheriff. Sheriff McMillan's body was shipped home on a train, and the city, which had been decorated for a huge Fourth of July celebration, was plunged into mourning. The killing only strengthened the resolve to catch Railroad Bill. He was finally caught in a store some time later and shot to death. His body was brought back to Brewton and to other places where it was put on display. Sheriff McMillan's pistols are now on display at the museum that is named after his grandson, Thomas McMillan.

Brewton has only grown in the last century, adding new businesses while holding onto the lumber business. T.R. Miller Mill is still in operation, and south of town, Georgia Pacific has a huge mill, which is the largest employer in the area.

A history of the area would not be complete without telling the story of the many floods that have visited the area over the years. All of the downtown area is of historical nature, but it is all in a flood zone. Most of the store owners downtown have learned to deal with the floods, and most of them have chosen to remain. Every time a flood is expected, friends and neighbors of the store owners come out to help move things to higher shelves. That is what Brewton and East Brewton are all about. They help each other, and the only thing that comes between the two towns, besides Murder Creek, is the football game played between W.S. Neal High School in East Brewton and T.R. Miller High School in Brewton. The game received the name "the Battle of Murder Creek" from a sportscaster and it stuck. Both schools would rather beat each other more than any other opponent of the season. It always brings out some strange situations, because there are many "mixed" families that have to take one side or the other.

One

Historical Scenes in Brewton and East Brewton

Brewton is 126 years old and in many ways is as up-to-date as any small town. In other ways, it remains the same, at least on the surface, as it was so many years ago. East Brewton, although incorporated less than 100 years ago, was actually settled before Brewton.

There are 27 businesses in downtown Brewton that have been declared eligible to be in the Alabama Historical Registry. Although the town has suffered from many flooding situations and at least three major fires, it has always continued to survive and in some cases to find new growth. In a time when the downtown areas of small towns have had to compete with shopping centers, Brewton maintains its downtown area and uses it to promote its history and image.

In recent years, the town has used its history to redefine the downtown area. The business owners and managers have come together to work for the good of the community. East Brewton, too, has joined with its sister city. Today, the two small towns have banded together and share the Greater Brewton Area Chamber of Commerce and other entities for the good of both towns.

The attitude of most of the citizens of the area is to embrace and remember the past while at the same time moving forward to make Brewton and East Brewton the best small towns they can be.

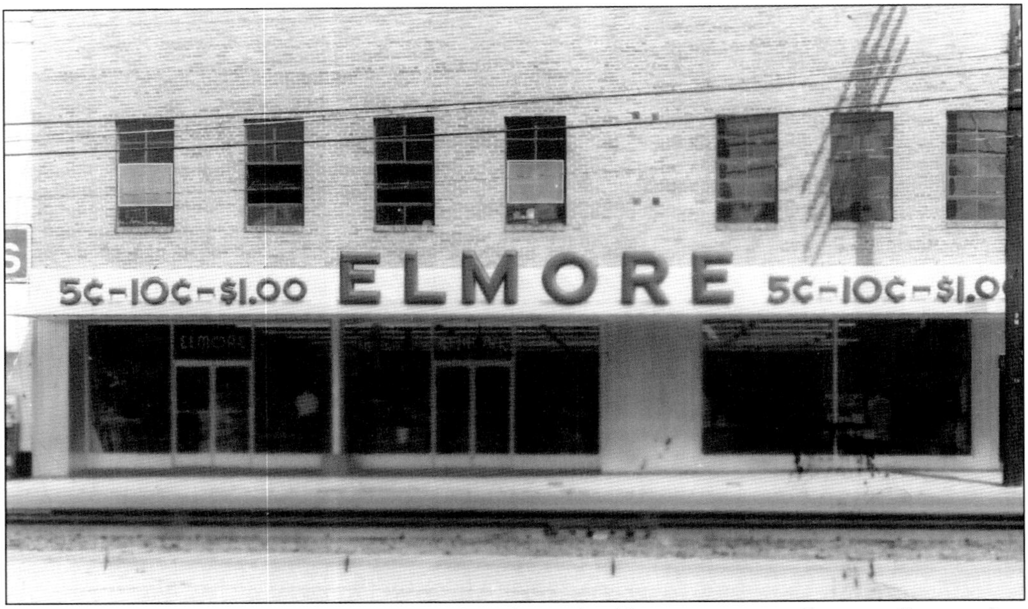

What has been known for some time as the Elmore building was originally a small store that was on city maps by 1898. At one time, it was enlarged to include the store beside it and made into Rogers Mercantile, which operated for many years. V.J. Elmore moved in during the 1940s and was open until 1972. Since that time, the building has been turned into several office and business spaces known as Elmore Place. (Courtesy of Robert Crenshaw.)

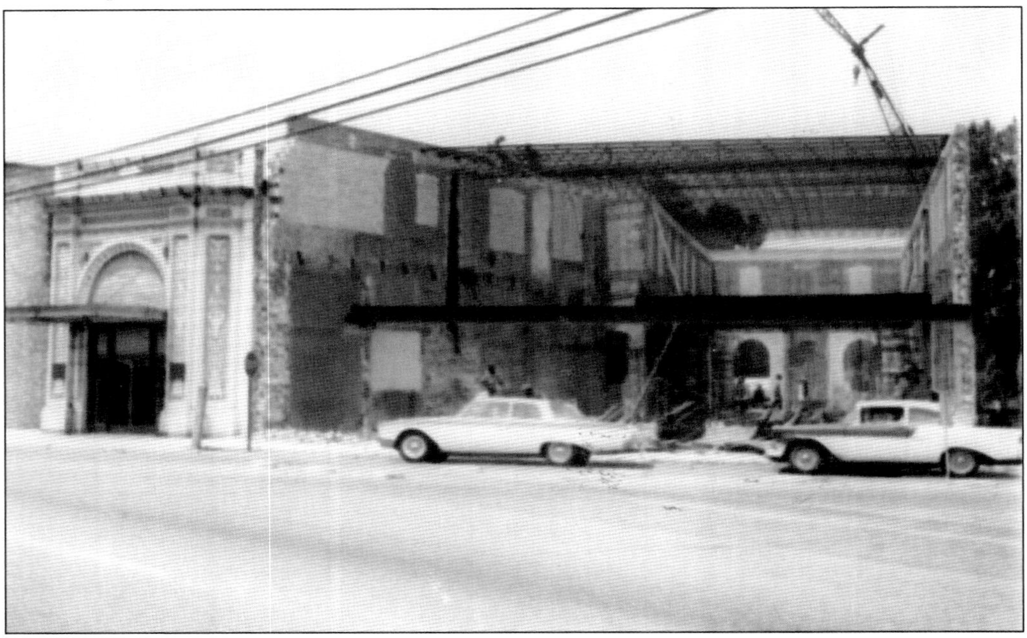

Lovelace Hotel, which operated from 1910 to 1963, was torn down, and the space was converted into a lobby and office area for the Bank of Brewton. The hotel was a hot spot for people to gather and had space for a ballroom. Many young ladies attended their first dances at the Lovelace Hotel. (Courtesy of Robert Crenshaw.)

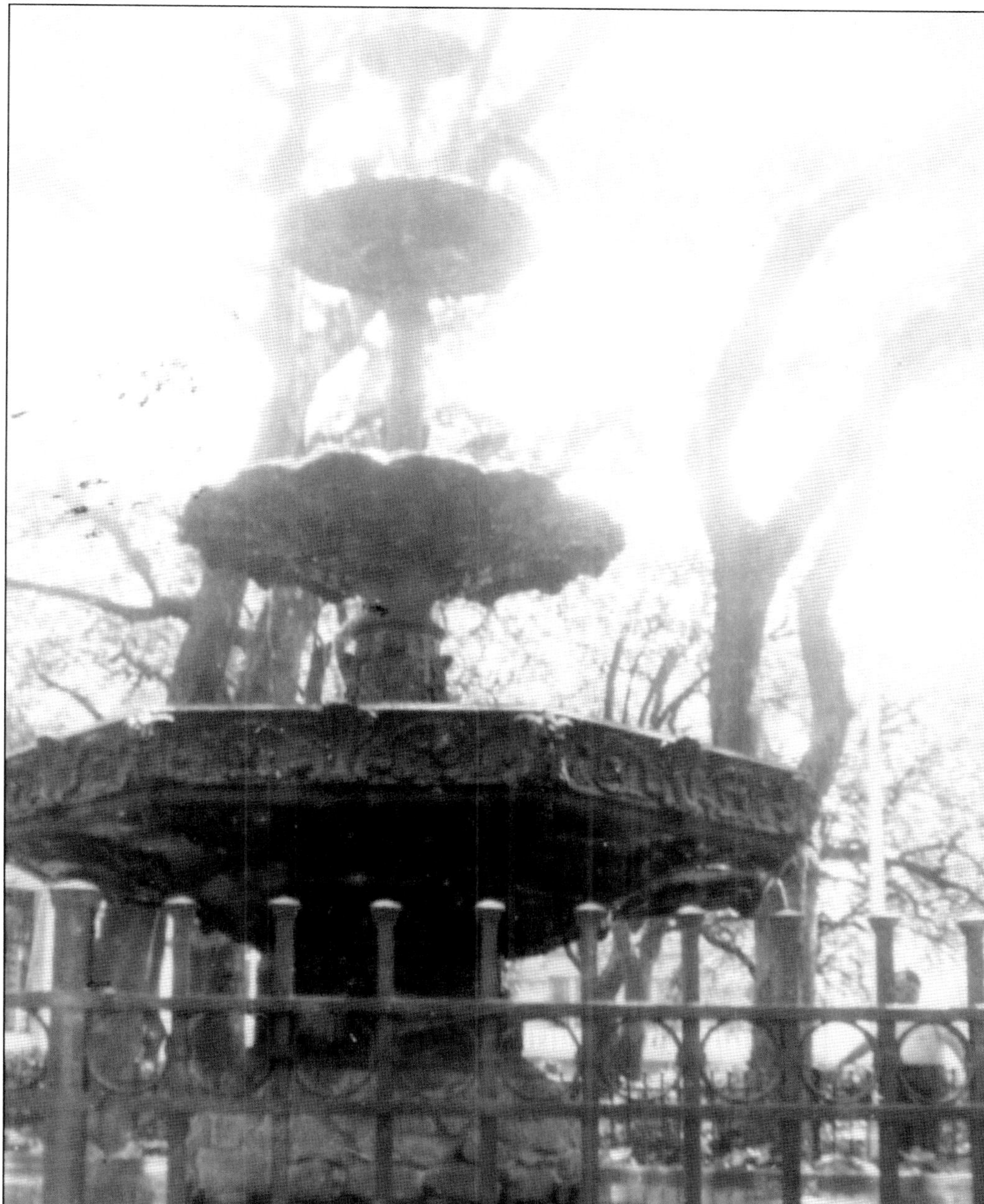

When the swampy watering hole for cattle and livestock became a sore spot for the citizens of Brewton, it was converted into a park, and today, it is known as City Park. This fountain originally sat about where the present fountain is. In later years, this fountain was taken down and a gazebo was built over the place. In 2009, the park underwent a restoration with a new fountain, city clock, and new gazebo. The old gazebo was moved to the Dogwood Hills Golf Course, where it joined another gazebo and a splash fountain that attracts crowds of children during the summertime. (Courtesy of Robert Crenshaw.)

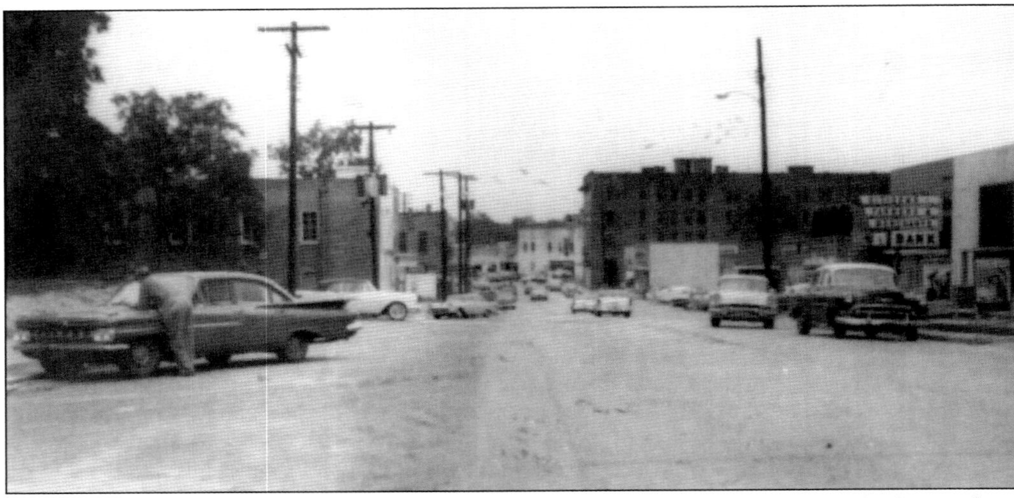

This photograph was taken in front of the Escambia County Courthouse. It looks south on Belleville Avenue to the intersection of Belleville and St. Joseph Avenue. The Masonic lodge is on the left, along with what is known as "Old Willie's." On the right are businesses leading down to the Bank of Brewton. (Courtesy of Robert Crenshaw.)

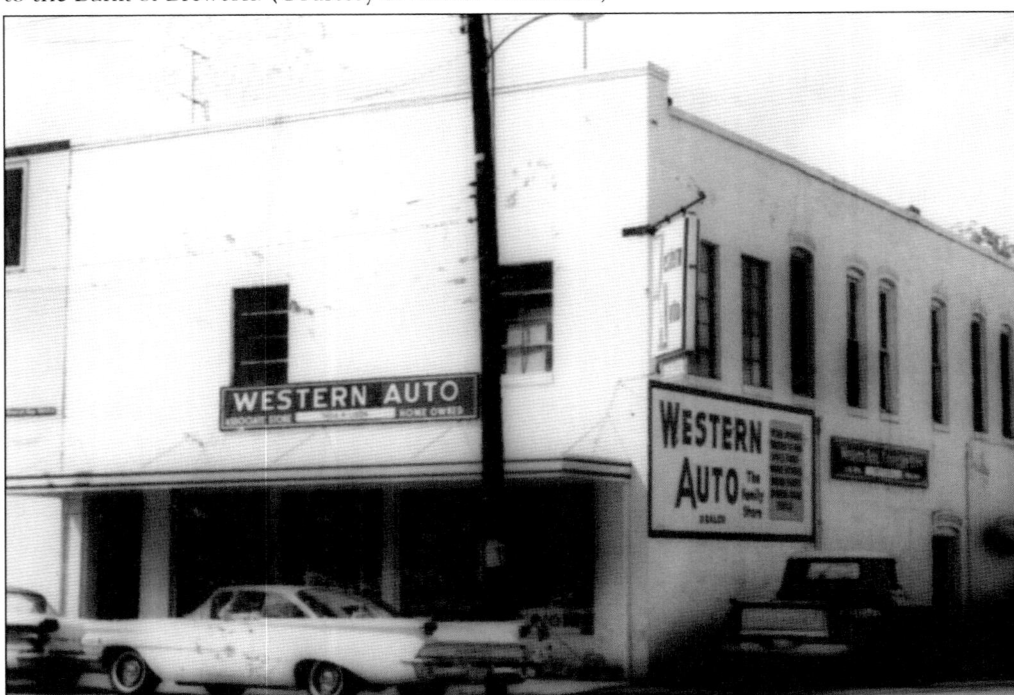

There was a building at the corner of St. Joseph Avenue and Mildred Street as early as 1893. It was originally used as a general store. Around 1910, Brewton City Hall offices were located upstairs, while the first floor became the home of Brewton Fire Department. It became Western Auto after 1939, when city hall moved into another building. Today, this building and those next to it have been torn down to build a minipark with a mural depicting the town history painted by Dothan artist Wes Hardin. (Courtesy of Robert Crenshaw.)

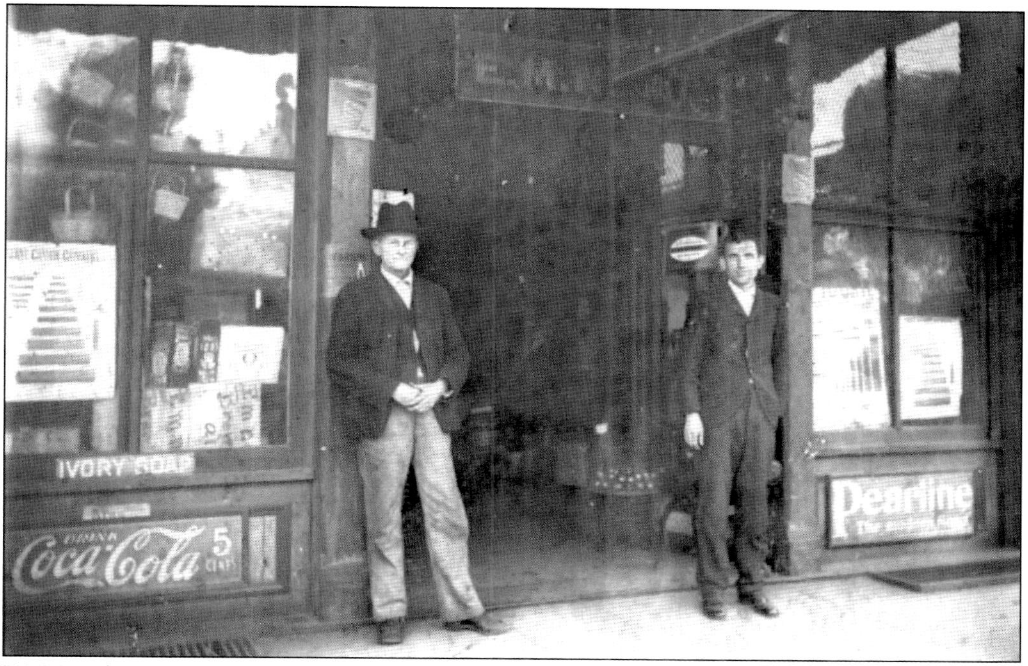

E.M. Neal Store was located on St. Joseph Avenue in the historical district. E.M. was the son of W.S. Neal, who was an early advocate for education in this area. He has been honored for that interest by having the elementary, middle, and high schools in East Brewton named after him. (Courtesy of Escambia County Historical Society.)

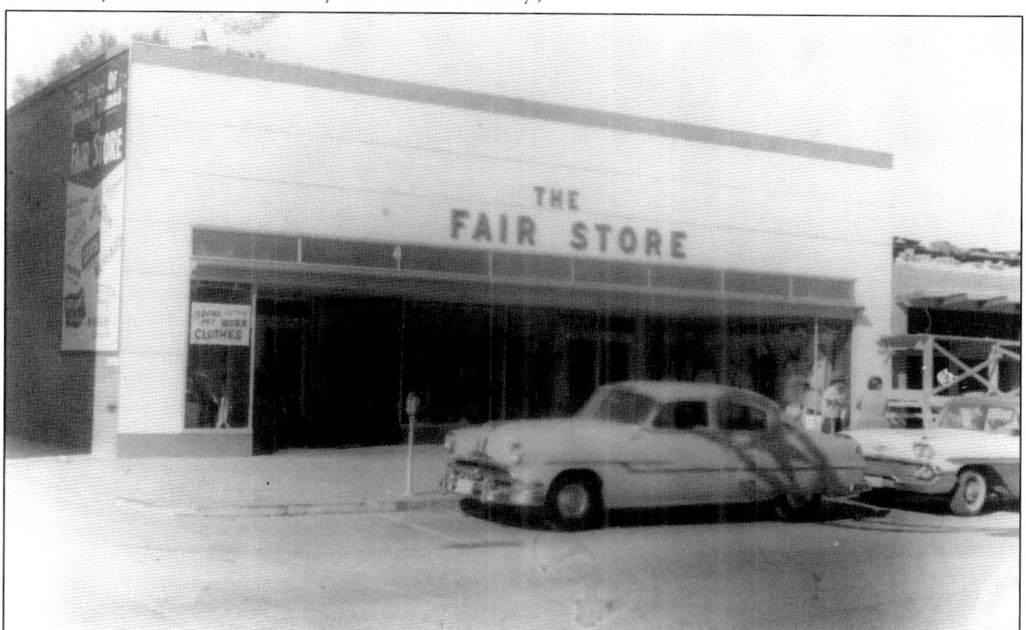

The Fair Store was one of the major department stores in downtown Brewton. This photograph was taken when the store was located across Bob Teller Drive from the Bank of Brewton. The building was later turned into a skating rink but, in 2011, it sits empty. (Courtesy of Robert Crenshaw.)

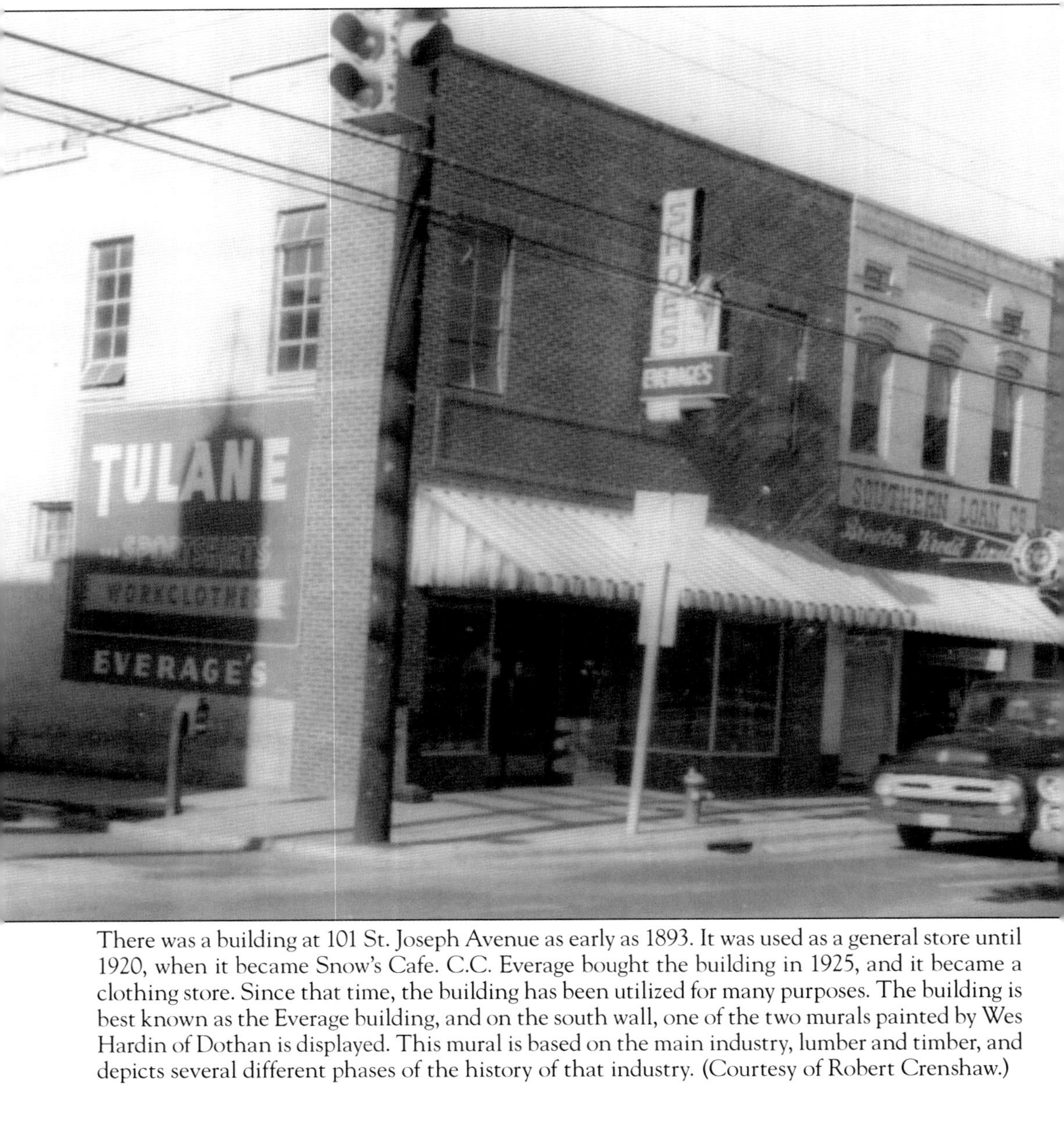

There was a building at 101 St. Joseph Avenue as early as 1893. It was used as a general store until 1920, when it became Snow's Cafe. C.C. Everage bought the building in 1925, and it became a clothing store. Since that time, the building has been utilized for many purposes. The building is best known as the Everage building, and on the south wall, one of the two murals painted by Wes Hardin of Dothan is displayed. This mural is based on the main industry, lumber and timber, and depicts several different phases of the history of that industry. (Courtesy of Robert Crenshaw.)

This building was erected in 1924 to house the Brewton Motor Company. It was the only Ford dealership in this area for many years. It was used as a dealership until 1978, when Peach Motors moved to a new site. Since that time, it has been used as a motorcycle shop, and Down to Earth is there in 2011.

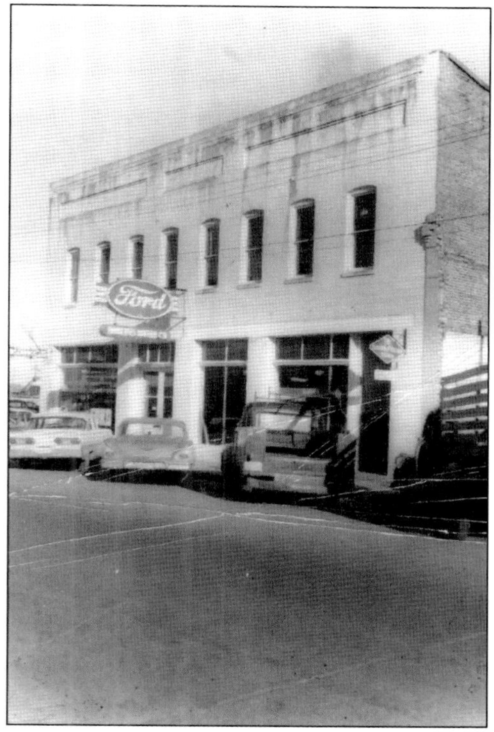

Scott's Garage was about where Church's Chicken is now located. It was handy for those attending ball games across the road during the years of minor league baseball in Brewton. It was also where the high school played ball. The first night games were played here after lights were installed. It was a perfect spot to while away some hours on a summer day. People could run across to the garage and buy a snack. This building and several others were torn down. The area is in a flood zone, and landscaped parking lots have taken the place of the buildings. (Courtesy of Frank Scott.)

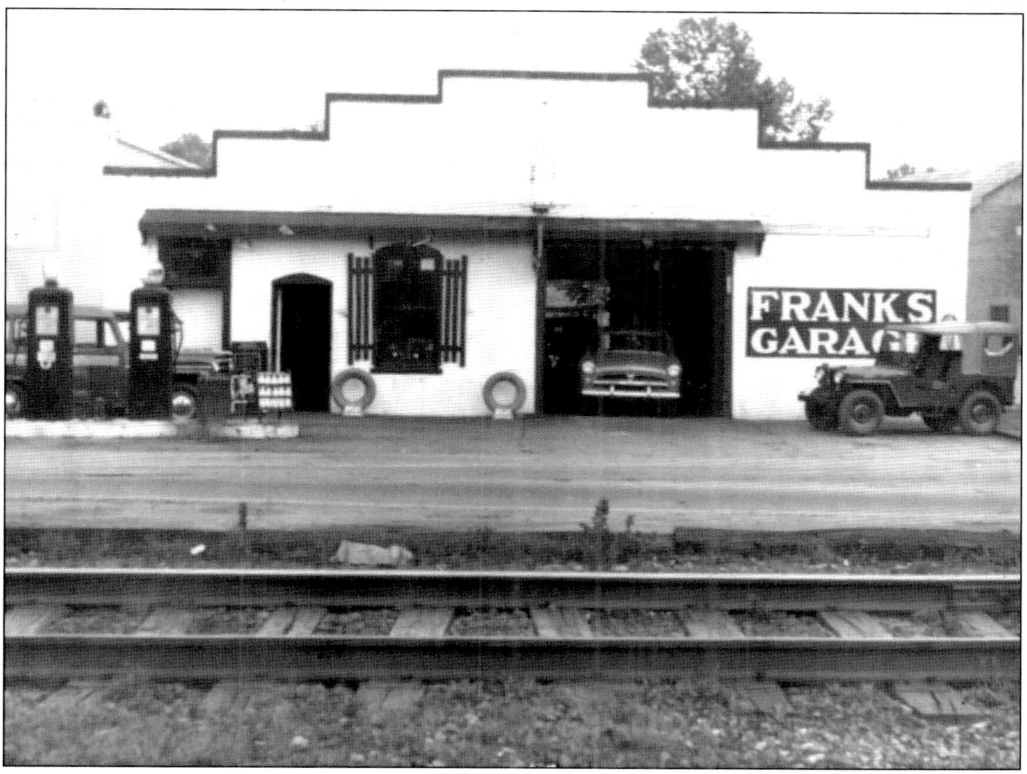

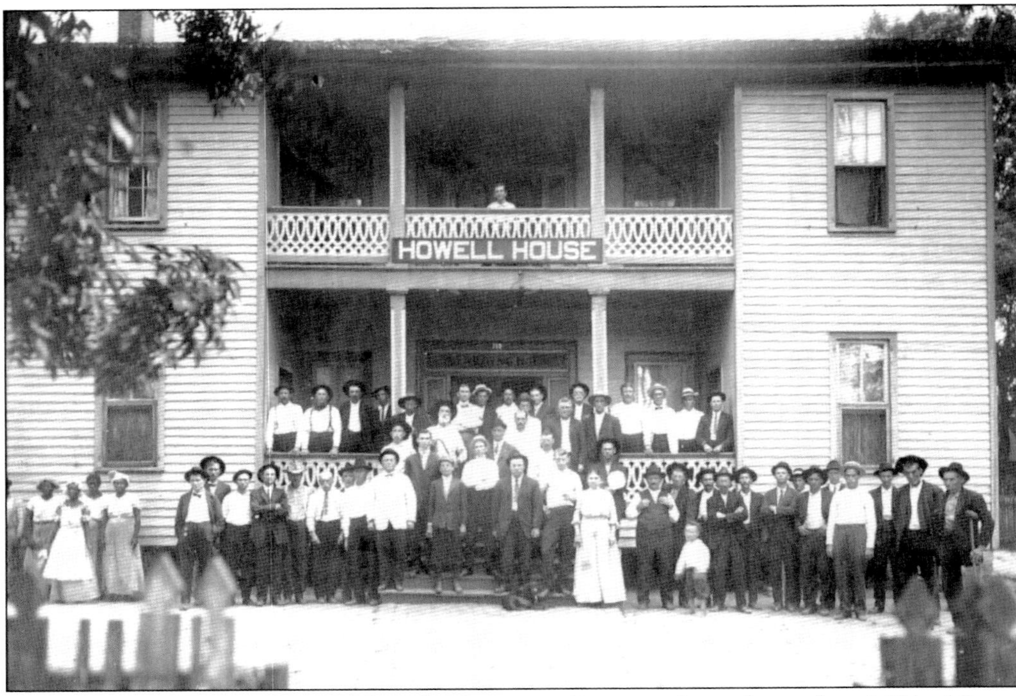

Howell House was one of several boardinghouses in Brewton. It was located on Mildred Street between what is now Moye's Office Supply and Murder Creek. This is the second building, and it is believed to have been across Mildred Street from the current fruit market. At one time, it may have been located where Watson-English Hardware store was for many years. It is mentioned in an old newspaper clipping of the 1895 football team as being on the property now owned by Buddy Crenshaw. (Courtesy of James Wilson.)

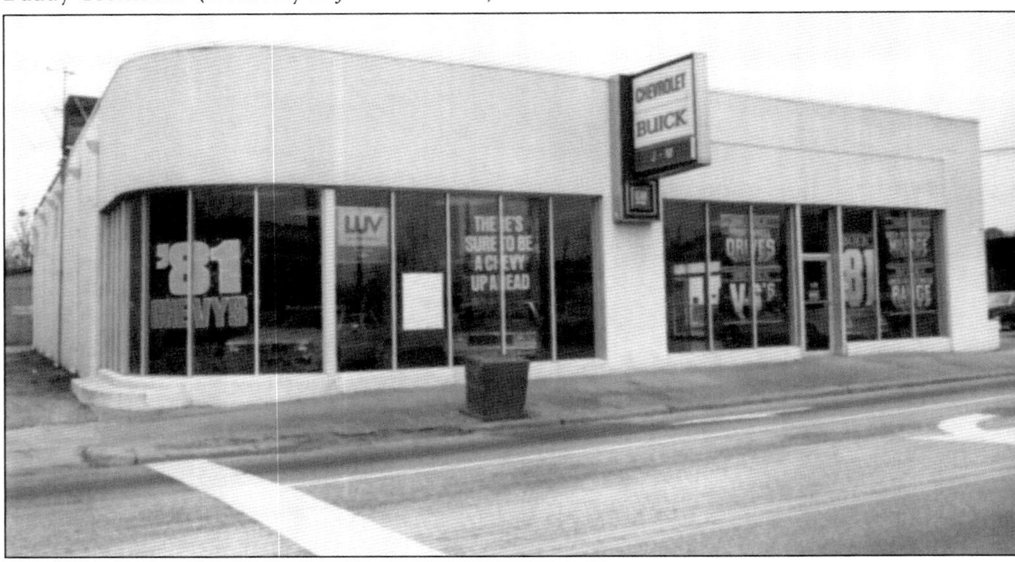

This building, now owned by Brewton Iron Works, was the J.M. Chevrolet dealership (which stood for Jernigan McMillan). This photograph was taken in 1981. The many signs in the windows show that the 1981 model was probably brand new. (Courtesy of the *Brewton Standard.*)

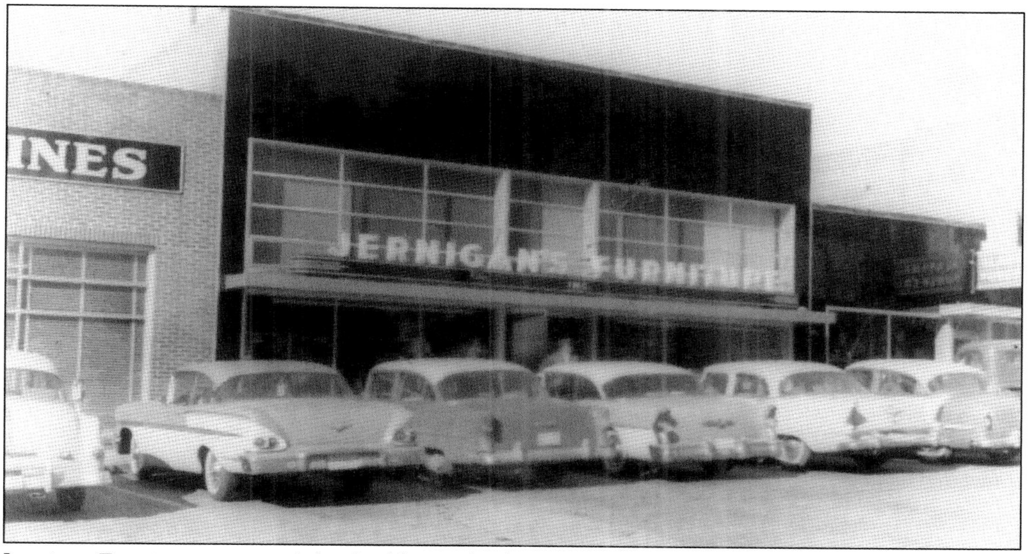

Jernigan Furniture occupied this building, which now is part of Paris Market. It has been used for several businesses over many years, including a drugstore. Paris Market is the retail store of Natural Decorations, Inc. (NDI). NDI is a local manufacturer that supplies flowers and arrangements to some of the best hotels and homes in the United States. The business is owned by Joe and Carol Gordy, well-known horticulturalists. Today, tour buses bring people to tour the factory, see some of the beautiful homes, and visit the downtown area. (Courtesy of Robert Crenshaw.)

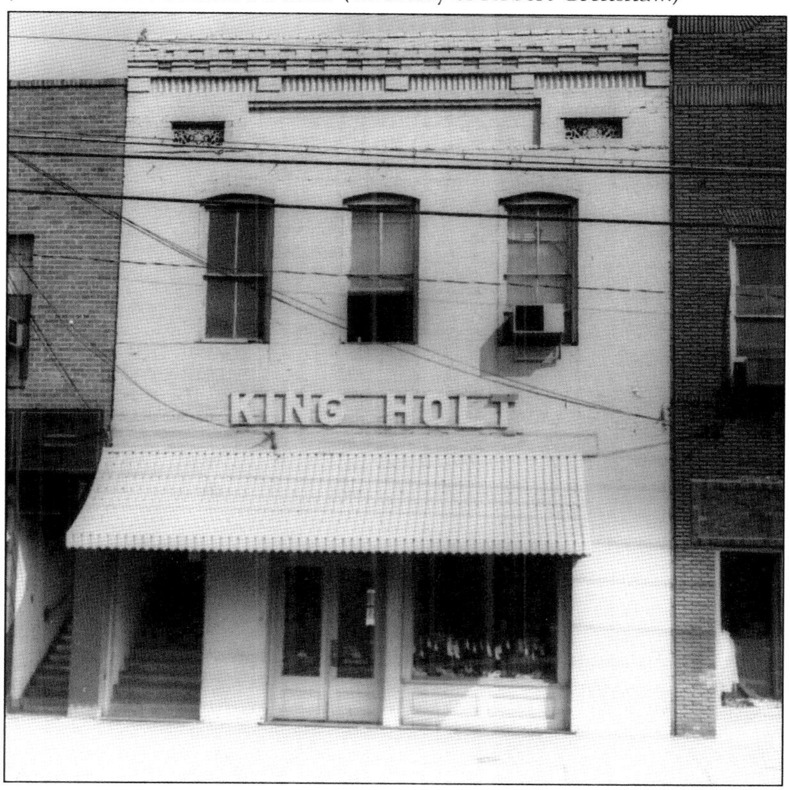

The King Holt business was one of many located along the west side of St. Joseph Avenue. It sold a variety of items and apparently was there for many years. The location was next to the Bank of Brewton. (Courtesy of Robert Crenshaw.)

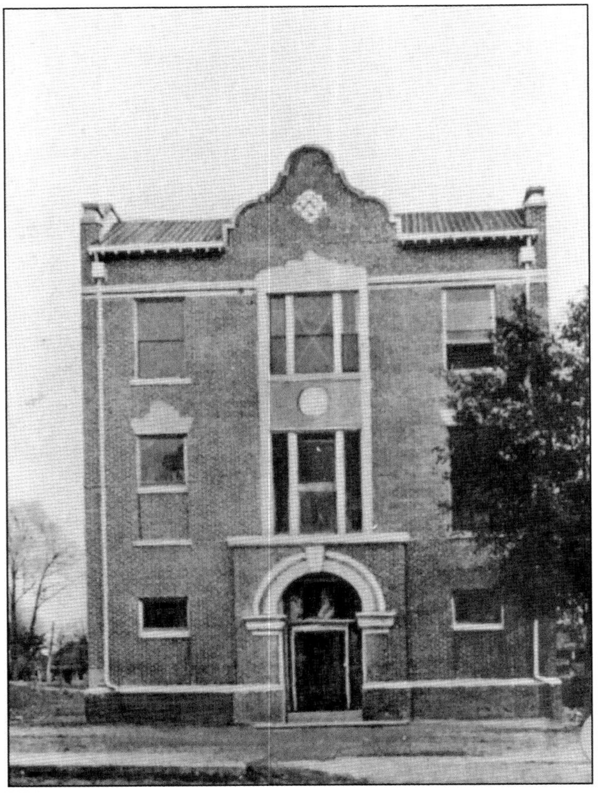

The Masonic lodge building is pictured as it looked in 1920. It was built in the early 1900s and has been used for various things over the years. It was once a three-story building before a fire burned the top floor. The building housed the first offices of Dr. Robert Low as well as the office of the *Brewton Standard* newspaper. The outside no longer looks like the old Masonic lodge, but the stairway inside is original. (Courtesy of Yancey Lovelace.)

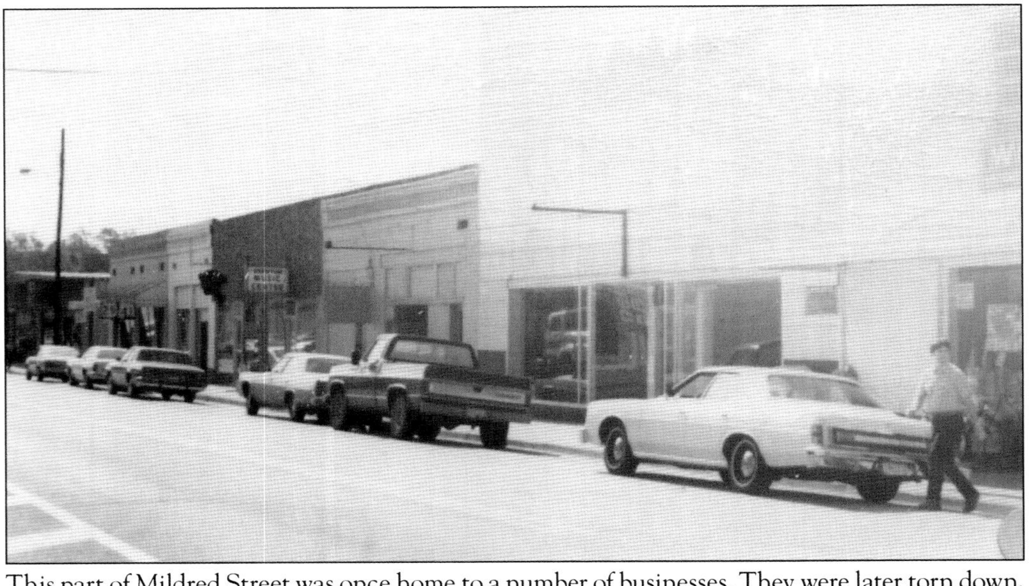

This part of Mildred Street was once home to a number of businesses. They were later torn down, and today the space is used as part of the Mildred Street Park. The beautifully landscaped area is home to one of two murals in the downtown area. Brewton has several parks in the downtown area, including the Mildred Street Park, City Park, and Burnt Corn Creek Park, the site of the annual Blueberry Festival.

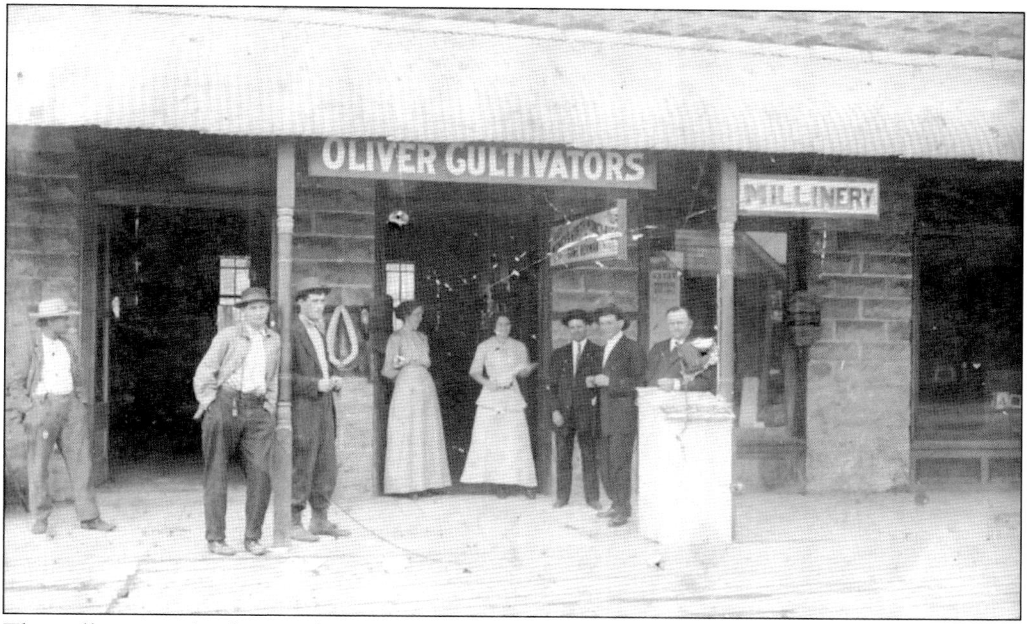

The millinery and cultivator businesses would appear to have shared quarters in Brewton at one time. No one remembers where the store was located. It seems to be made of blocks, and there were only two other places in downtown Brewton made of blocks, Old Willie's and a residence that stood on Lee Street.

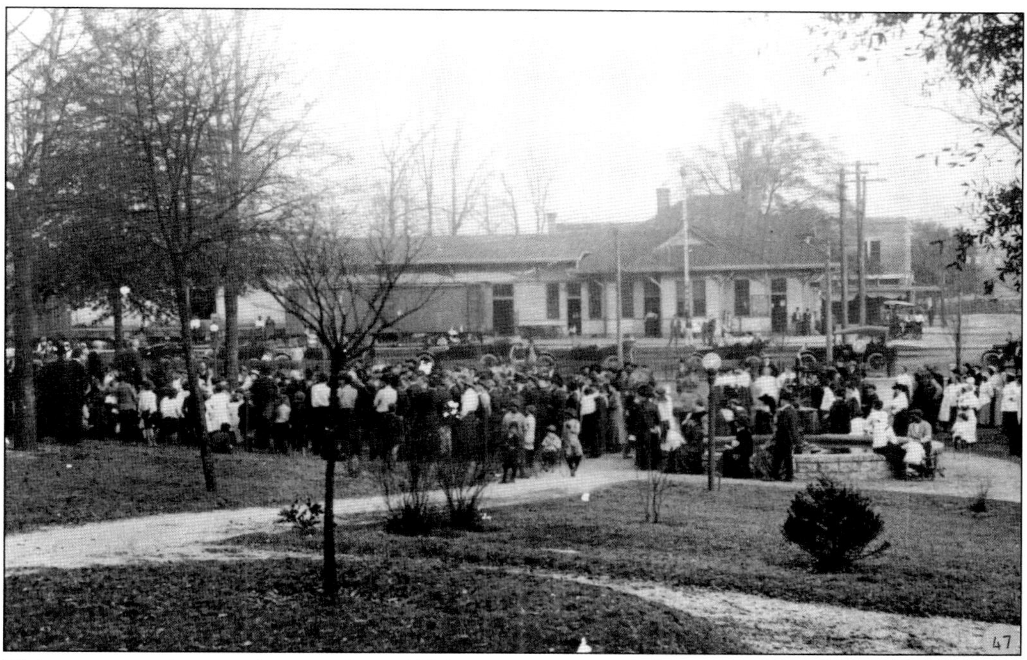

This space, used as a park since about 1908, was once a swampy area used by livestock and horses. This photograph was taken of some event about 1925. It has been the site of many events, including more recently the Movie in the Park, which is held several times a year. People sit on the ground or in their lawn chairs and watch family films on a large inflatable screen.

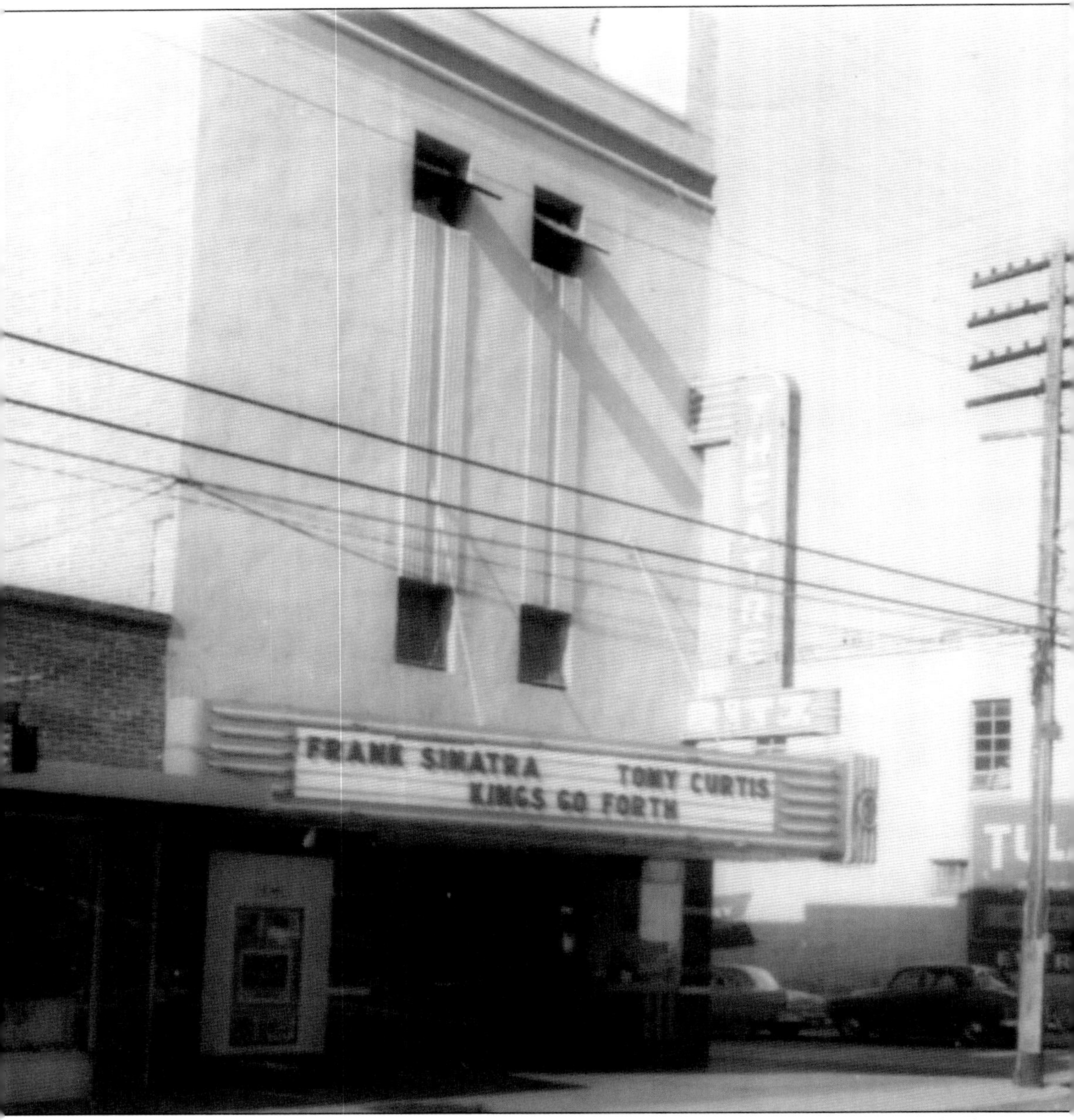

The Ritz Theater was a busy place from 1936 until 1987. The place opened to great fanfare in 1936. On the first anniversary of the opening, the *Brewton Standard* devoted a whole section of the newspaper to where not only movies but also live shows were shown. The employees were not too shabby either—they had uniforms—and many youngsters enjoyed it for many years. Today's citizens talk often of the need to once again have either a movie theater or a bowling alley for the youngsters of the town in order to help keep them out of trouble. Brewton at one time had a bowling alley. (Courtesy of Robert Crenshaw.)

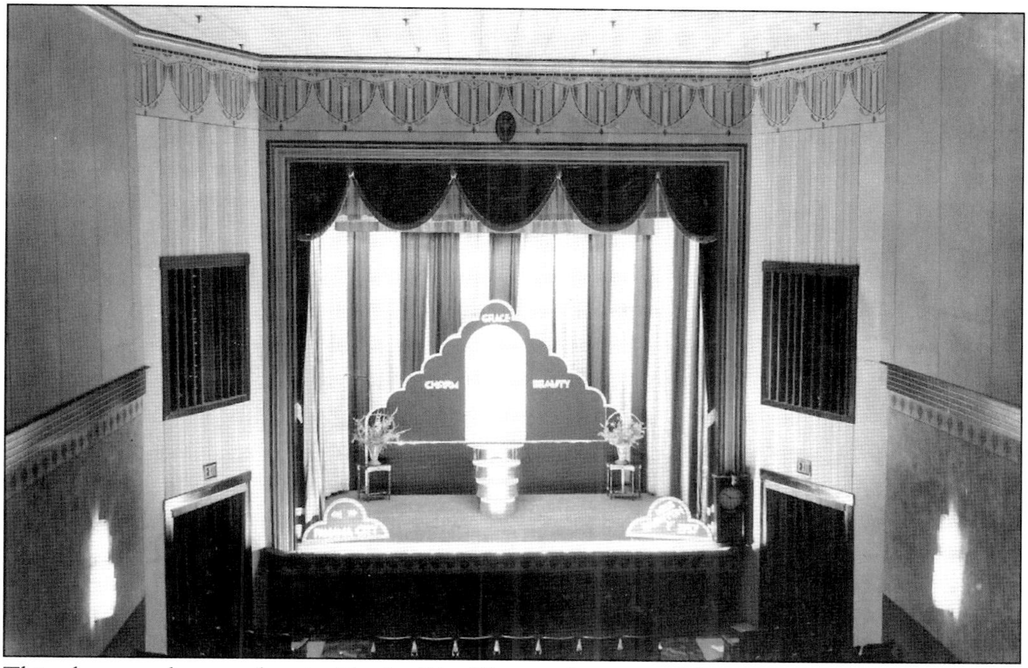

This photograph was taken inside the Ritz Theater. It was used for movies and live shows and, in this case, a Miss Brewton contest. There is not a date on this photograph, but it would have been taken after 1936, when the theater opened. (Courtesy of Scott Hillman.)

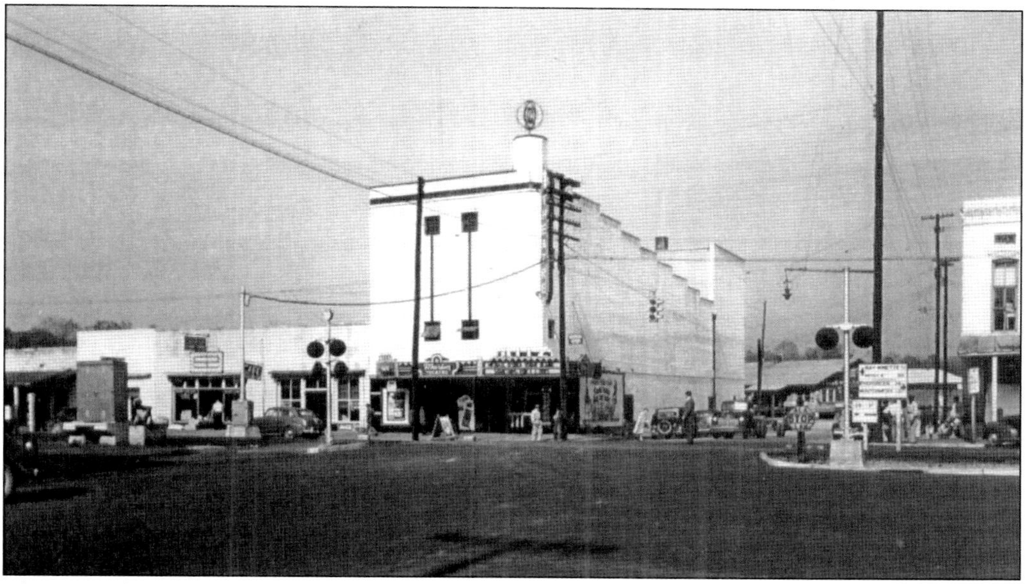

The Ritz Theater was a familiar sight in Brewton and was a gathering place for youngsters for many years. Today, the building is gone. The flashing ball that once sat at the top of the theater tower was saved and now occupies the top of a modern message center. On New Year's Eve, young and old gather at Burnt Corn Creek Park to listen to music and to watch the "blueberry" drop from the top of the message center. At the stroke of midnight, those brave enough to face the cold get a beautiful display of fireworks.

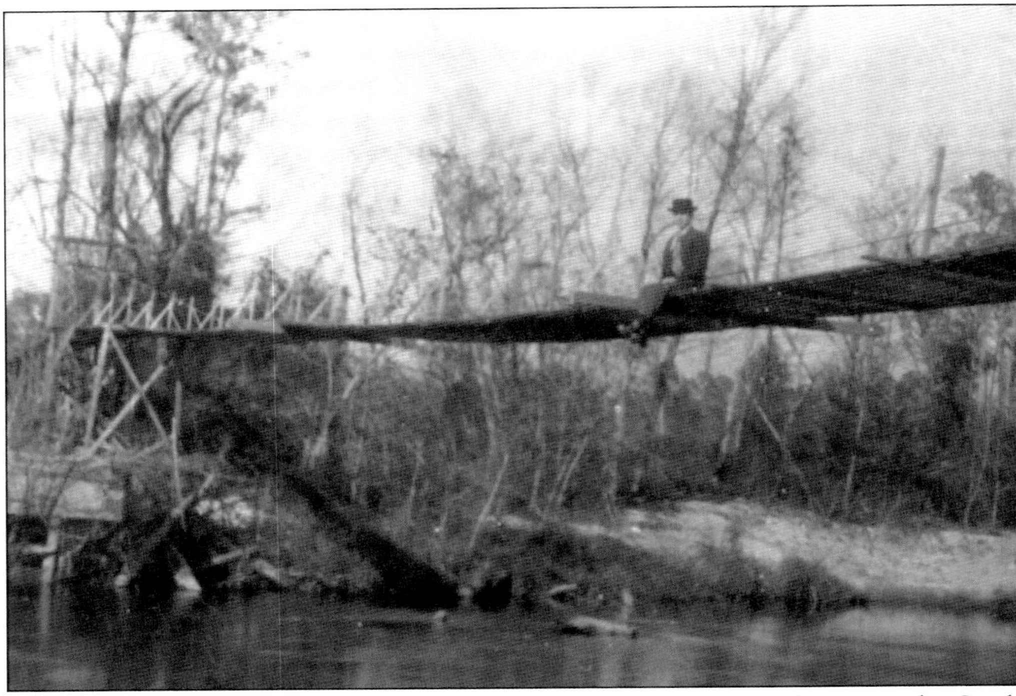

This swinging bridge was where the workers at T.R. Miller Mill crossed over Murder Creek. This photograph was taken in 1913. The man sitting on the bridge is Mr. Brusear, the telegraph operator in Brewton. (Courtesy of James Wilson.)

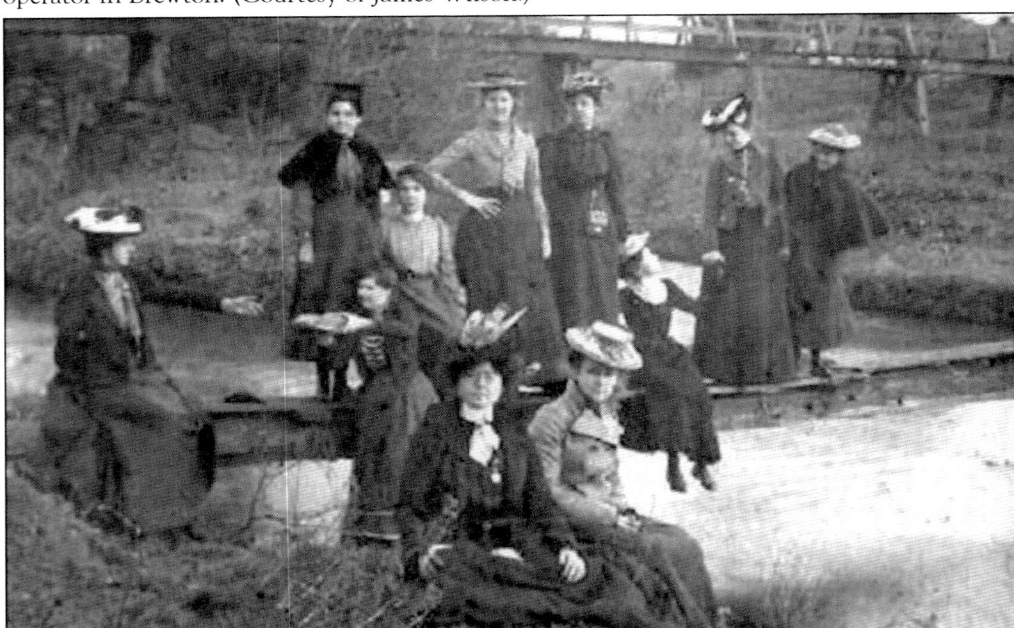

Murder Creek has played an important role in many things over the years. Whether it is flooding or going through a dry spell, it seems to always be something to discuss. These ladies are dressed in their finery and gathered at a footbridge at the creek. (Courtesy of James Wilson.)

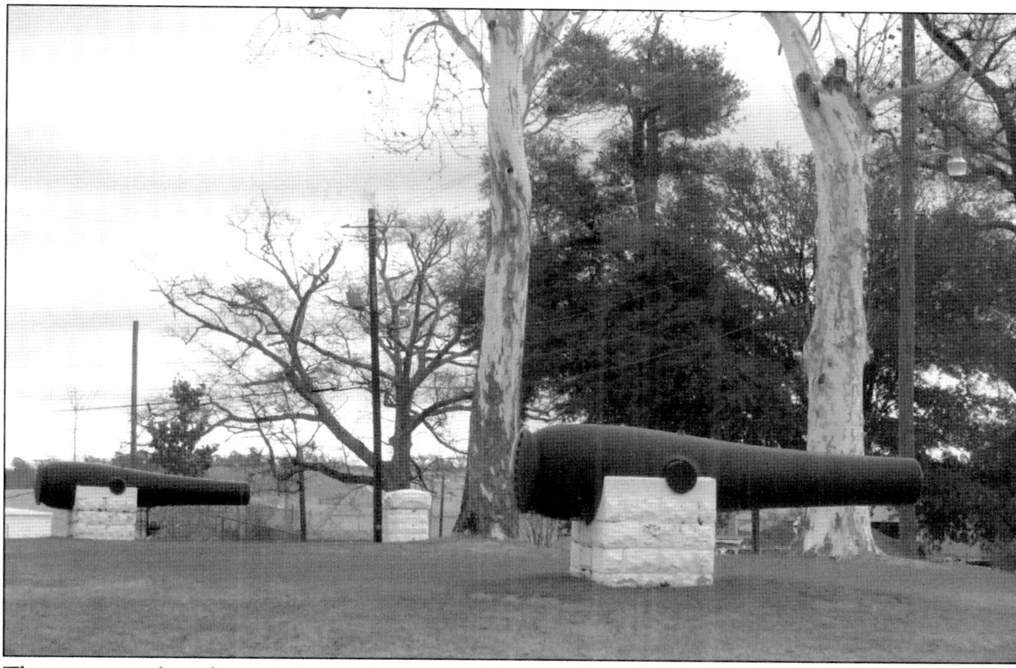

These cannons have been sitting on the corner of the courthouse lawn since 1905. They were apparently never fired, and they came to Brewton from Fort Barrancas in Pensacola when the fort was getting rid of old weapons. They still attract children, who sit on them during parades downtown.

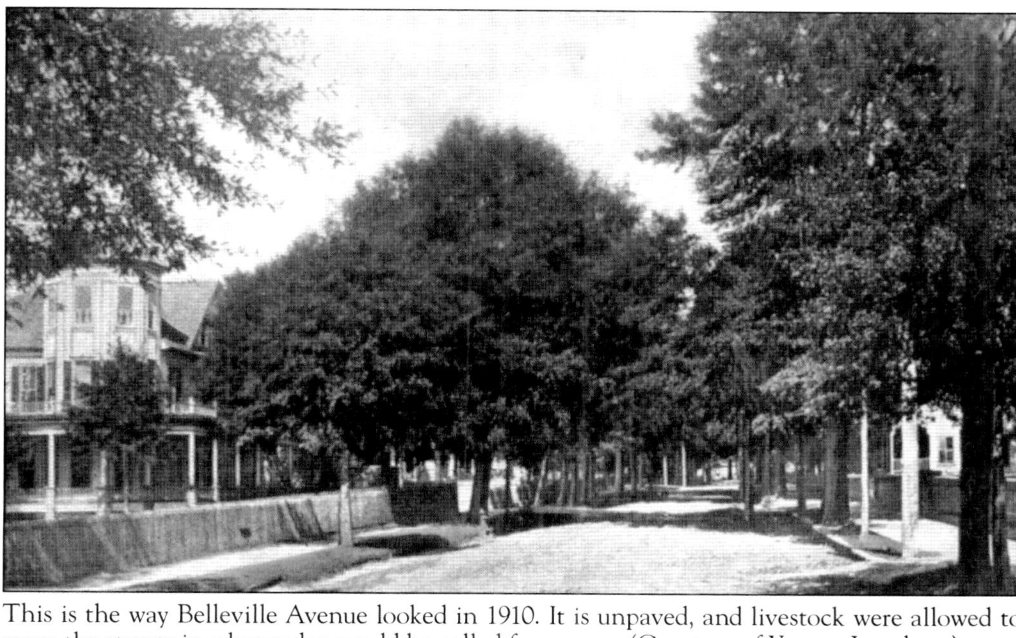

This is the way Belleville Avenue looked in 1910. It is unpaved, and livestock were allowed to roam the streets in what today would be called free range. (Courtesy of Yancey Lovelace.)

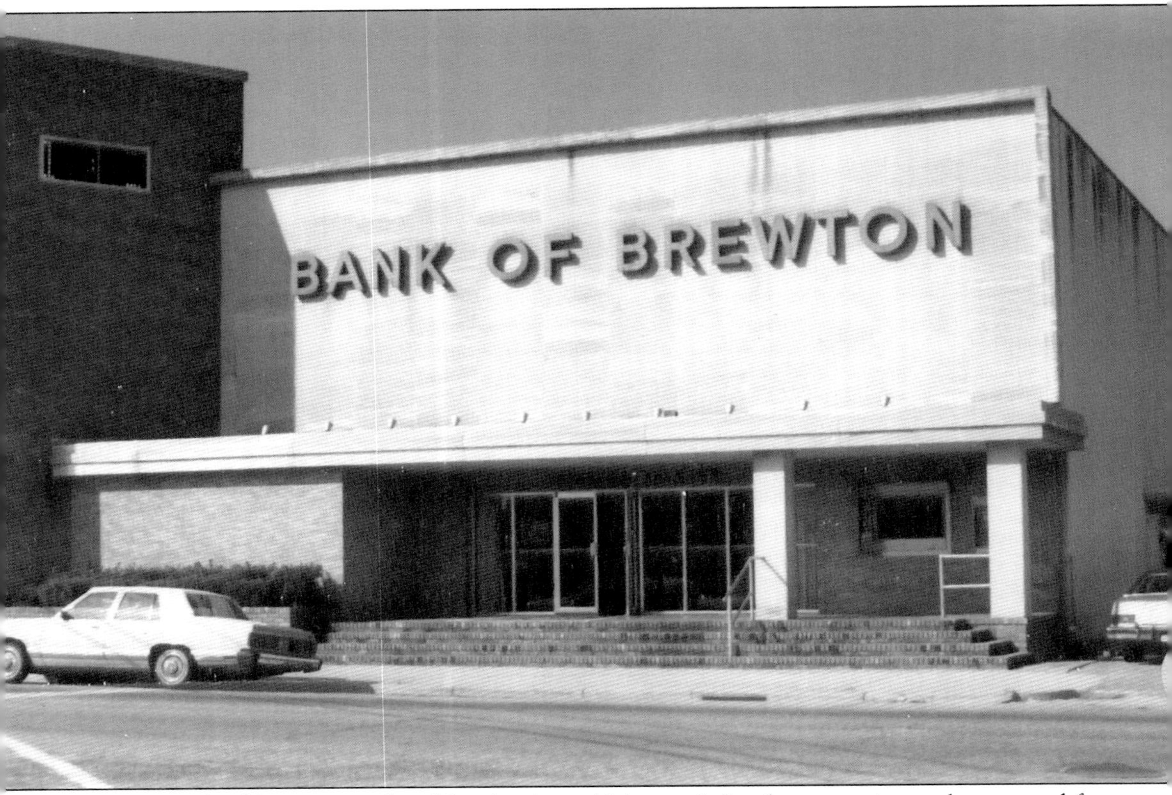

The Bank of Brewton is the oldest bank in Alabama. It has been continuously operated from the time it opened in 1889. It was originally located in one of the buildings down the street. In 1912, a new bank building was constructed at the corner of St. Joseph and Belleville Avenues (formerly Parker Street). The front facade, which was put up at the time, is the same as it is today, almost 100 years later. It is made up of green tiles and unusual designs, making it unique. When the Lovelace Hotel next door was torn down, the bank took over some of the space that had been the hotel. This photograph was taken about 1963. At that time, the time and temperature were displayed out front. It has undergone several other changes since that time. (Courtesy of Escambia County Commission.)

Charles L. Sowell came home from the Civil War after suffering the loss of one arm. He walked home with nothing to call his own. He went into the lumber business, and in 1889, he came up with the idea of building a bank to hold all his money. This would be the Bank of Brewton. (Courtesy of Bank of Brewton.)

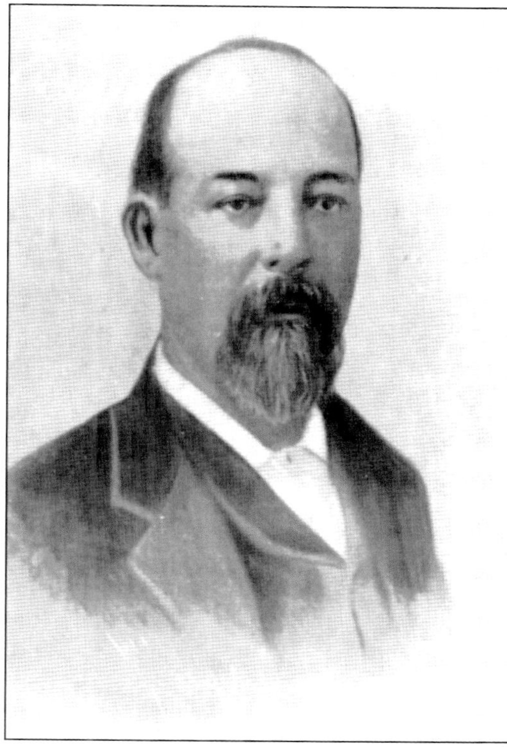

Brewton has always lived in the shadow of the railroad tracks that run through the middle of St. Joseph Avenue. The trains used to play a very important part in getting lumber shipped out and merchandise shipped in. Today, the trains come through and never stop.

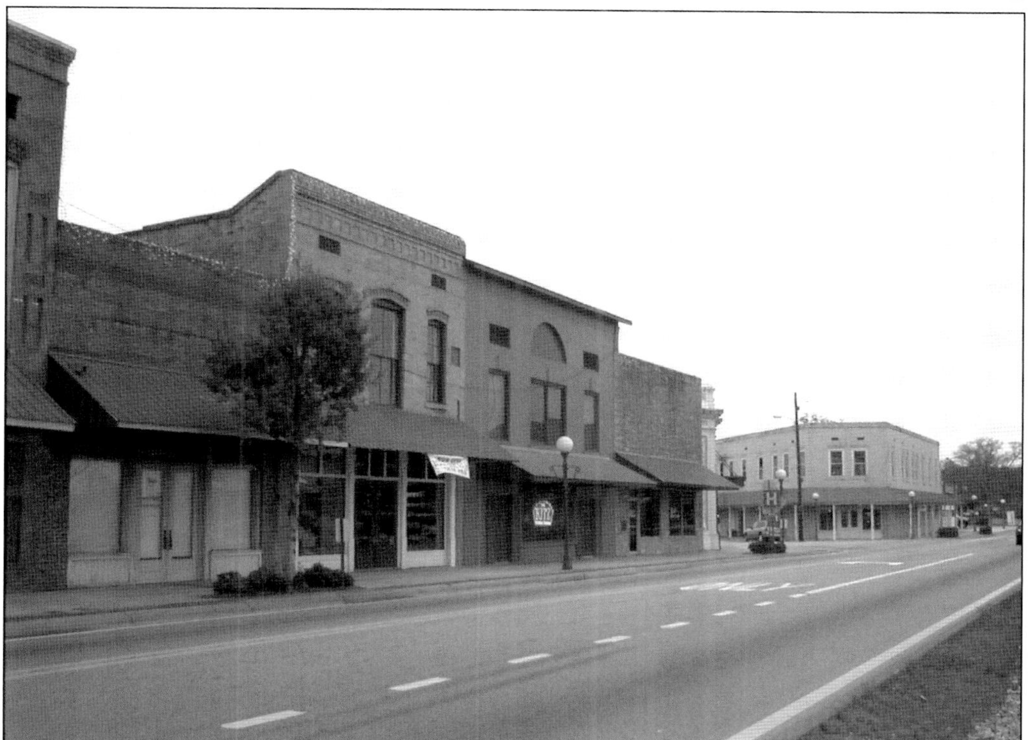

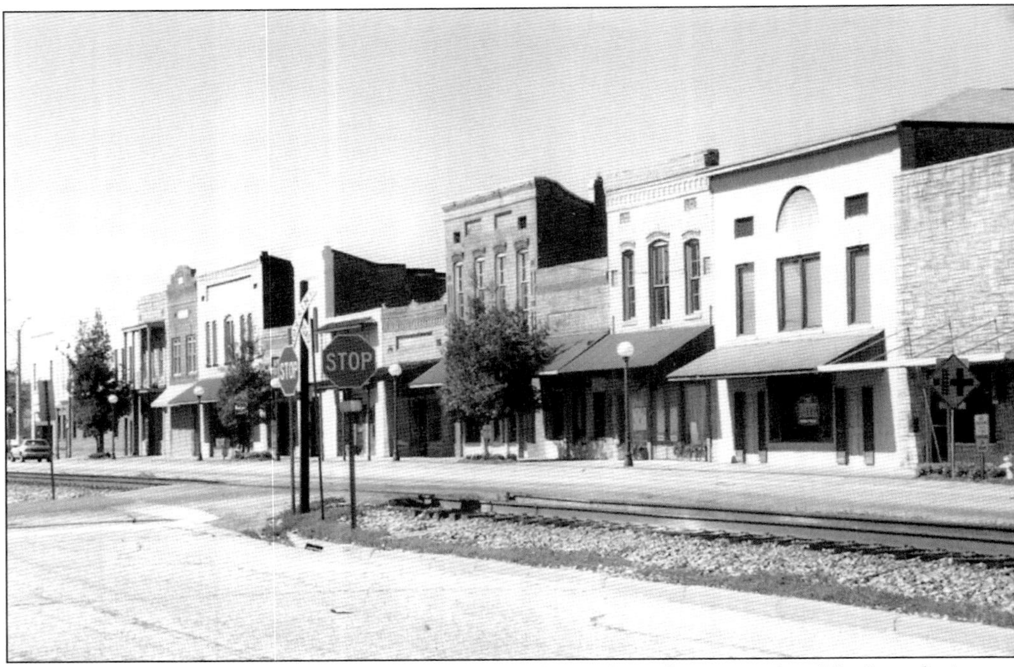

This photograph is a good view of the businesses located on the west side of St. Joseph Avenue in 1950. Many of them have had some changes, but for the most part, they look as they did in days gone by. (Courtesy of Escambia County Commission.)

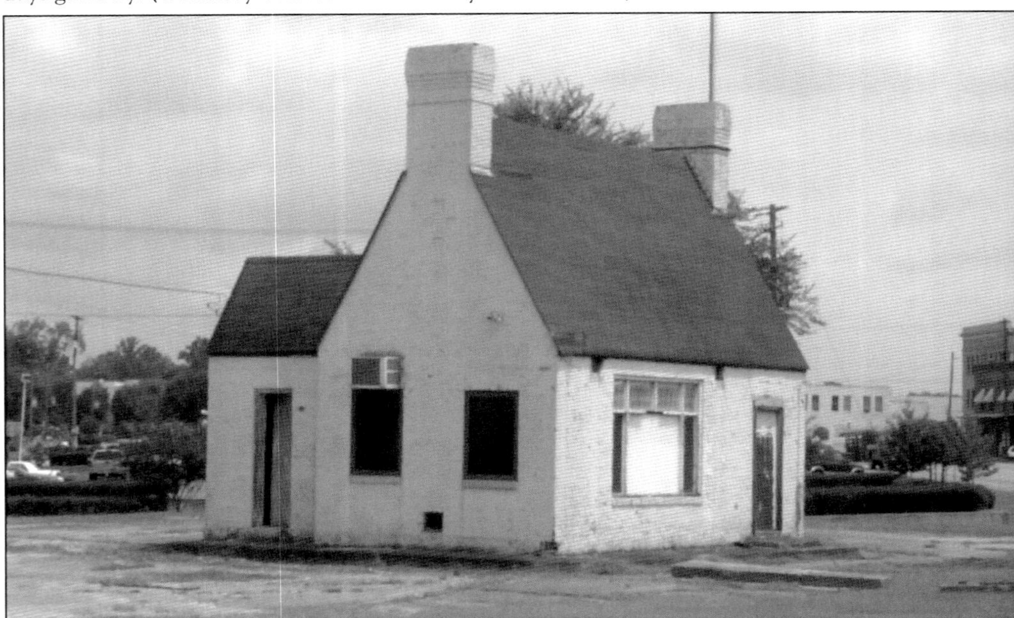

This was built as a Pure Oil station and bears the unique architecture that the Pure Oil Company used during the 1940s and 1950s. It later became so run-down that it was in danger of collapsing. Residents were very happy to see the building restored around 2006. For a short period of time after restoration, the building was used as an insurance office, but now it sits empty again.

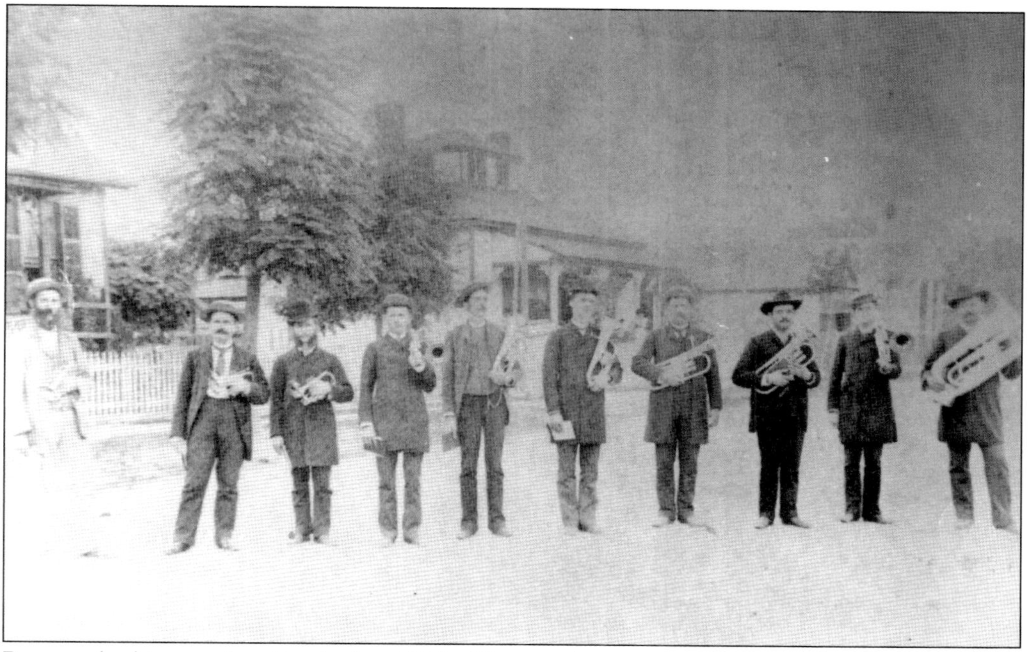

Brewton had its own band in the late 1800s. The members are, from left to right, A.V. Buck, C.W. Robbins, Dr. S.C. Henderson, J.H. Lovelace, O.P. Luttrell, Ed McGowin, W.A. Lovelace, Sumpter Lovelace, Harry Henderson, and C.F. Rankin. (Courtesy of James Wilson.)

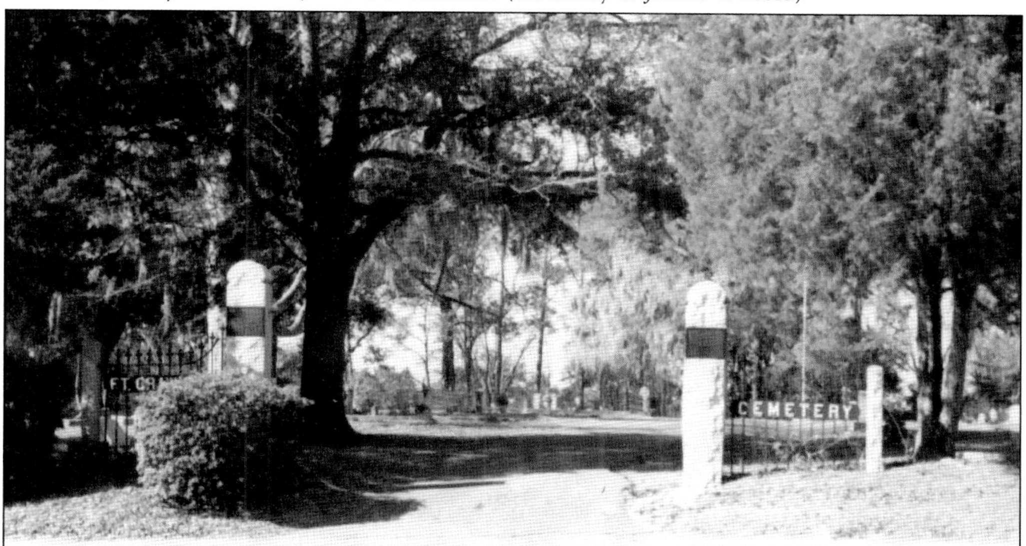

Both Brewton and East Brewton have historical cemeteries. This is Fort Crawford Cemetery in East Brewton. It is very old, and some believe that there were people buried there who were actually at the fort, which was built about 1816. This is the only remaining clue as to where the fort was actually located.

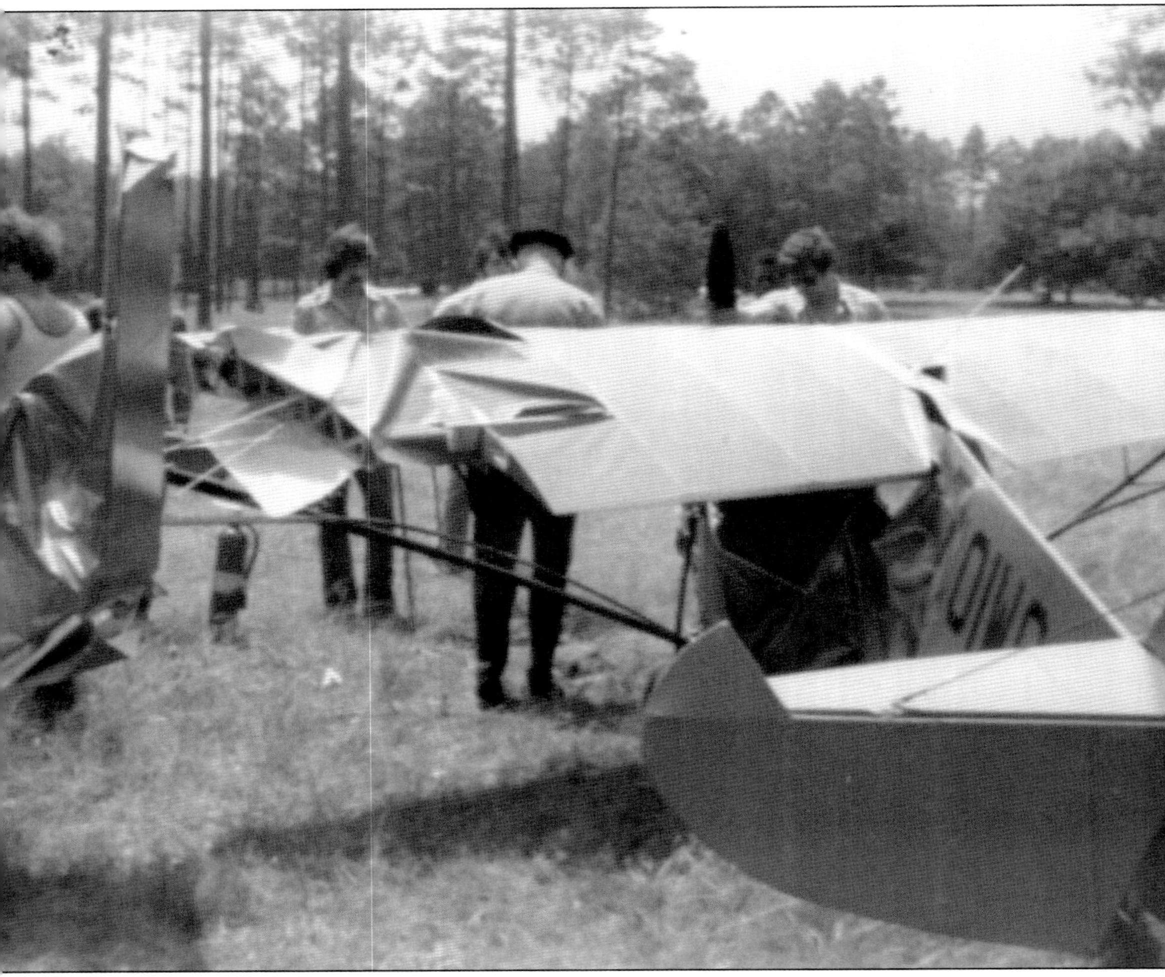

This airplane went down at the old airport. The airport was later moved to a new field south of East Brewton. This is also the site of the old Brewton Country Club. It is said that the golfers on the course would sometimes have to move out of the way of an incoming plane. Parts of the old Brewton Country Club were used after the new country club was built north of the city limits. Today, it has a golf course with a clubhouse, a swimming pool, playground, splash pad, and gazebos. The playground, splash pad, and gazebos are free to the public, and many children take advantage of them during the hot summer days. (Courtesy of Frank Scott.)

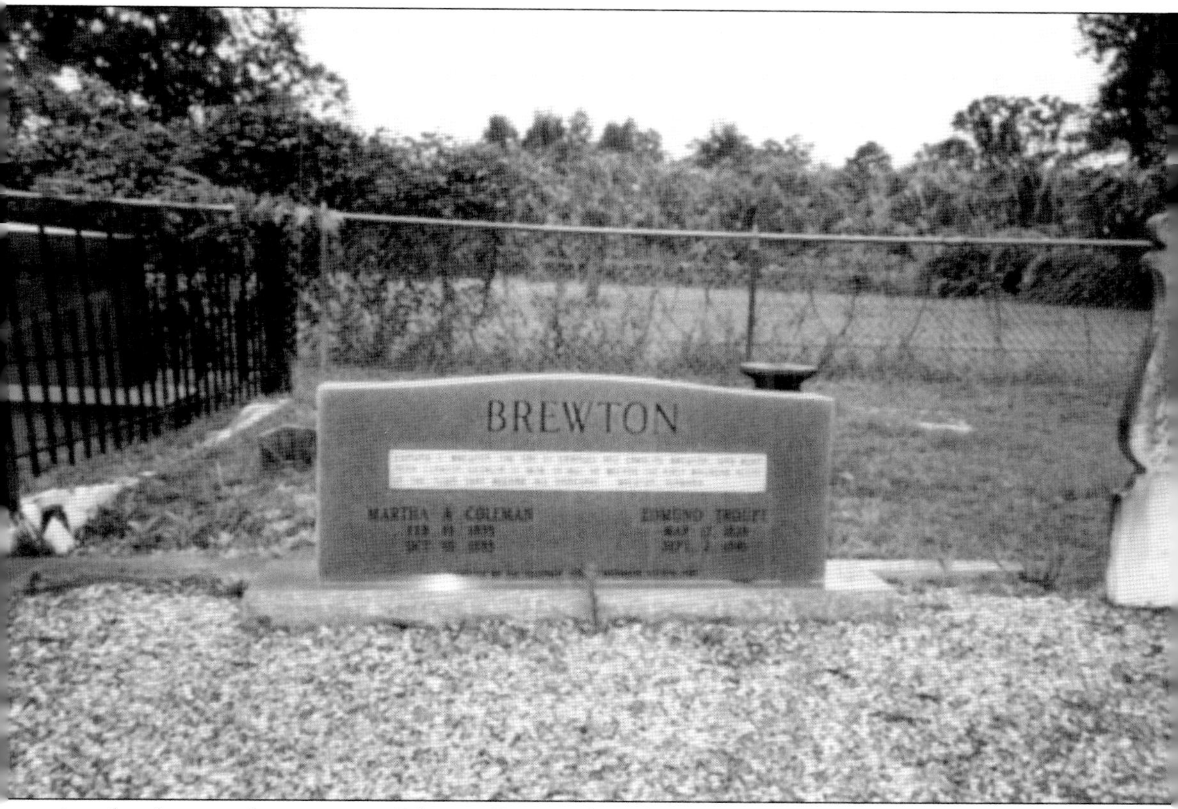

Another historical cemetery is Pilgrims Rest in the Alco section of Brewton. The remains of many of the yellow fever victims of 1883 are buried here. This modern tombstone marks the grave of Edmund Troupe Brewton, who many believe was the namesake of the city of Brewton. He migrated to this area of Alabama from Georgia. There once were many Brewton family members living here. Some people believe that the town was named for E.T. Brewton, while there are old records that say Brewton was named for the Brewton family. Whichever is the truth, it is clear that this family had a big influence on the area. E.T. is buried here with his wife, Martha Coleman Brewton, who died in the yellow fever epidemic of 1883.

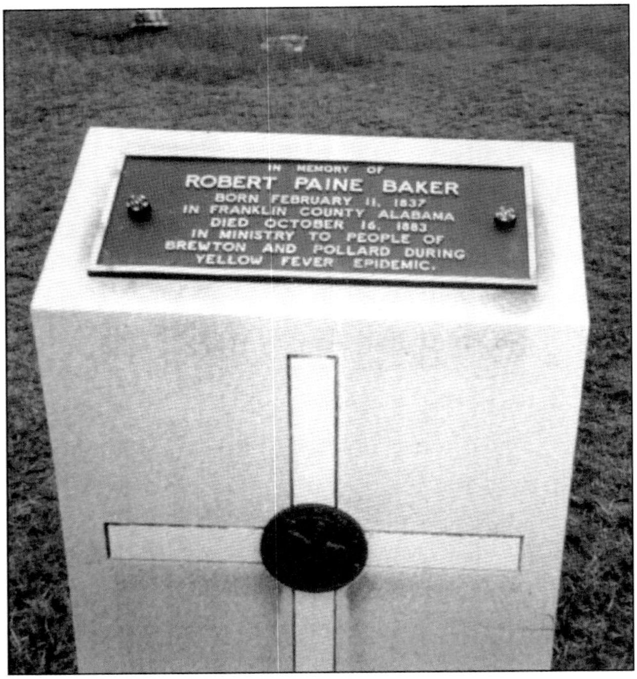

A monument was placed in Pilgrims Rest Cemetery to honor the Reverend Robert Payne Baker, who worked tirelessly to help yellow fever victims. He worked to tend the sick and caught the disease himself. It was a dark time in the history of the area. In just a few months in the late summer and early fall, 28 people died and 42 had the disease but recovered. The town was quarantined, and people had no one to help. Some who died left loved ones who were near death too. Those who were not ill evacuated the town and moved to a campsite nearby. With the coming of cooler weather, the number of those dying began to drop.

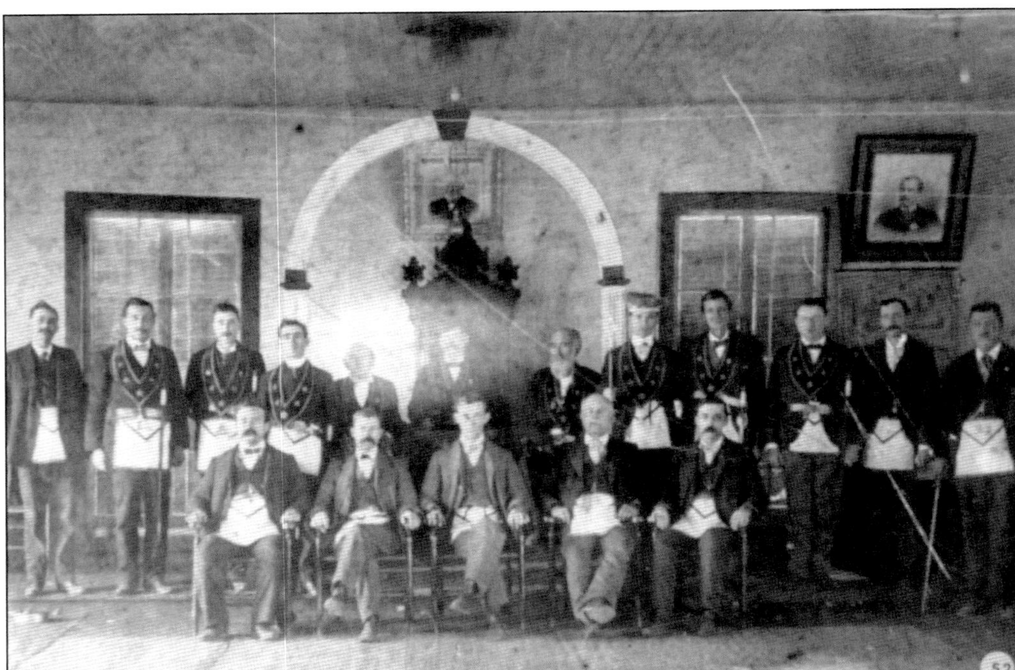

Norris Lodge 301, the local group of Masons, was organized many years ago. Today, the lodge is still very active in Brewton. They still meet in the Masonic lodge located on Belleville Avenue in downtown Brewton. (Courtesy of Charles Blair.)

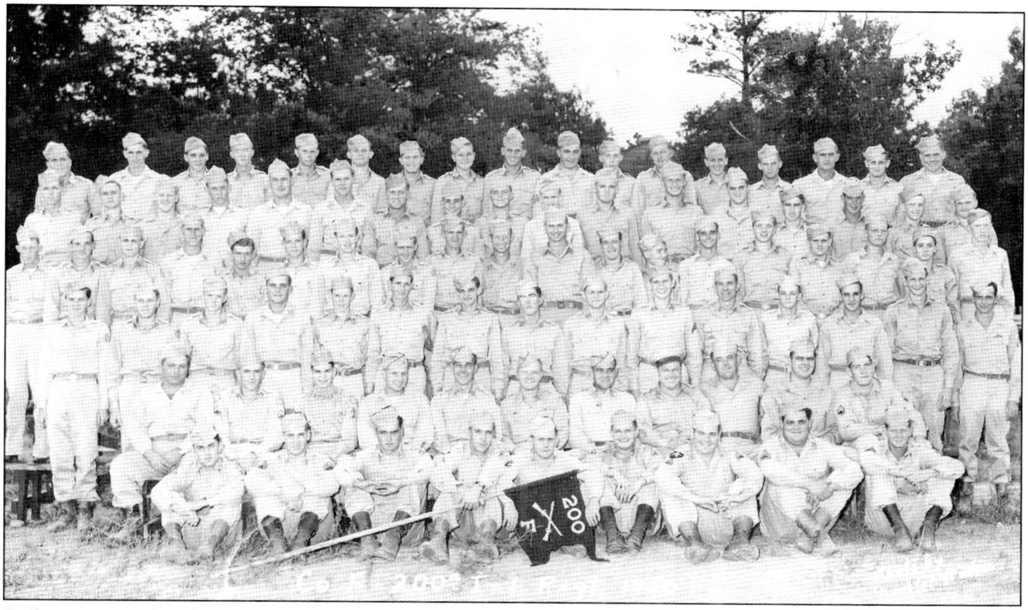

In January 1951, this group of young men of the Alabama National Guard was mobilized during the Korean War. They left Brewton and traveled to Fort Jackson in South Carolina. Many of them never actually went to Korea but about 20 of them did. Only one soldier in this unit did not make it back; Don Bryant was shot by a sniper. Today, the local National Guard armory is named after Bryant. (Courtesy of Charles Blair.)

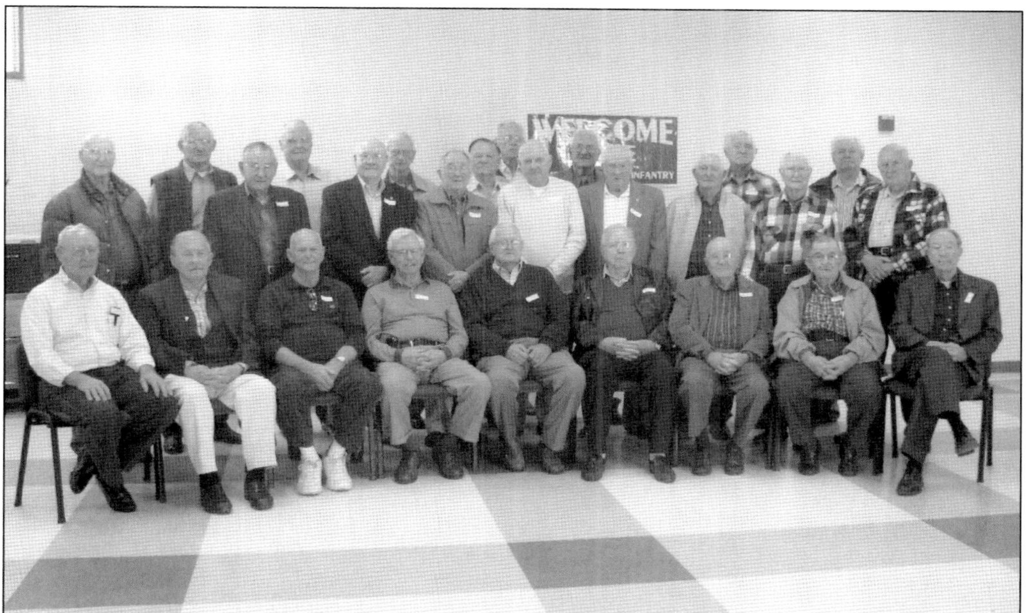

This group of the 1951 National Guard met in Brewton in January 2011 to celebrate the 60th reunion. The unit members had left their homes and families to answer the call to duty. This reunion turned out to be a success, and the men hope to get together again. Many stories were told and enjoyed about those days so long ago. (Courtesy of the *Brewton Standard*.)

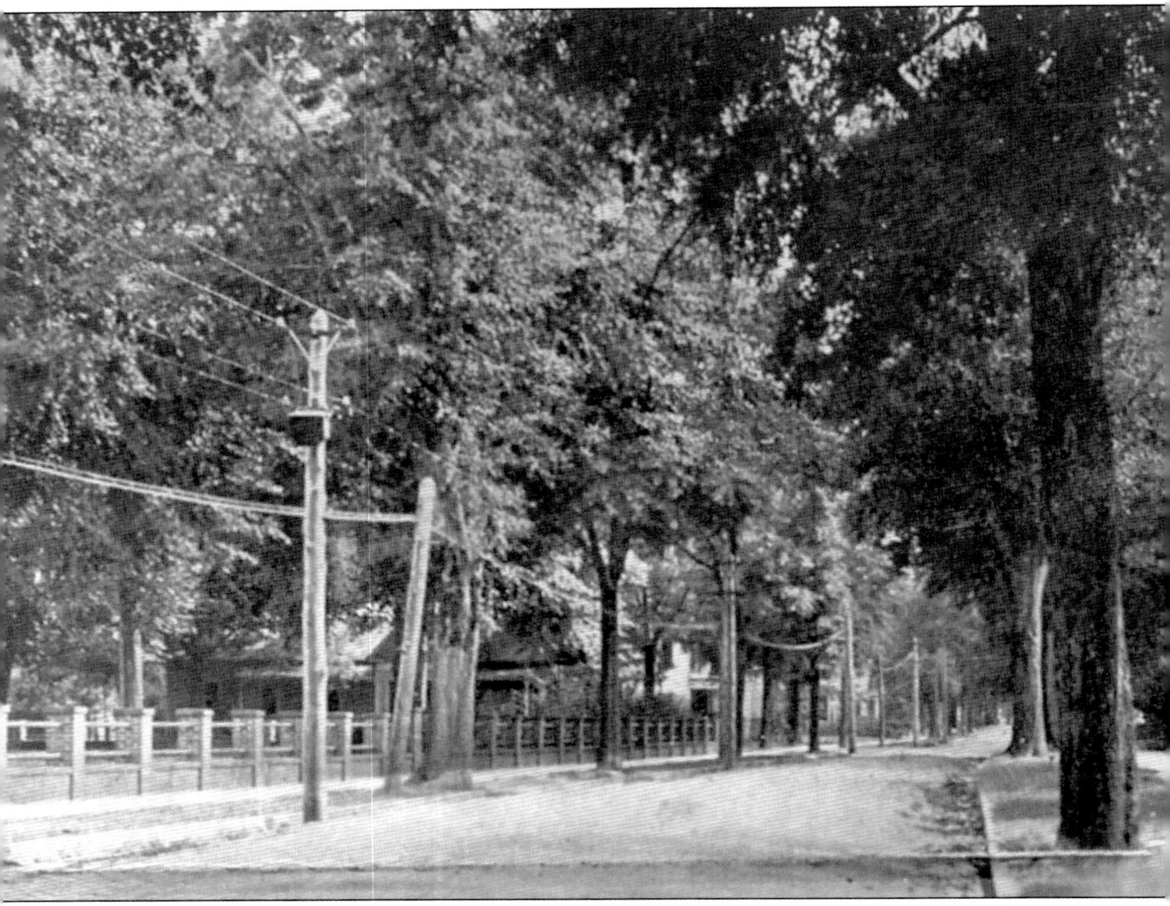

This is an early photograph of Belleville Avenue, which at the time was known as Parker Avenue. Notice the unpaved street. The photograph was taken about 1910, and the downtown streets were not paved until about 1924. It was not unusual to see animals and children in the streets, as they were the best place to play. Animals were allowed to roam in the streets. (Courtesy of Yancey Lovelace.)

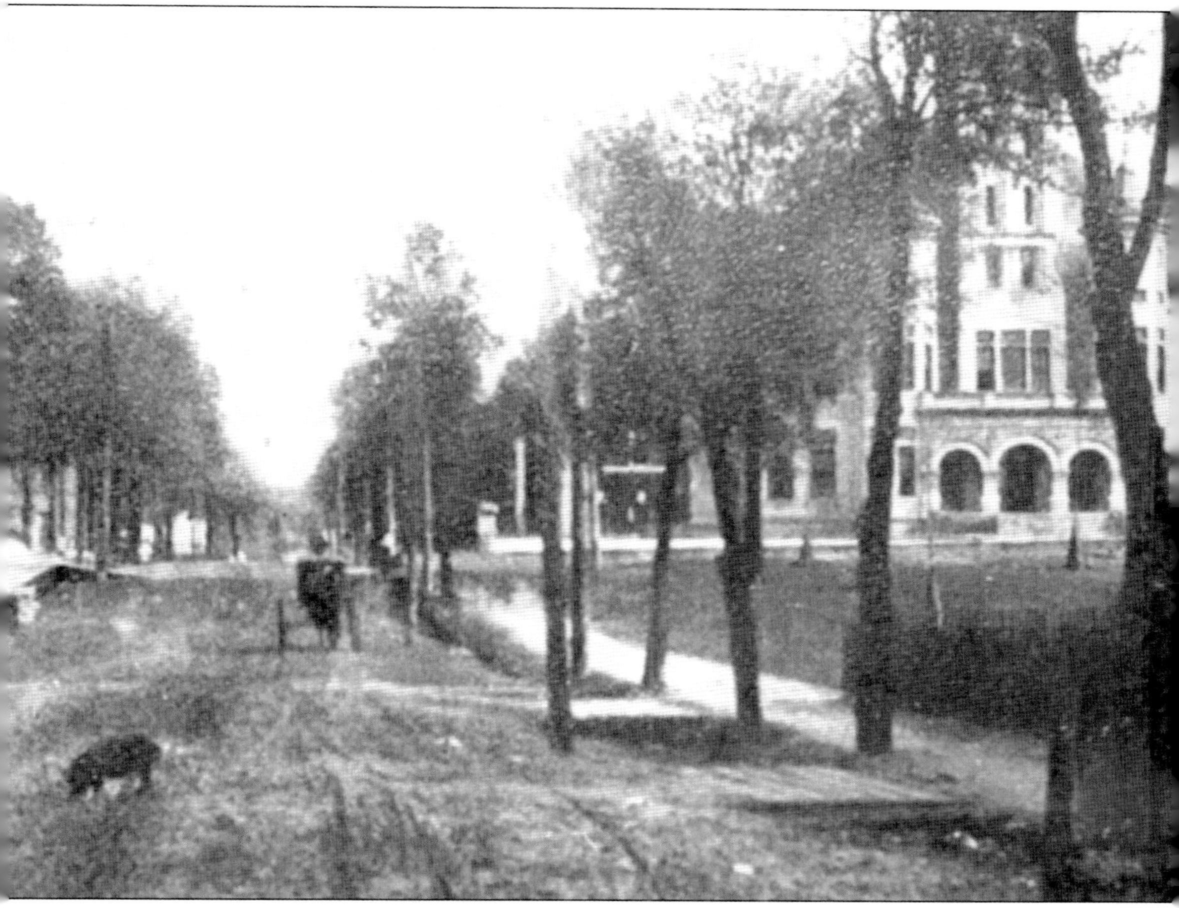

This is another photograph of Belleville Avenue. Notice the presence of the pig in the street. At the time, there were no laws against livestock running wild in the street. As the city has grown, those laws have of course changed. Brewton has some rather comical laws on the books, but the majority of them are based on actual events. There is one stipulation that says it is against the law to drive a motorboat down the street. This may sound silly, but the law was based on the fact that it was believed a motorboat caused a backwash that broke store windows during a flood. (Courtesy of Yancey Lovelace.)

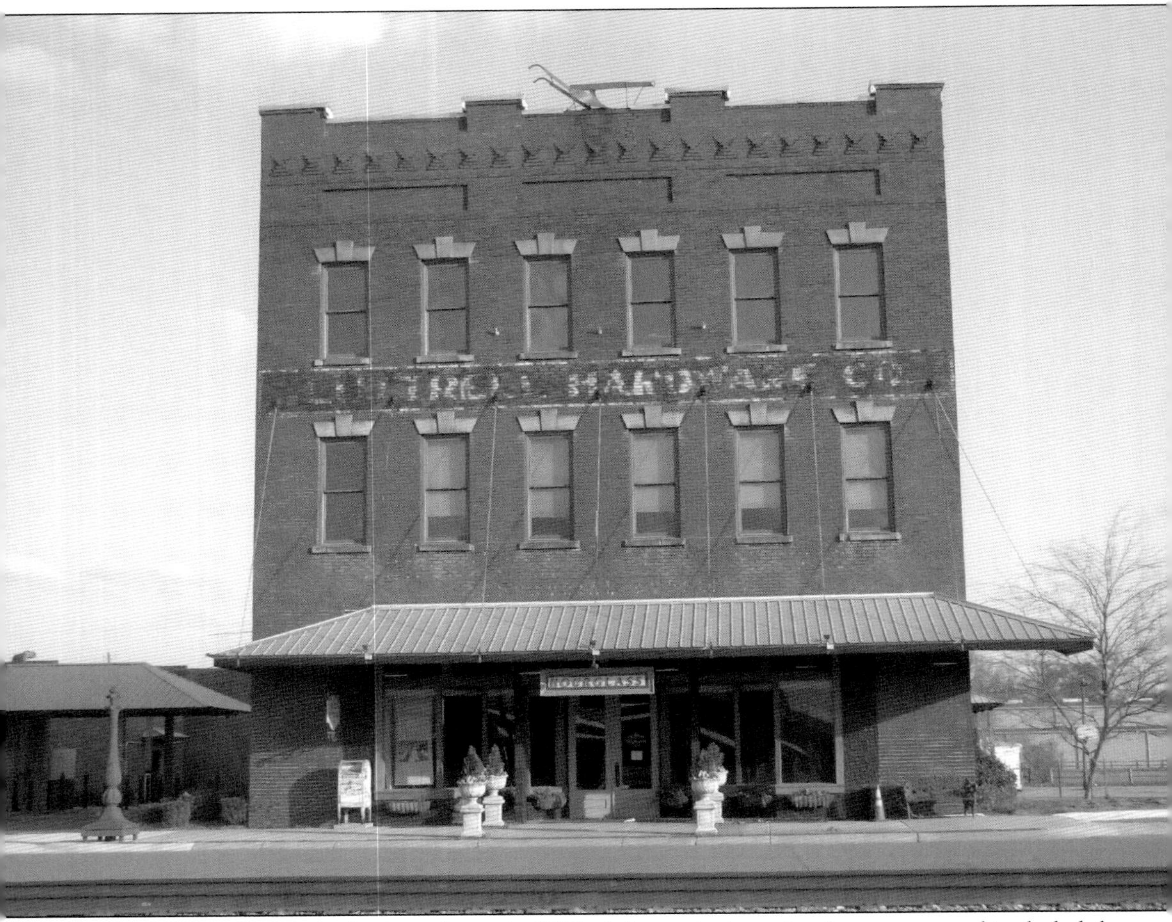

Luttrell Hardware was built in the early 1900s. It housed a large hardware store and included the space where coffins were stored until needed. When Brewton was part of the Alabama-Florida AAA baseball team, some of the players were housed in this building. It became the Pensacola Mill Supply later on, and today it belongs to Terrence and Becki Breckenridge. They used it as an antique store, and today it is used by the Breckenridges for special events. Note the plow on top of the building. It has been up there since the start of the business. (Courtesy of Barbara Carden.)

Two

Church and Faith

Brewton and East Brewton have many churches of many different denominations that live in harmony. Most of them are Methodist and Baptist, but there are plenty of others. Around 1854, the original Pilgrims Rest on Alco Drive was organized in the Alco area. In 1878, some members began to talk of moving into downtown Brewton. This brought about a problem that resulted into a split in the church. Some members built the First Baptist Church of Brewton on Belleville Avenue near the Brewton Collegiate Institute. That church has grown. The other group of members of Pilgrims Rest moved north of Brewton and became North Brewton Baptist Church.

Brewton First United Methodist Church had its beginnings in 1879 in the downtown area but moved into a new building farther up Belleville Avenue about 1950. Perhaps one of the most recognized churches in Brewton is the building that was at one time the Universalist church. The first sanctuary was built in 1886, and the present structure took its place in 1896.

First Methodist Church in East Brewton was organized in 1906, while East Brewton First Baptist began its services in Taylor Hall, which was one of the buildings left from the old Downing Shofner Institute. Many others have followed, such as Baptist Hill Missionary Baptist Church, First and Second St. Siloam Baptist Churches, The Church of Jesus Christ of Latter-day Saints, several Church of Christ organizations, and others.

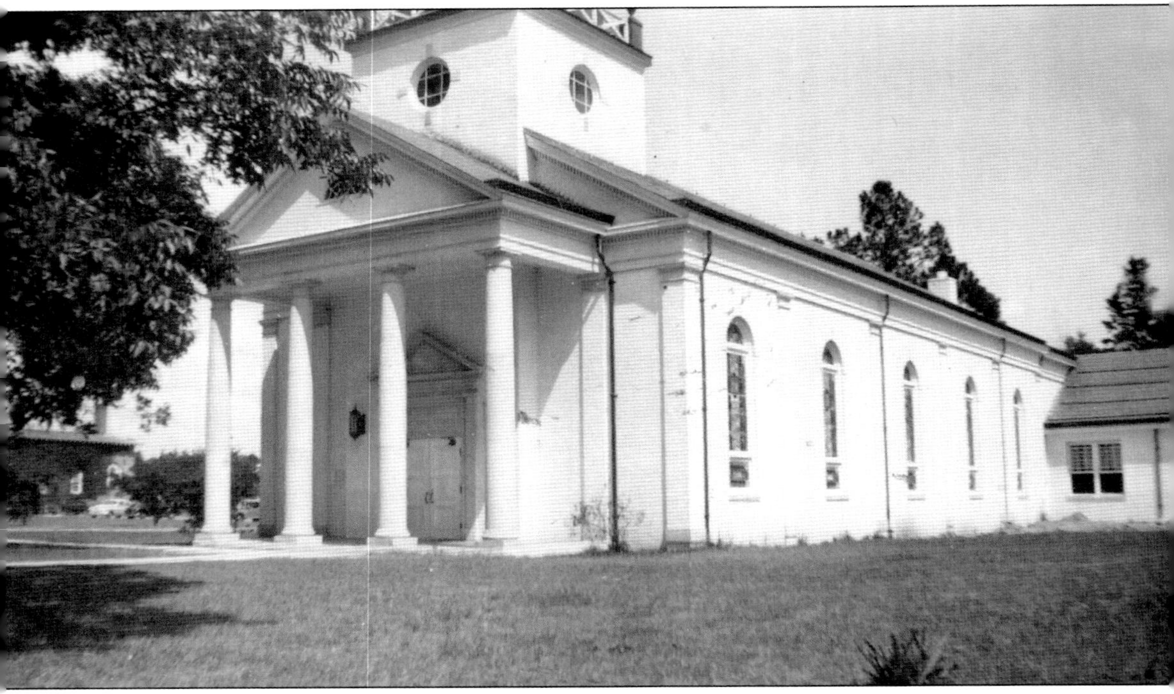

This building was constructed in 1949 as the First United Methodist Church of Brewton sanctuary. The first service was held here in January 1950. The church was originally located in downtown Brewton in a flood zone, but this site, at the corner of Underwood Street and Belleville Avenue, was well out of the flood zone, and there was space to expand. The church suffered a fire in 1961 that destroyed much of the sanctuary, including the pulpit, organ, and altar. A ground-breaking ceremony took place in 1964 to mark additional building. Today, the church has classrooms, office space, a fellowship hall, and a kitchen. (Courtesy of Robert Crenshaw.)

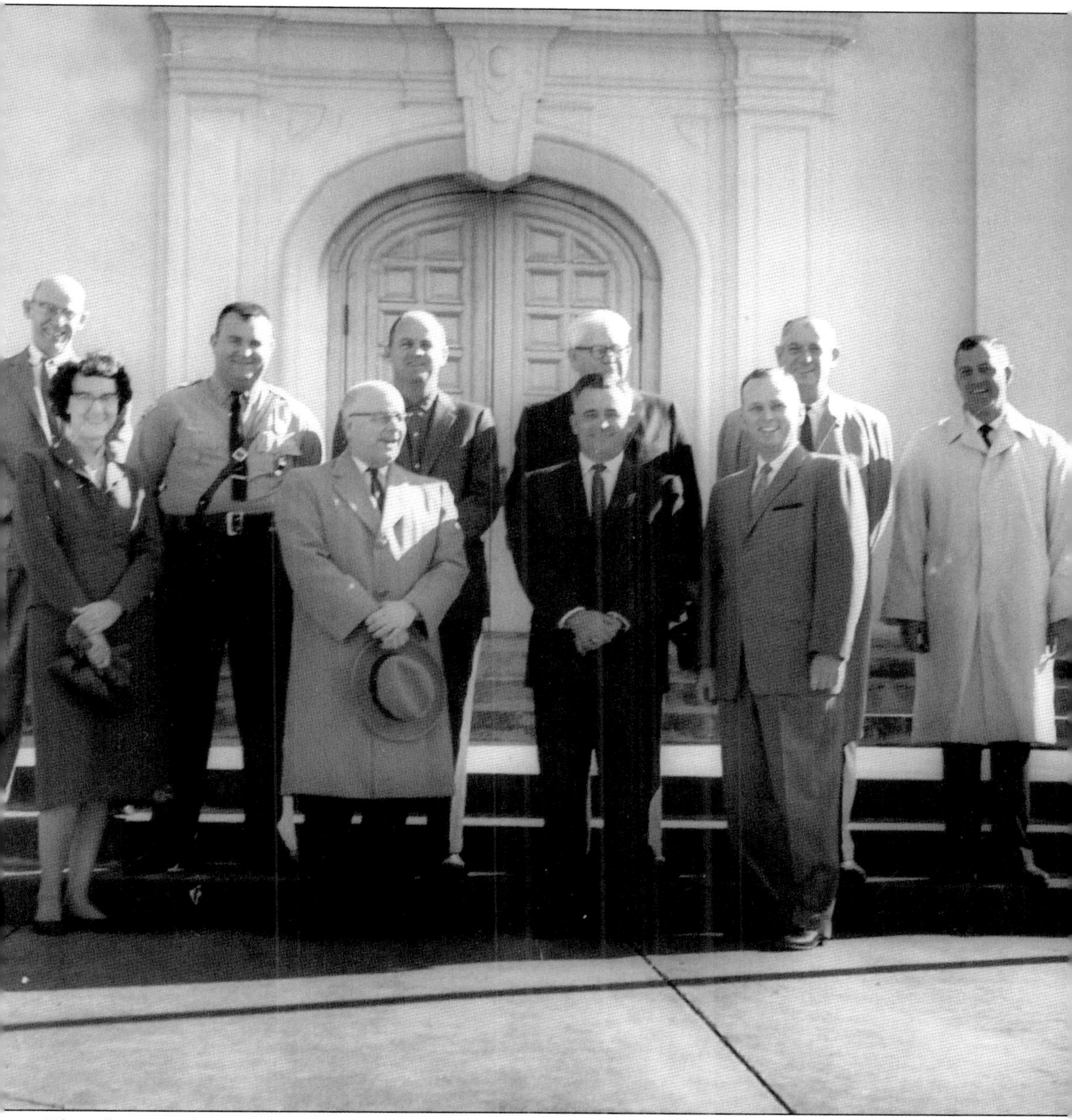

This photograph was taken on the front steps of First Presbyterian Church of Brewton on Belleville Avenue. The reason for the photograph is unknown, and the subjects were not all members of the church. The church has unique design features that give it a decidedly old-world look. It was built of brick and stucco on the corner of Belleville Avenue in 1924 on property donated by W.T. Neal. The only identified people in the photograph are (front row, from left to right) Hazel Byrd, Philip "Pop" May, and Lee Otts. (Courtesy of Robert Crenshaw.)

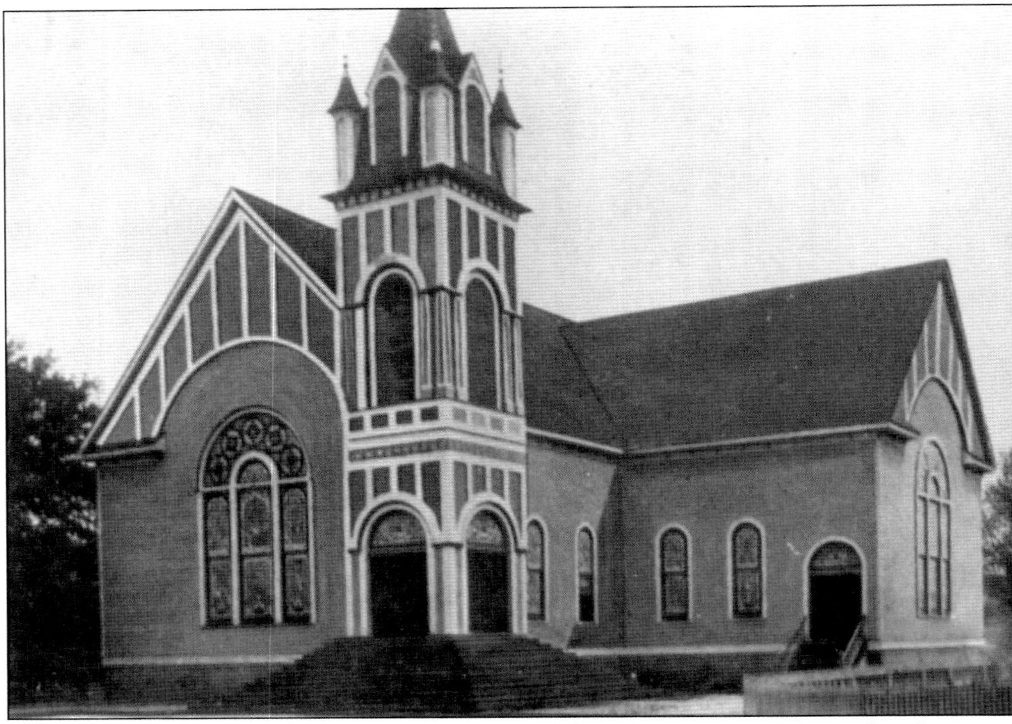

First Baptist Church of Brewton was built on Belleville Avenue in 1911. It burned to the ground in 1912, and another building took its place. Today, it is known as Bell Chapel and is used as a part of the current church, which was built in 1966. (Courtesy of Robert Crenshaw.)

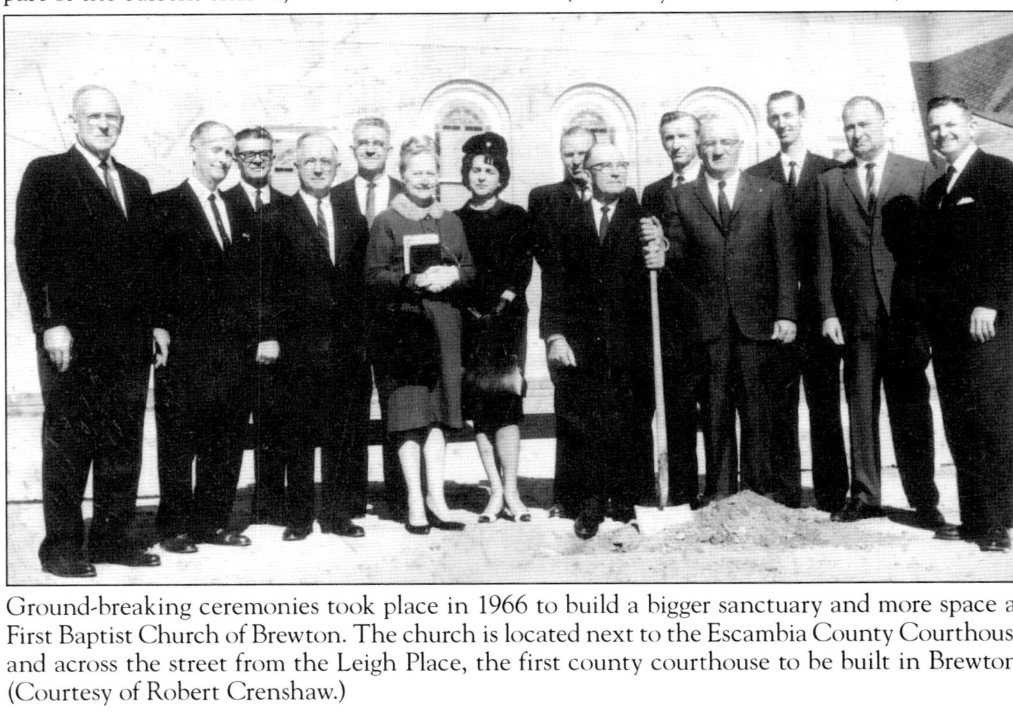

Ground-breaking ceremonies took place in 1966 to build a bigger sanctuary and more space at First Baptist Church of Brewton. The church is located next to the Escambia County Courthouse and across the street from the Leigh Place, the first county courthouse to be built in Brewton. (Courtesy of Robert Crenshaw.)

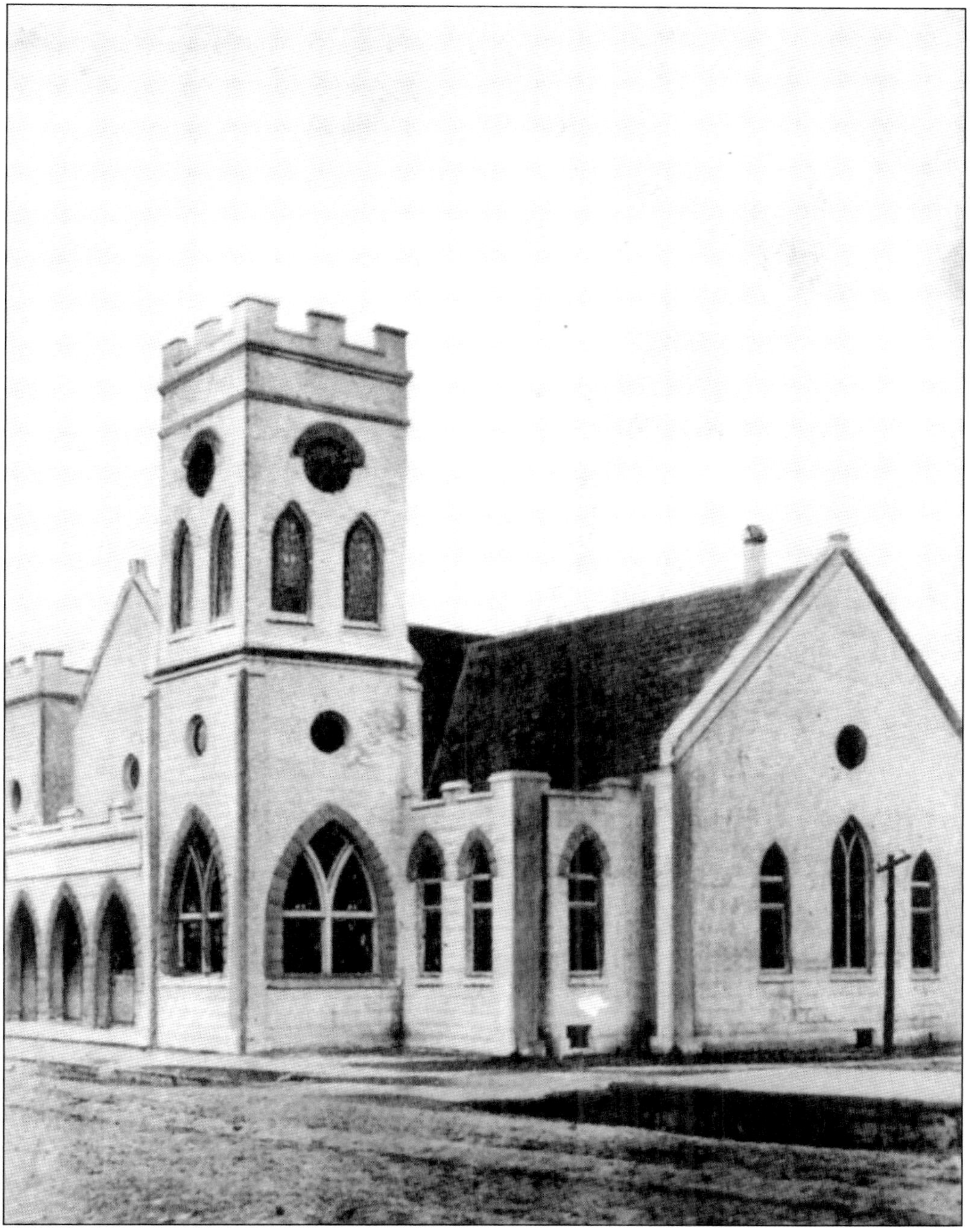

The First United Methodist Church of Brewton was first located in downtown Brewton in a flood zone. A lot was bought from J.W. and Mildred Coleman, whose family had originally owned the property the Lovelace Hotel was built on. In fact, there was a hotel there earlier that was known as the Coleman Hotel. After suffering through many floods, the church was moved north on Belleville Avenue.

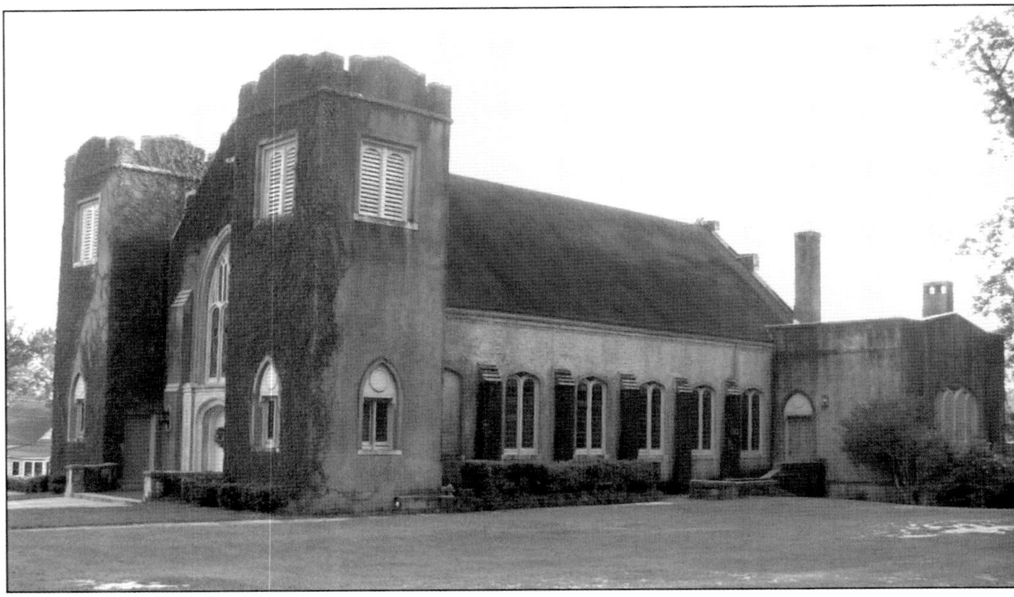

The Universalist church was built on the corner of Belleville Avenue and Blacksher Street. It has an old-world feeling, with ivy climbing the walls of the beautiful building. This photograph was taken of the north side of the church, which was built in 1896 on the site of an earlier wood structure.

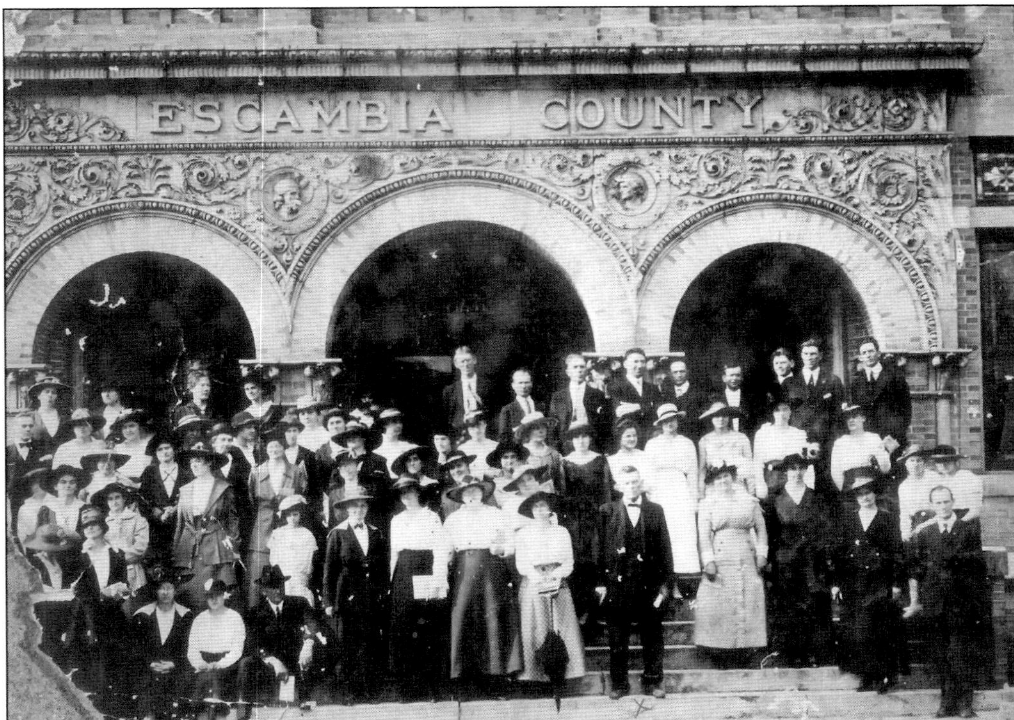

This early photograph of the Escambia County Courthouse must have been taken when the courthouse was first built or shortly thereafter, judging by the clothing worn by the people. (Courtesy of the Escambia County Historical Society.)

First United Methodist Church in East Brewton is more than 100 years old. This photograph was taken of the church in the early days. The church, now bricked and refurbished, is still used by the congregation. Members met on the occasion of the 100th anniversary and held a celebration in honor of the church. A new church was later built nearby, but the original is still used by the congregation. (Courtesy of the *Brewton Standard*.)

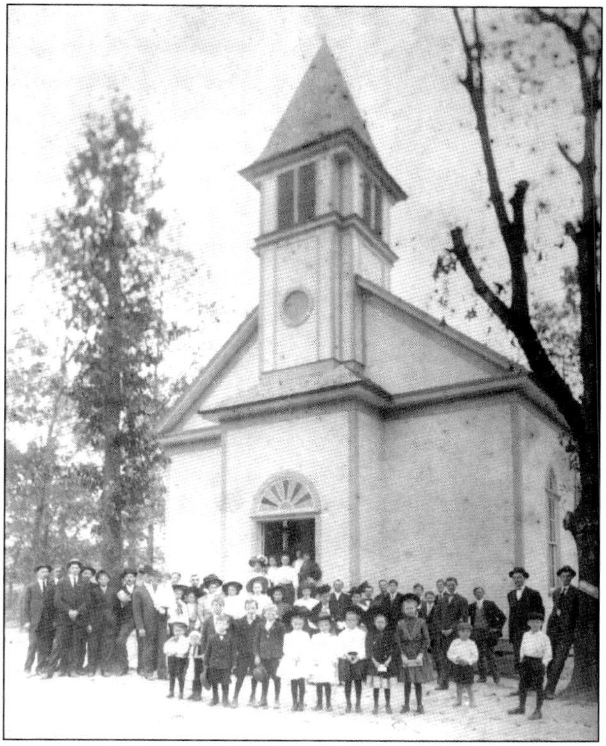

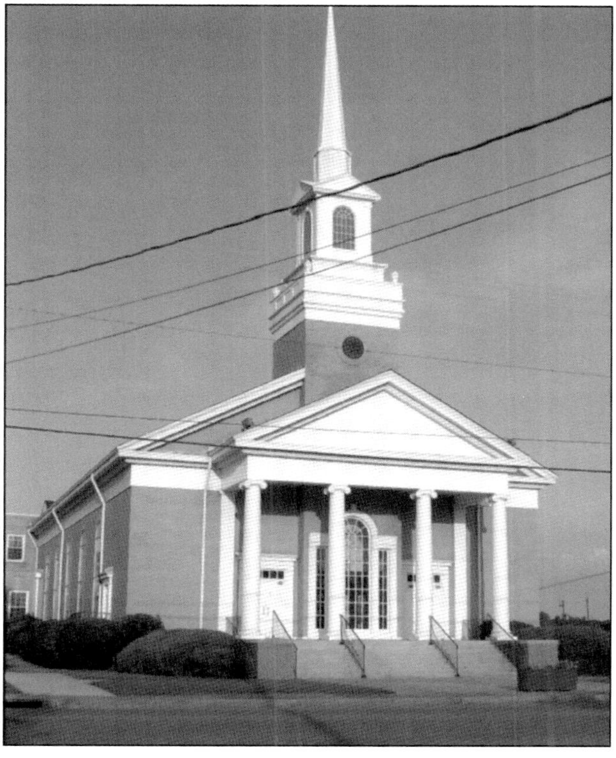

First Baptist Church of Brewton had its beginnings in Alco in 1854 and was known as Pilgrim's Rest. In the late 1880s, some of the congregation wanted to move into Brewton, while some did not. The church split with one group building on Belleville Avenue (First Baptist Church of Brewton) and the other group started North Brewton Baptist Church. Today, both churches enjoy a large membership.

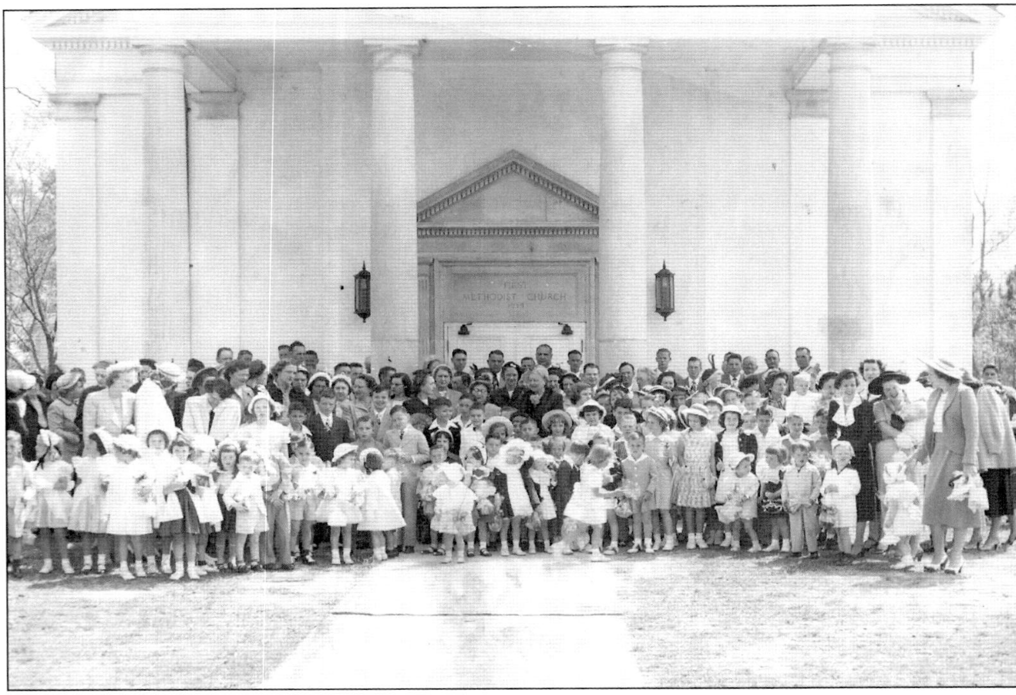

Church members gather at First United Methodist Church of Brewton in 1951 to celebrate some occasion. (Courtesy of Robert Crenshaw.)

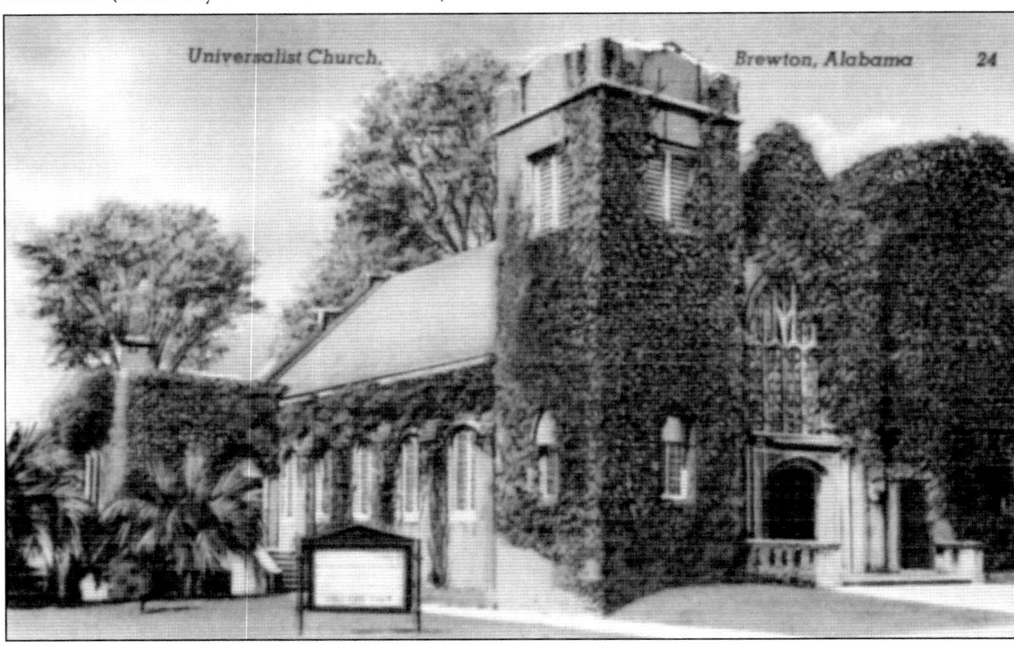

This was the Universalist church built in 1886. It is no longer used by the Universalist congregation, but today it is being utilized by the members of the Cornerstone Community Church. This church has old-world beauty and charm, from its ivy-covered walls to the stained glass window and the use of beautiful wood on the inside.

Three

City and County Government

Both Brewton and East Brewton operate with a mayor and city council, all of them elected by the residents of the two towns. Brewton City Hall once was located on the second floor of the building later occupied by Western Auto. The first floor was used by the fire department. In 1939, a new city hall was built with the help of the Works Progress Administration. It housed the police department as well as other offices. The building is today Hope Place, where several services are offered to the public. Today, the old National Guard armory, located next to Alabama Power, houses the services offered by the city. Brewton Fire Department is located on St. Nicholas Avenue next to the city barn. East Brewton's first city hall was located about where the car wash is on Forrest Avenue. That building came down and was replaced by a new brick building, which was later also torn down, and a new and modern facility is located farther down Forrest Avenue. It houses the city clerk, police department, and a city courtroom.

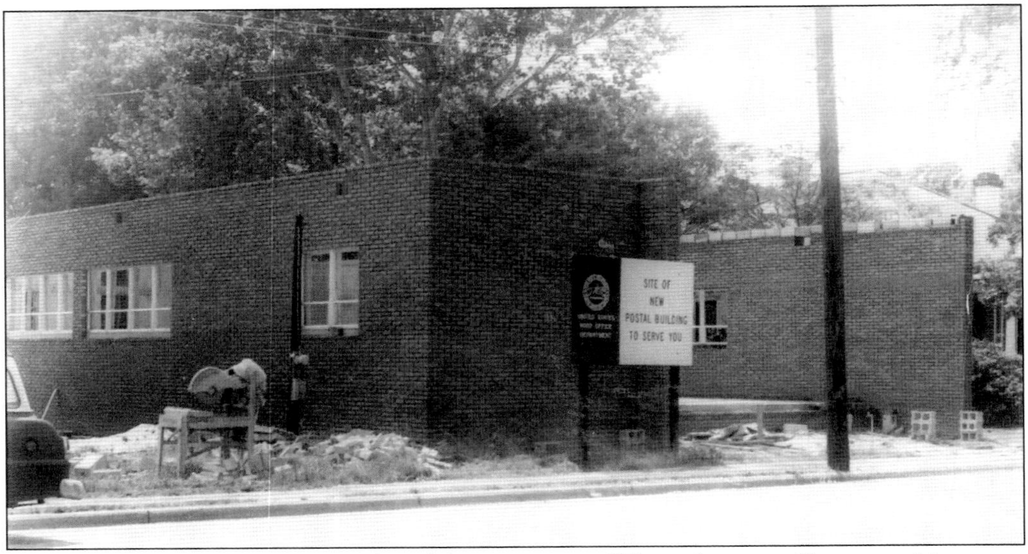

This was built as a post office and used for some years. When the post office moved into new quarters a little north on Belleville Avenue, the Escambia County School Board took over the building, and it is still there today. (Courtesy of Robert Crenshaw.)

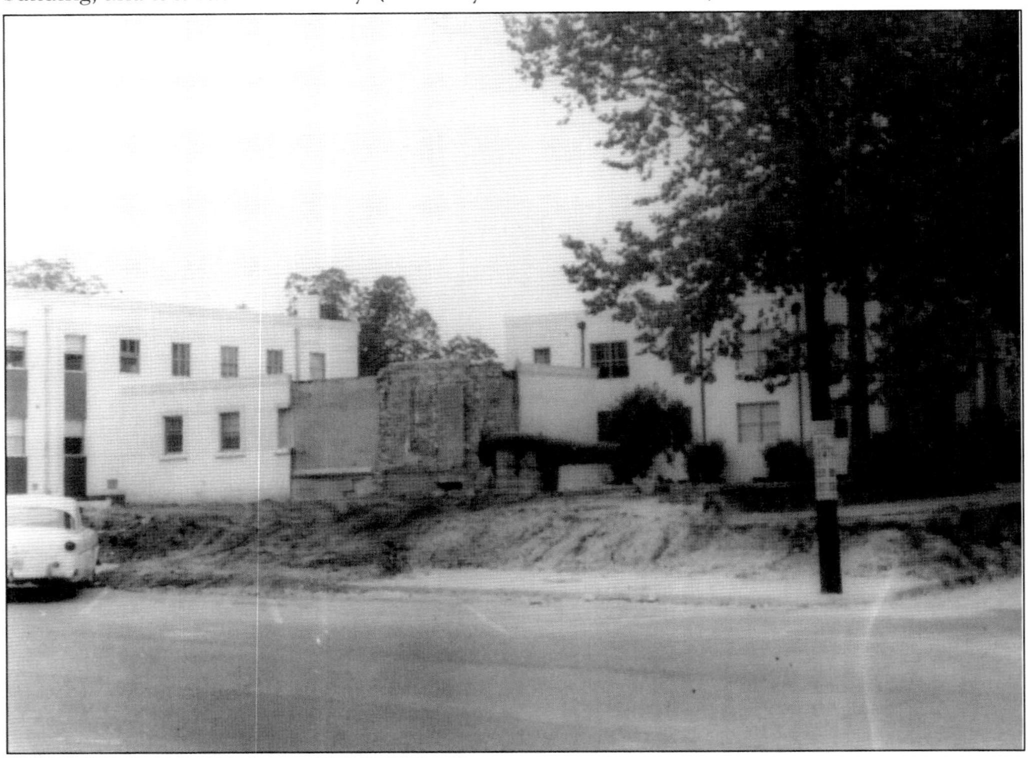

The second courthouse building to stand on this site was opened in 1960. In this photograph, there is still some construction going on. This is the current courthouse in use today. A part of the old courthouse was left and incorporated into the one that opened in 1960. (Courtesy of Robert Crenshaw.)

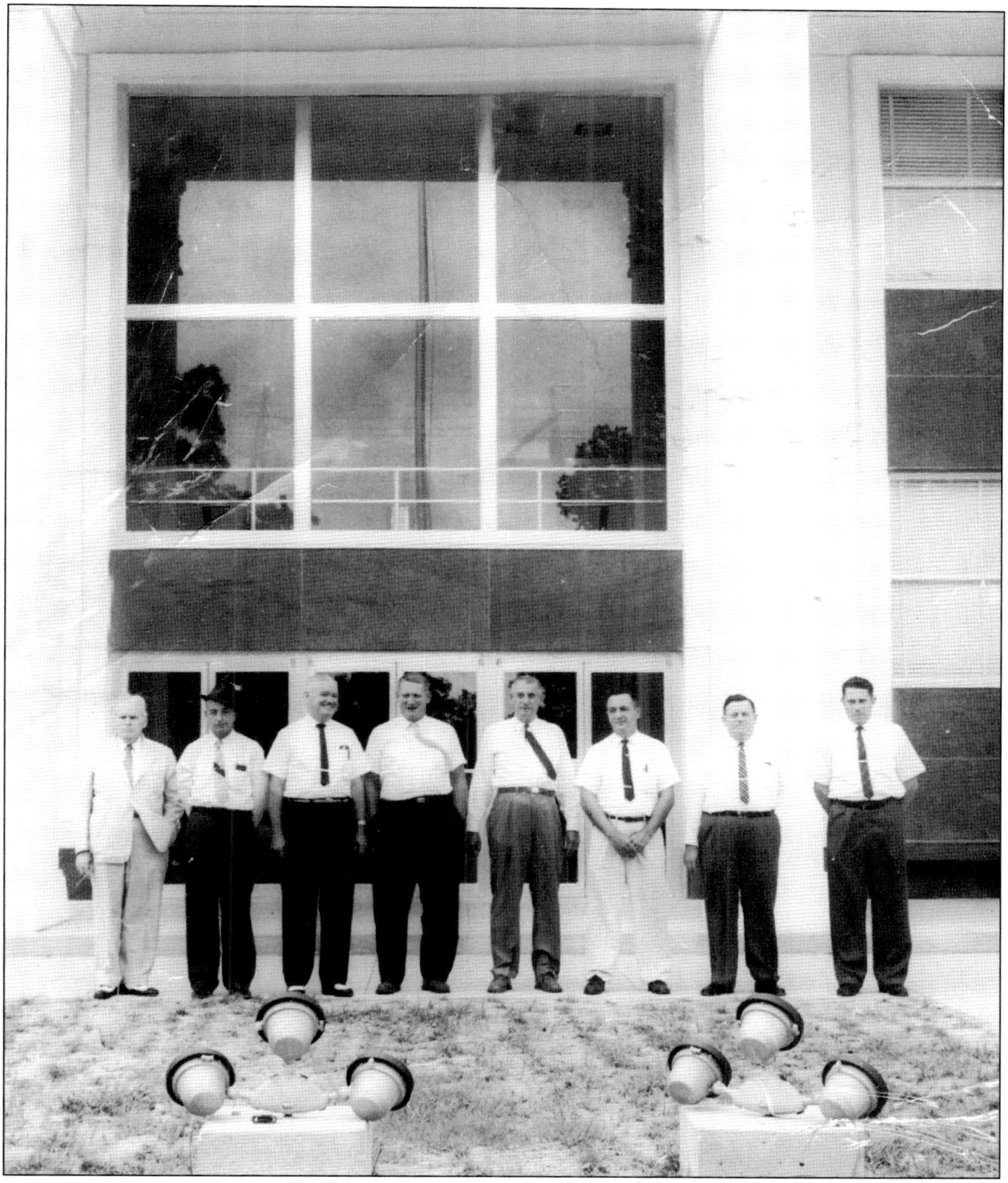

When the new courthouse opened in 1960, county officials posed in front of the building. They are, from left to right, Judge Archie Elliott, Harry Weaver, Skim Horton, Red Vickery, Reo Kirkland, Roy Stokes, Brooks White, and G.S. "Scotty" Byrne. (Courtesy of Robert Crenshaw.)

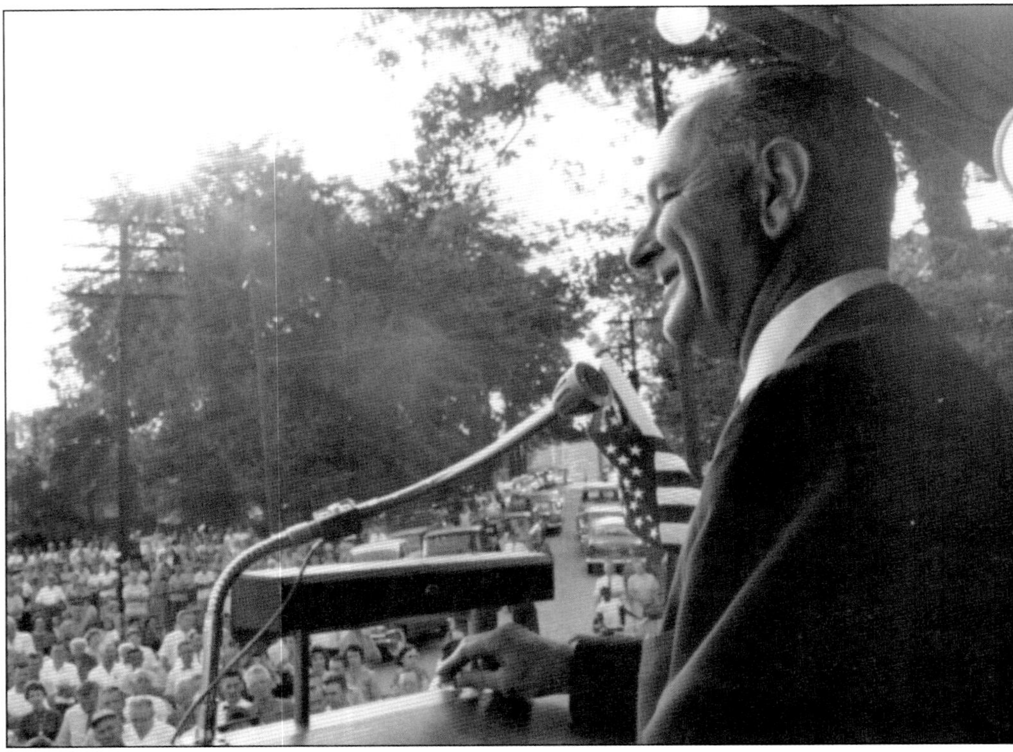

Pres. Lyndon B. Johnson made a stop as he passed through Brewton by train. The time frame is not known, and it was probably an unannounced visit. This was when the passenger train used to stop to take on passengers or to drop them off. (Courtesy of Robert Crenshaw.)

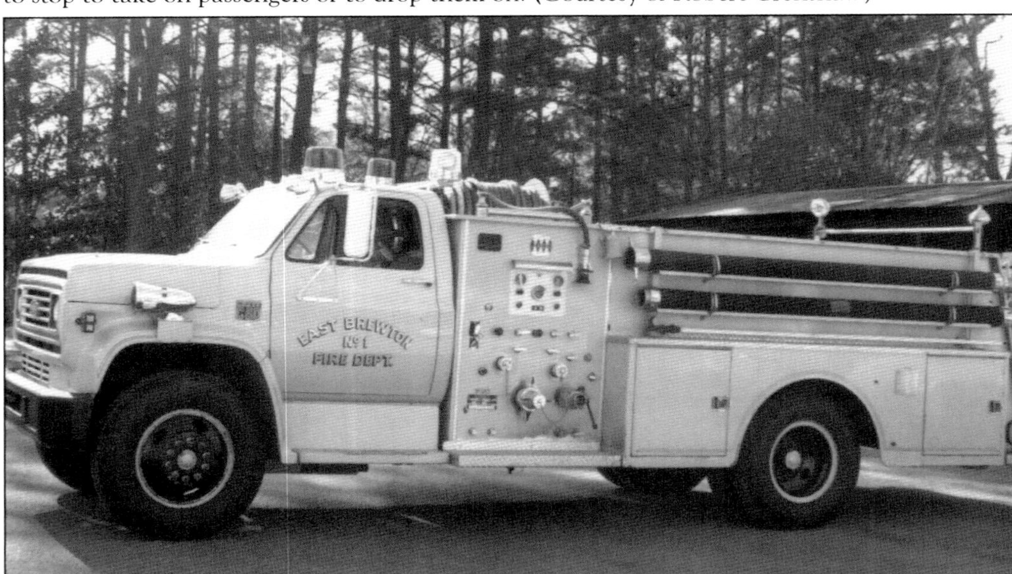

East Brewton Fire Department is run with mostly volunteers, and they were very proud to have this fire truck. The fire department may not be large, but the dedicated men and women who give their time are a credit to the city. (Courtesy of the *Brewton Standard*.)

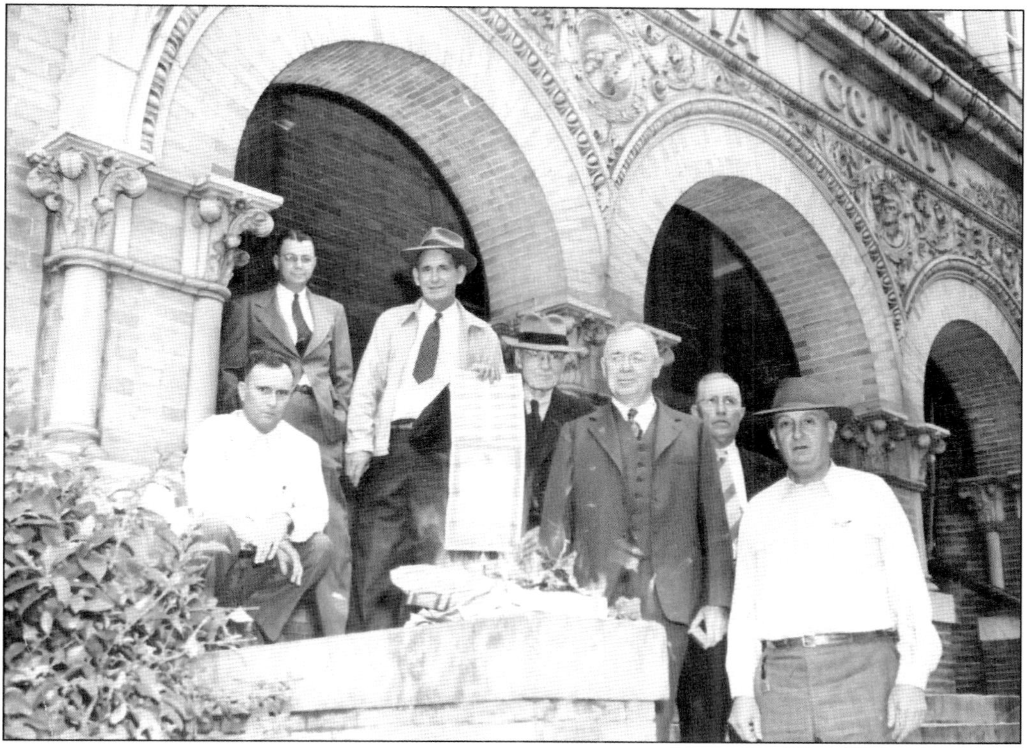

This group of men is standing on the steps of the south side of the Escambia County Courthouse that was built in 1902 and torn down in 1960. They are not named but would have been some of the residents of the county. (Courtesy of Robert Crenshaw.)

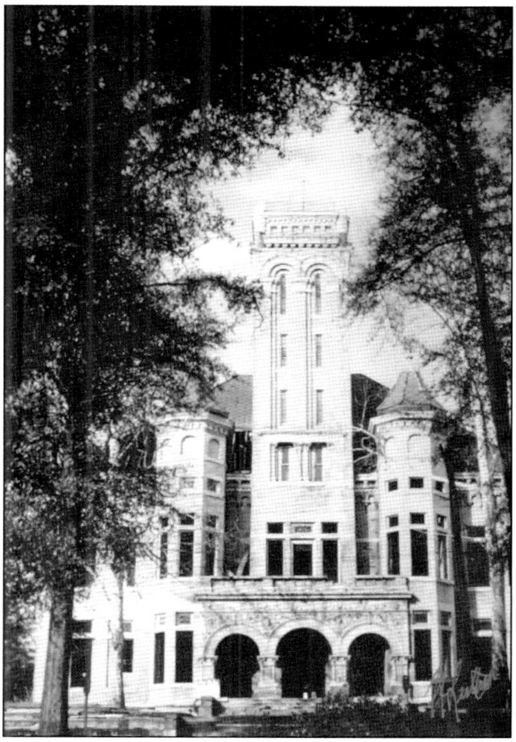

This photograph of the Escambia County Courthouse (1902–1960) shows the entrance on Henderson Street. It was taken after the tower spire had been removed. This was the second courthouse to be built in Brewton. The current courthouse sits on the same site. In fact, a portion of the old courthouse was incorporated into the new one. (Courtesy of Scott Hillman.)

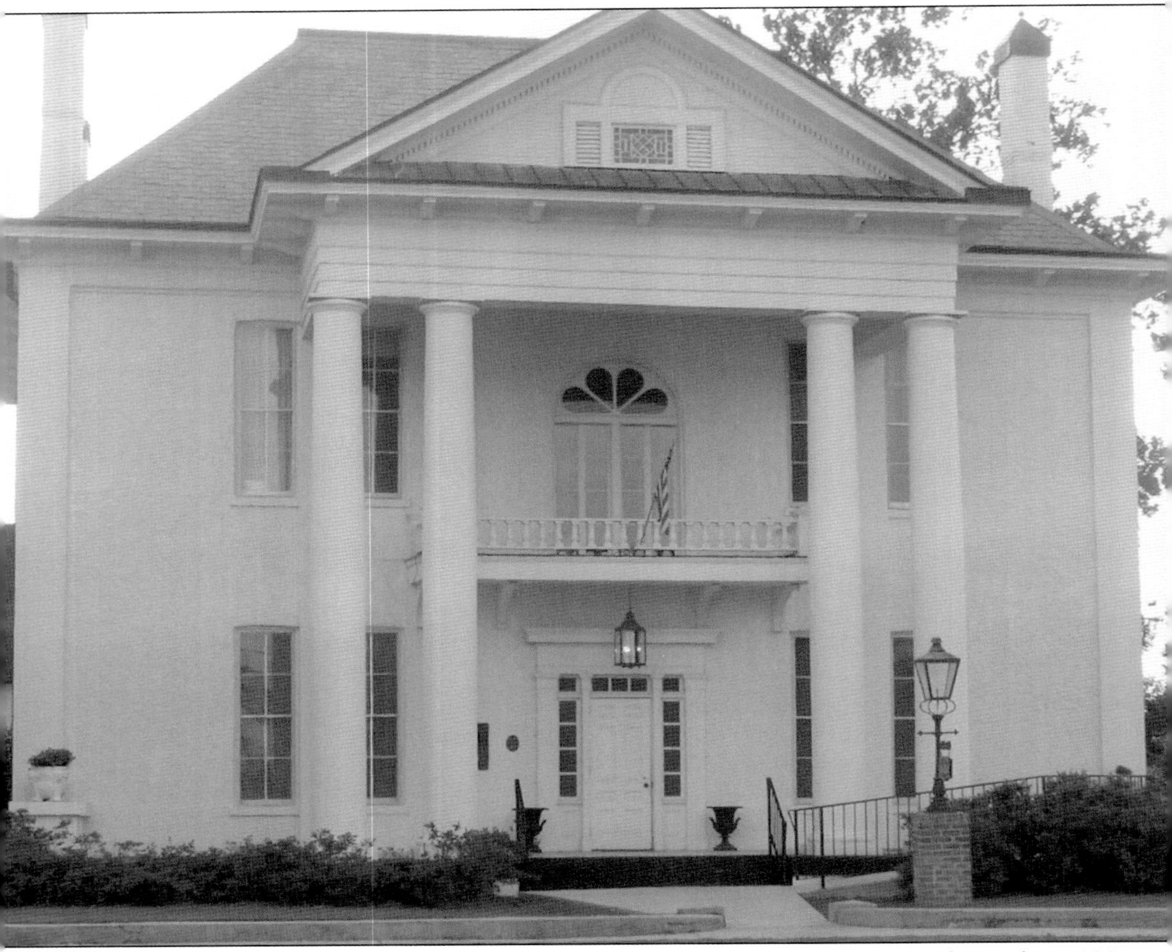

Leigh Place is pictured as it looks today—not bad for a building that was condemned in 1900. It served as the first courthouse after the county seat was moved to Brewton from Pollard. The move was not a happy one. There was much talk between those who voiced their opinion about the county seat relocation. It got so bad that a couple of good stories came out of it. It was called a regular cat fight by the newspapers, so the people of Pollard supposedly loaded a rail car with stray cats and shipped it to Brewton. On the other hand, those from Brewton went down to Pollard and stole the record books. It is said that they left Pollard in such a hurry that some county record books were dropped along the way.

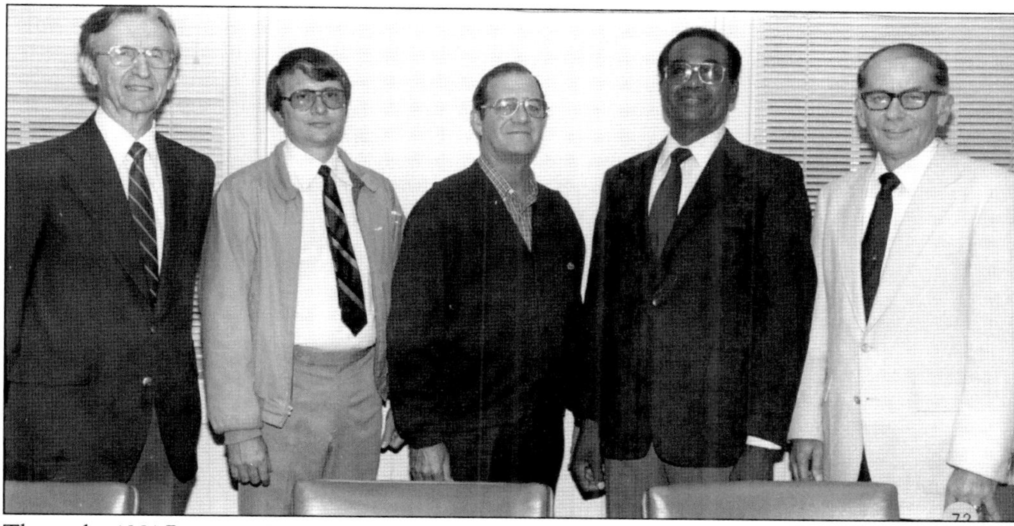

This is the 1981 Brewton City Council. Pictured from left to right are Bryars Byrd, John Gleaton, Gene Hudson, unidentified, and Mayor Ray Sherrer. (Courtesy of the Escambia County Commission.)

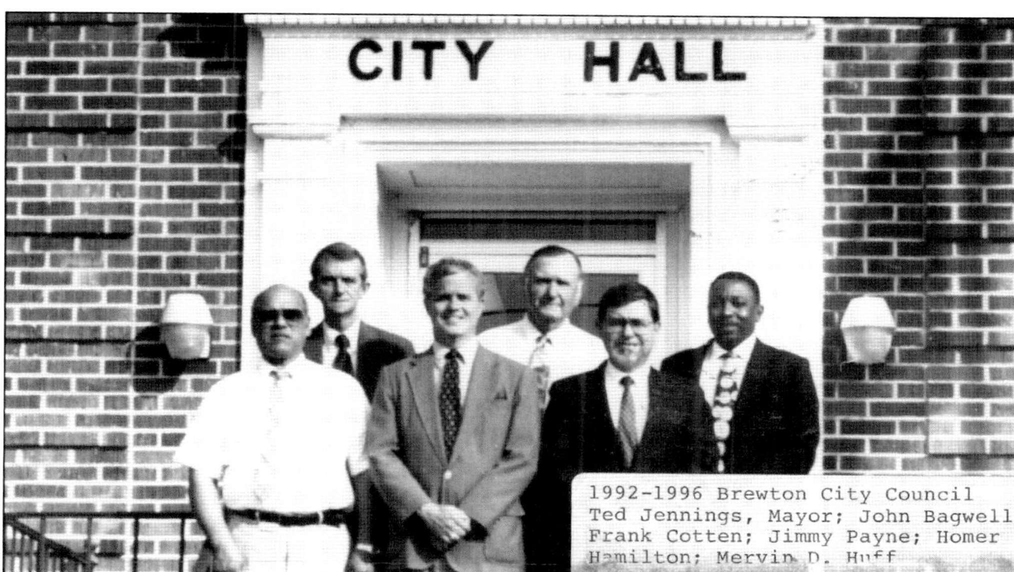

The 1992 Brewton City Council members are, from left to right, Jimmy Payne, Frank Cotten, Mayor Ted Jennings, Mervin Huff, John Bagwell, and Homer Hamilton. (Courtesy of the Escambia County Commission.)

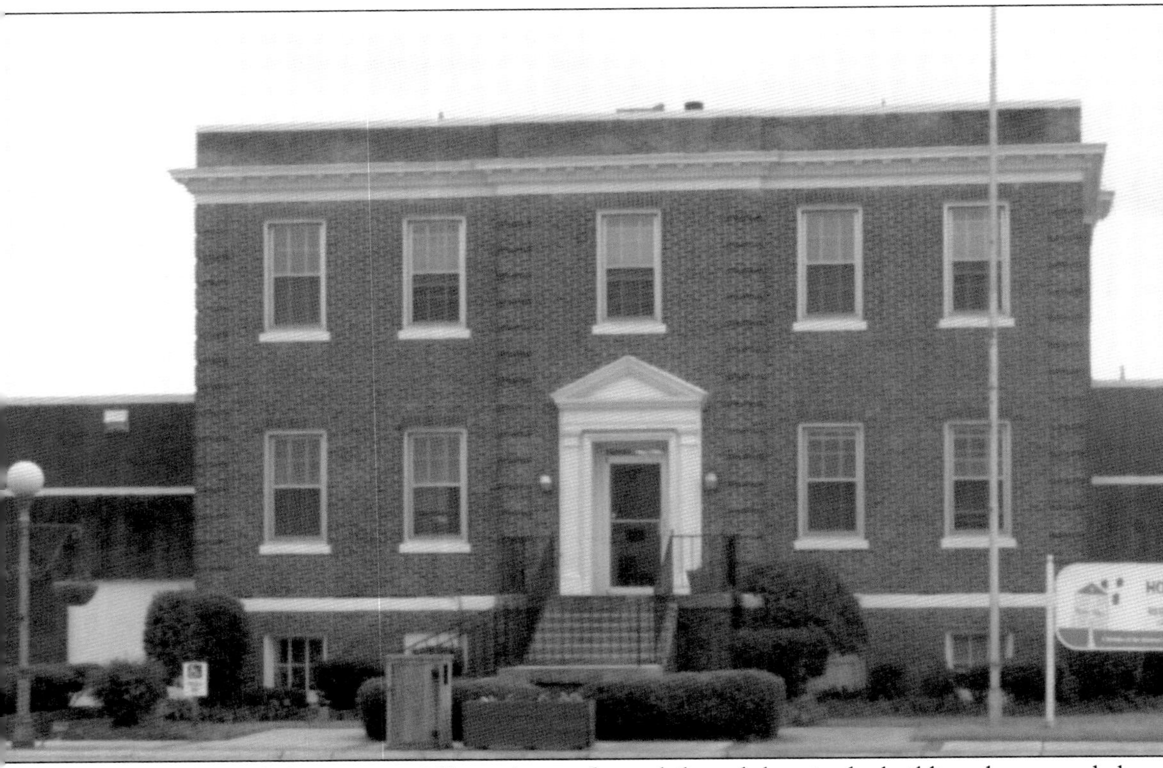

Brewton's city fathers met in different homes for a while and then in the building that preceded Western Auto on the corner of St. Joseph Avenue and Mildred Street. In 1939, with the help of the WPA, this city hall was built, and the city offices did business there for many years. Later, the old National Guard armory on Douglas Avenue was converted to become the present city hall. (Courtesy of Escambia County Commission.)

Four

Education, Backbone of Future

Brewton has its own city school systems, while the schools in East Brewton are part of the Escambia County School System.

Education in Brewton began in small buildings and made the big move to Brewton Collegiate Institute, which opened in 1886. It housed all grades to begin with, but in 1925, the high school moved to a three-story building that was located on the Belleville side of the same lot where the current Brewton Elementary School stands. In 1941, a new building for the elementary grades was built on the corner of Belleville Avenue and Underwood Street across the street from the three-story building. In 1970, after integration, the old Booker T. Washington School became the home of Brewton Middle School. In 1976, a new elementary school was built on the previous location of the campus of Miller High School. Today, a new middle school is under construction a couple of miles north of Brewton, giving students the space they need.

East Brewton schools were all named in honor of W.S. Neal, who was an advocate of education. The high school is on Andrew Jackson Street in East Brewton, and the middle school and the elementary school are both on Williamson Street.

Before integration, African American students attended Booker T. Washington School on Liles Boulevard and then Southern Normal School. Today, Southern Normal has been bought by Alabama State University and is used for various programs. Last but certainly not least is the location of an excellent community college in the Alco area that is the bridge between high school and a four-year college. Jefferson Davis Community College has a beautiful campus and is graduating students who are going on to great futures.

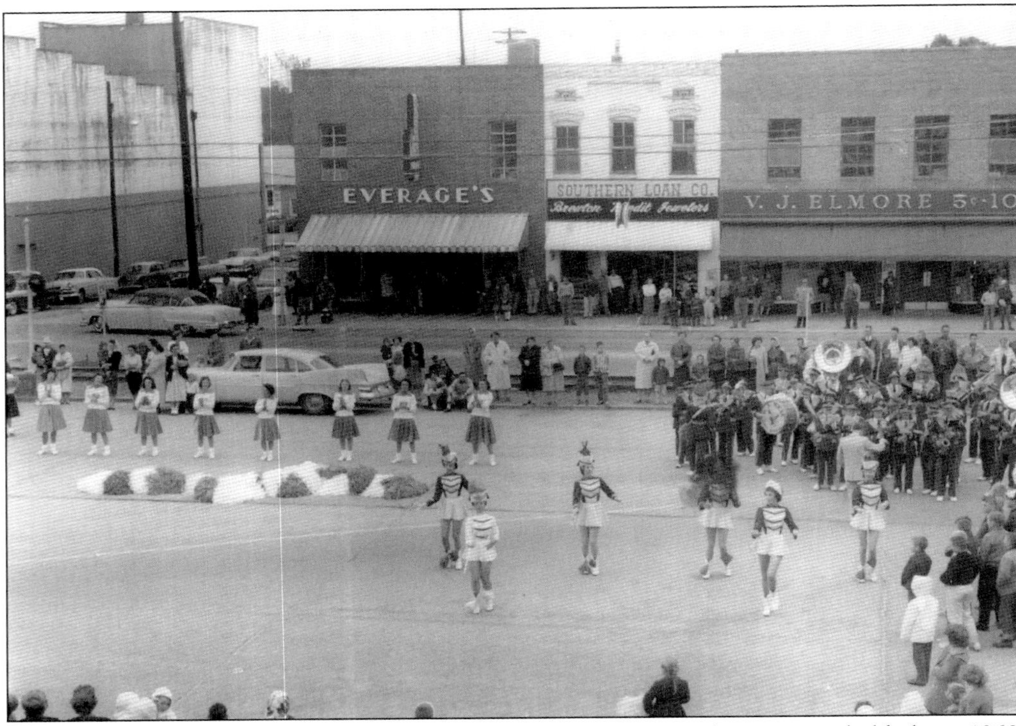

Brewton has several parades in downtown Brewton every year. This one was held about 1960, and the W.S. Neal Band is performing on the corner of the east side of St. Joseph Avenue and Mildred Street. (Courtesy of Robert Crenshaw.)

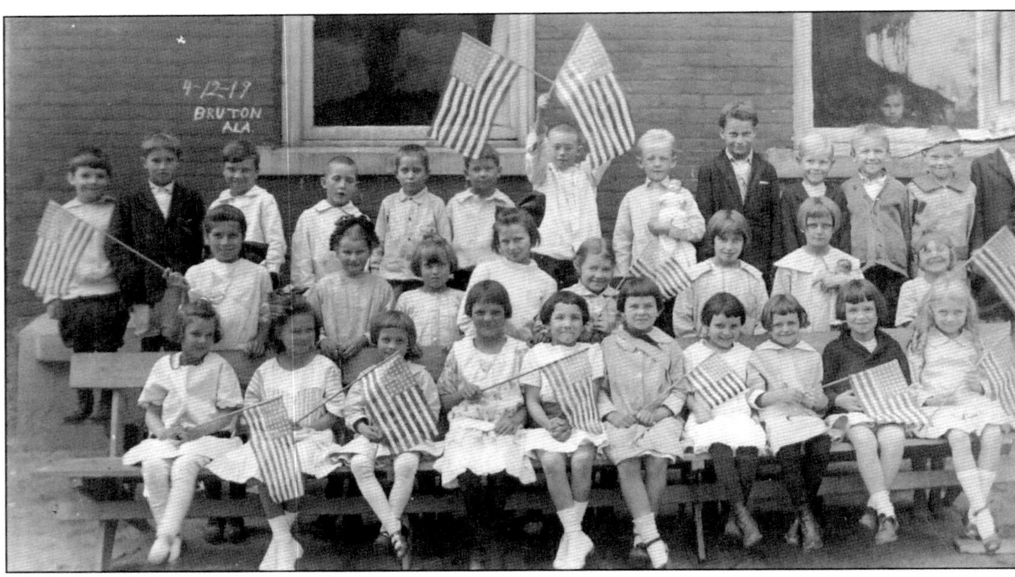

This group of children is pictured in front of the old Brewton Collegiate Institute (BCI) on April 12, 1917. BCI was a large building next to the courthouse. It opened its doors in 1886. It must have been a special day with all the flags the children are holding.

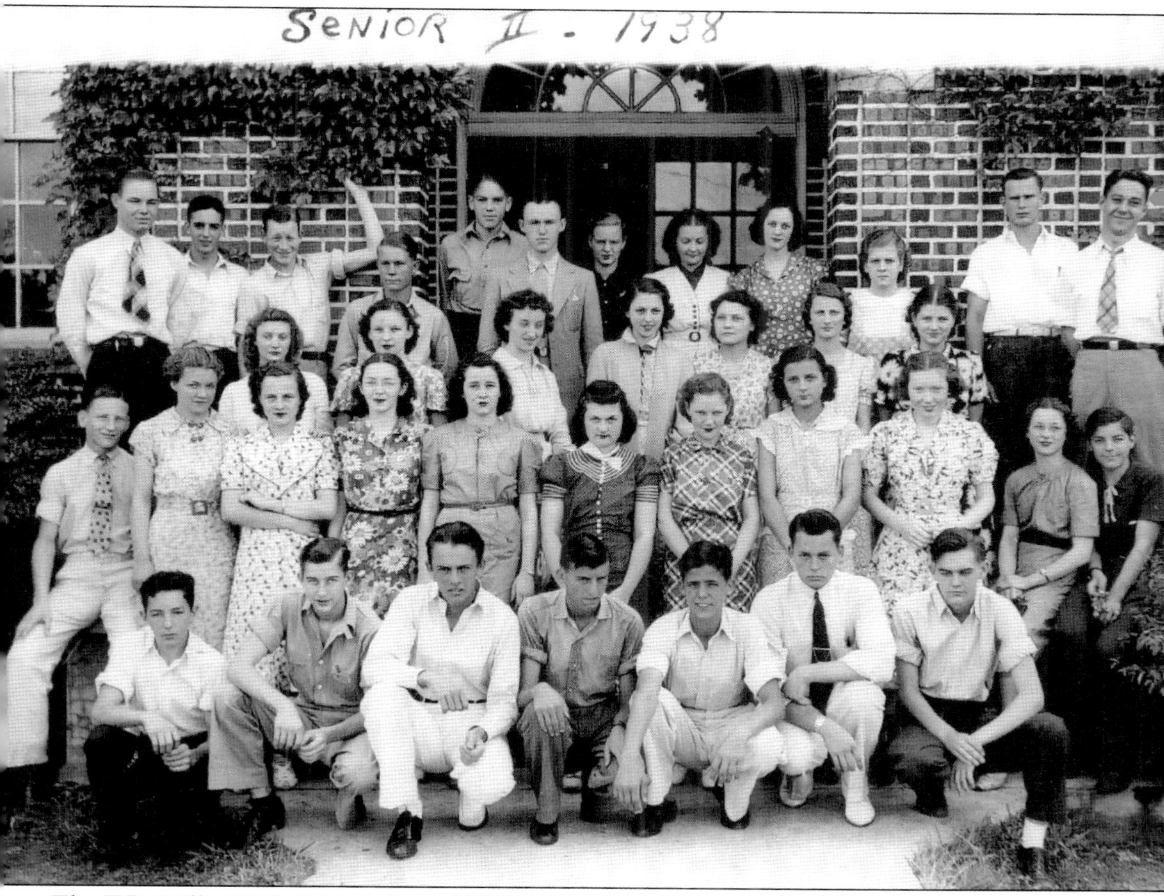

The T.R. Miller High School class of 1938–1939 is standing in front of the old Brewton High School on Belleville Avenue in this photograph. They are, from left to right, (first row) Bobby McCall, Marvin Kelly, Troy Brannan, Mac Weaver, Norman Dixon, Fred Key, and Bill Brooks; (second row) John David Enfinger, Dot Fitzgerald, Estelle Weaver, Maye McCall, Eunice Sims, Catherine Caffey, Lucille Temple, Mary Helen Hubbard, Wilma Jernigan, Edna Sims, and Fred Scott Larkins Jr.; (third row) Navalou Martin, Jane Kennedy, Manelle Holman, Dorothy Jernigan, Eddie Rea Hubbard, Rochelle Parker, and Jean Gillis; (fourth row) Charles Owens Jr., Mike Allen, D.P. Liles Jr., Glen Gillis, Lester Martin, Robert Snuggs, Virginia Alexander, Mildred Skinner, Betty Paul Beavers, Odelle Jordan, Goffrey Hawsey, and Jerry Tippins.

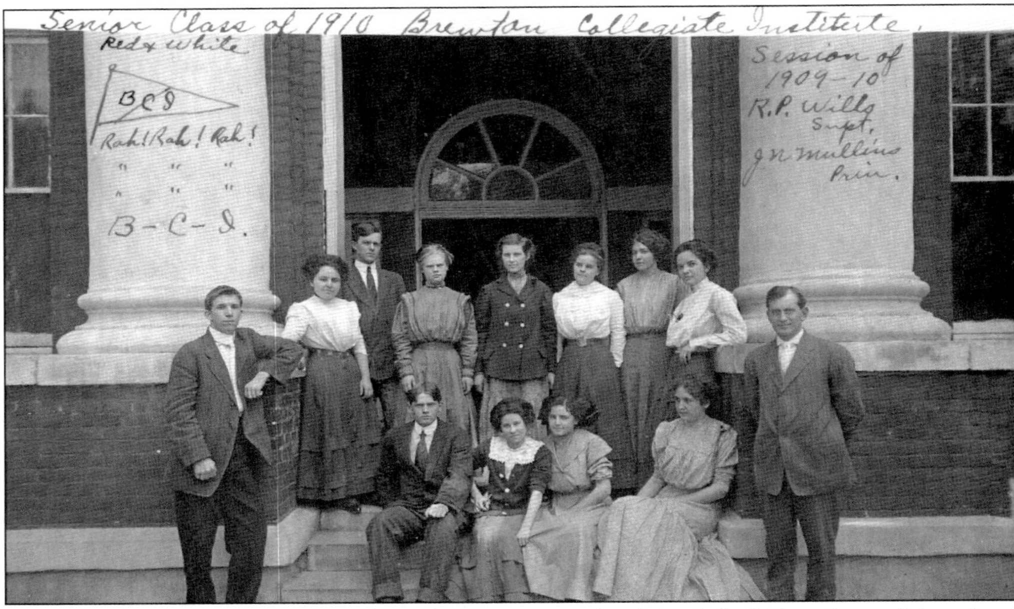

The Brewton Collegiate Institute class of 1910 is pictured on March 9, 1910, in front of the school, which was located next door to the courthouse (1902–1960). They are, from left to right, (first row) Roeder Morris, Charles Robbins, Anna S. Downing, Eleanor Davison, Rufus Mayo, and superintendent R.P. Willis; (second row) Minnie Mae Harold, Joe Sowell, Melba Robbins, Mary Stewart, Bernice Larkin, Bessie Wiggins, and Annie Corrie Park.

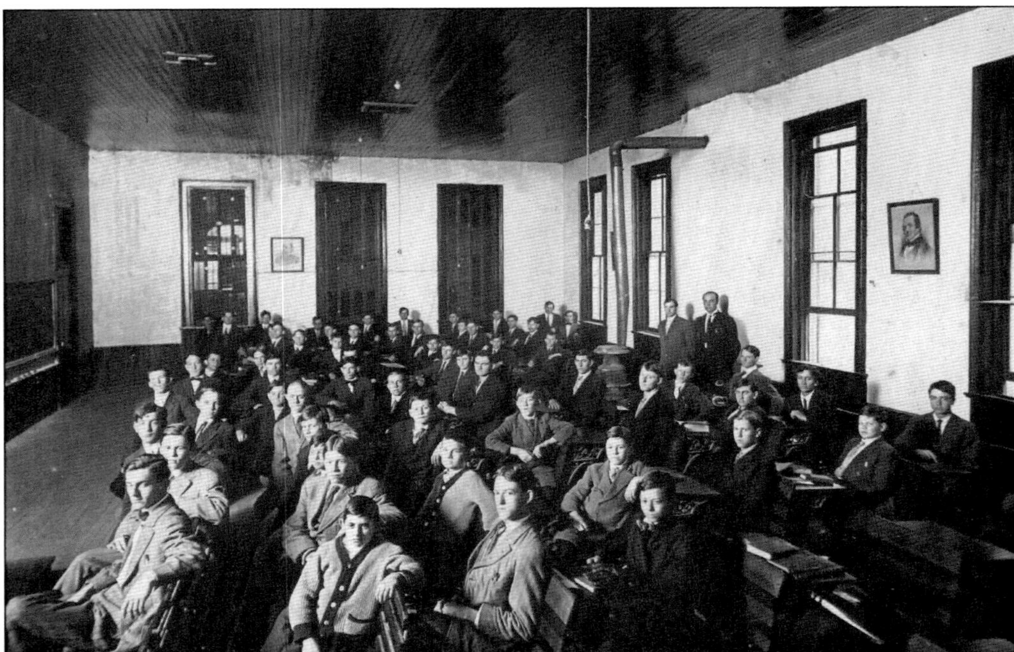

This is the boys' class at Brewton Collegiate Institute. Although both boys and girls attended classes, for some reason this included just the male student population.

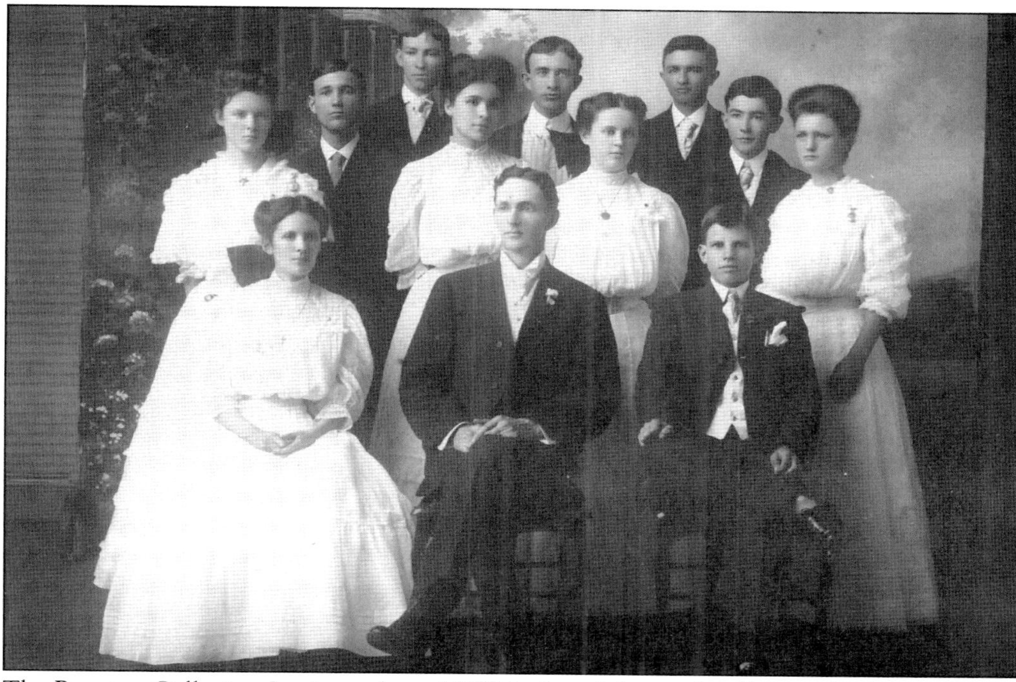

The Brewton Collegiate Institute class of 1907 is, from left to right, (first row) Alice Till, W.C. Griggs, and Wiley Downing; (second row) Virginia Jernigan, Rochelle Larkin, Corrie Luttrell, and Arvie Weaver; (third row) Finklea Davison, Greene Stokes, Tollie Strong, Gordon Parker, and Bof McCall. Not shown is Alma Harold.

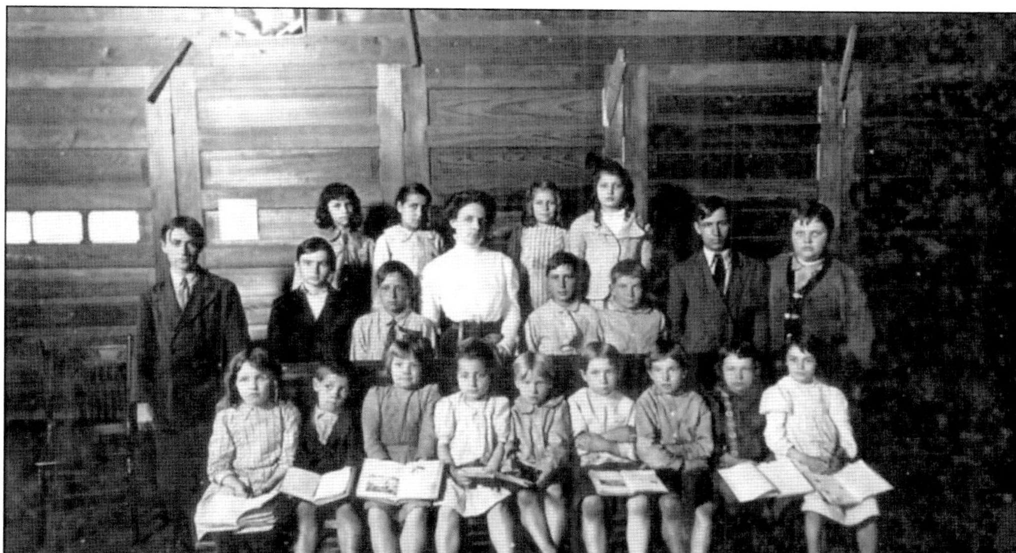

Alco School is pictured as it looked in 1912. The children are not named, but the teacher is known to have been Lucille Higdon Scott. This was one of the schools that would have sent students to the county school system until Alco was taken into the city limits of Brewton. The children would have then gone to the city school system. (Courtesy of the Escambia County Historical Society.)

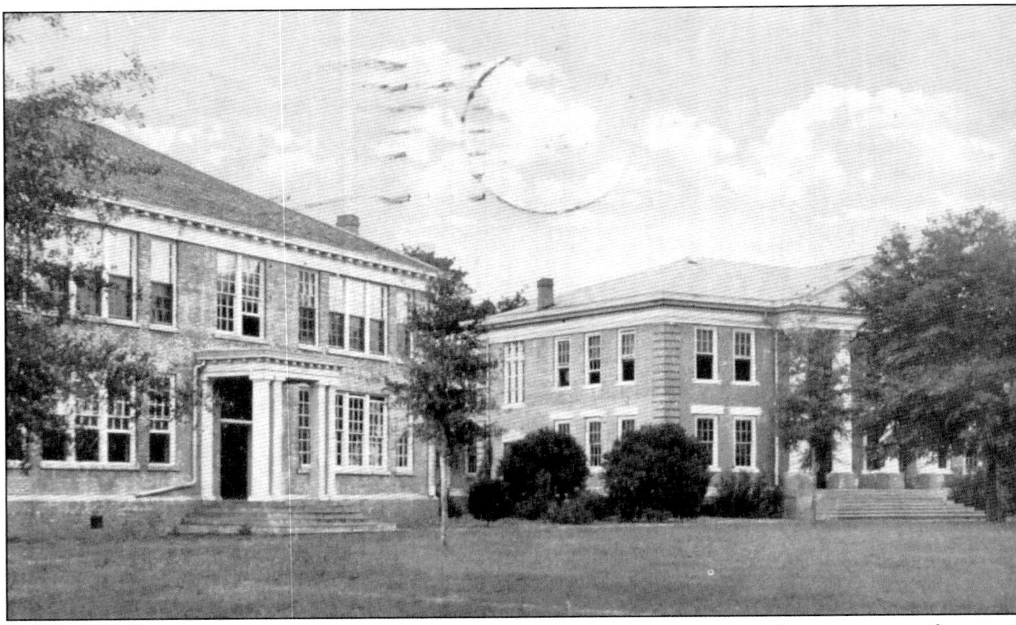

Taylor Hall, on the right, was added to the campus of Downing Shofner Institute for extra classroom space. It was one of the last of the buildings to be torn down. In its last days, it served as a temporary home for the East Brewton Baptist Church while the members were building a new church. (Courtesy of WilEllen Elliott.)

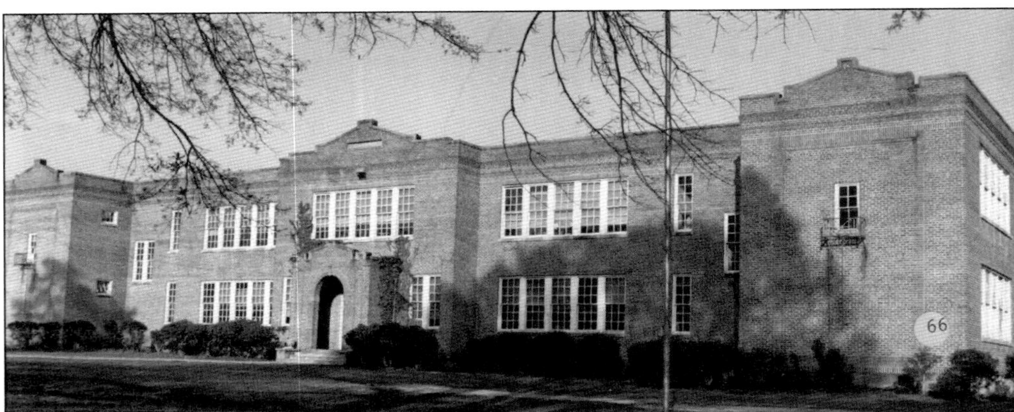

In 1924, the old Brewton Collegiate Institute had become too small to house the Brewton City School System. T.R. Miller offered a parcel of land on the corner of Belleville Avenue and Underwood Street on which to build a new school. In his honor, the school was named Miller High School. The first graduating class from this school was in 1926. It served as a school for grades one through 12 until 1936, when Brewton Elementary was built diagonally across the street. At that time, this building became T.R. Miller High School. When T.R. Miller moved into new quarters at its current site in 1962, the fifth through eighth grades moved into this building. In 1976, this building was torn down, and a new elementary school was erected on the same lot facing Douglas Avenue on the space that once was Rotary Field, which was used for athletics. (Courtesy of Scott Hillman.)

James M. Shofner was the driving force behind the building and operation of the Downing Shofner Institute. He actually ran the school for a number of years. He and his family lived in the only building left of the school on Shofner Street in East Brewton. Today, there are still a few who remember attending the school.

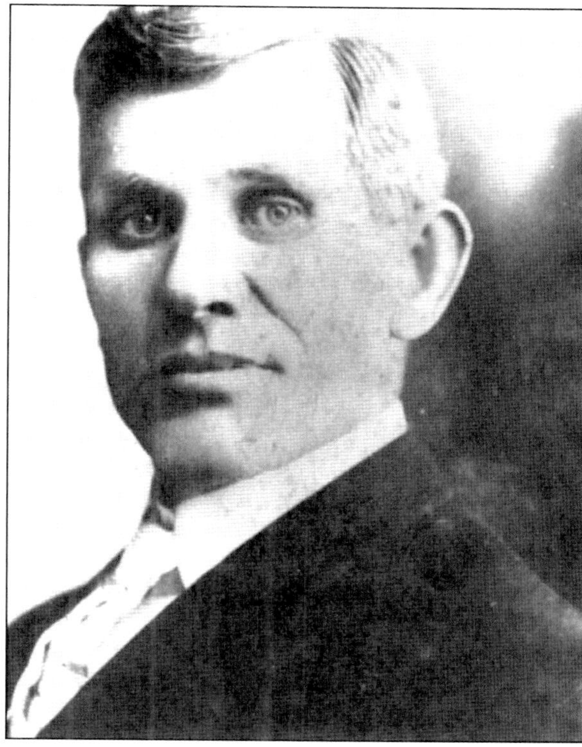

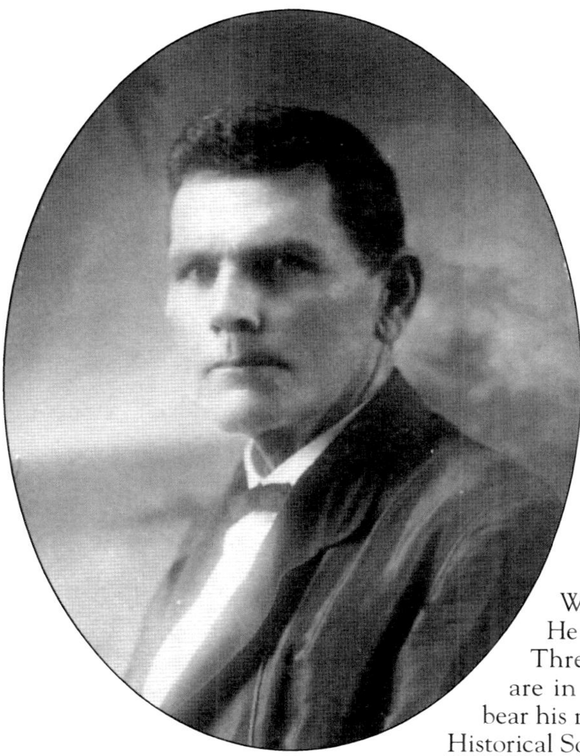

W.S. Neal was an early advocate of education. He spent most of his life promoting education. Three local schools in East Brewton, which are in the Escambia County School System, bear his name. (Courtesy of the Escambia County Historical Society.)

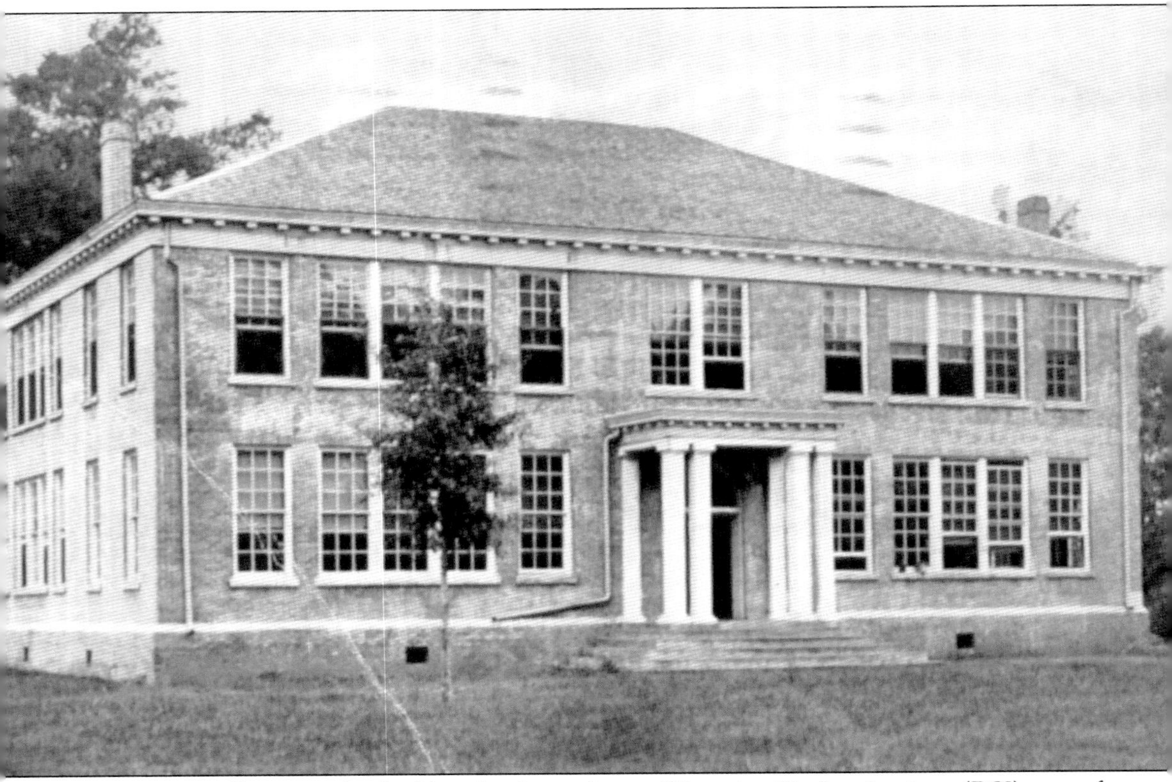

Wiggins Hall was another building for the students of Downing Shofner Institute (DSI) to use for classrooms. DSI was the dream of the Reverend James M. Shofner. He was a Methodist minister who wanted to provide an education to girls who were often not as educated as boys. The first building was constructed in 1908 and was soon followed by more. Shofner always had trouble financing the school, and eventually, he persuaded the Methodist Conference to lend its support. It continued to be a school until the 1940s. Today, there are no remains of the campus. The only building left is what the Shofner family used as their residence.

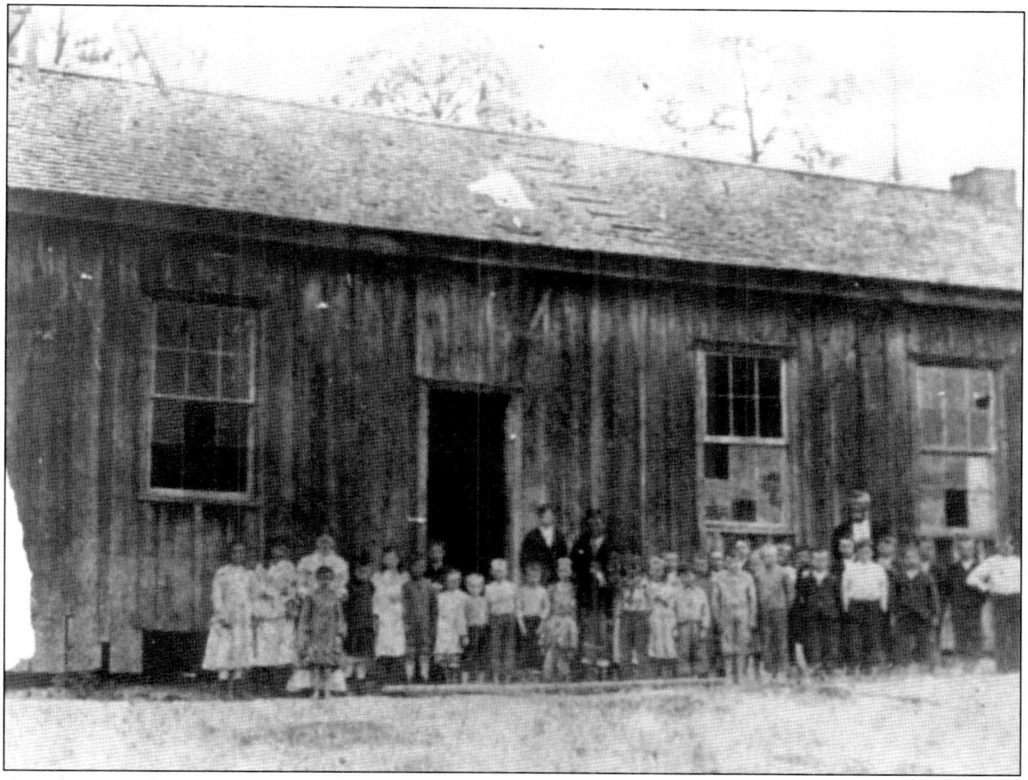

Granberry School was the first school in the Brewton area. It is said to have been built in the Eliza Brewton Field, which must have been somewhere in the vicinity of where the T.R. Miller Mill is today. (Courtesy of Barbara Carden.)

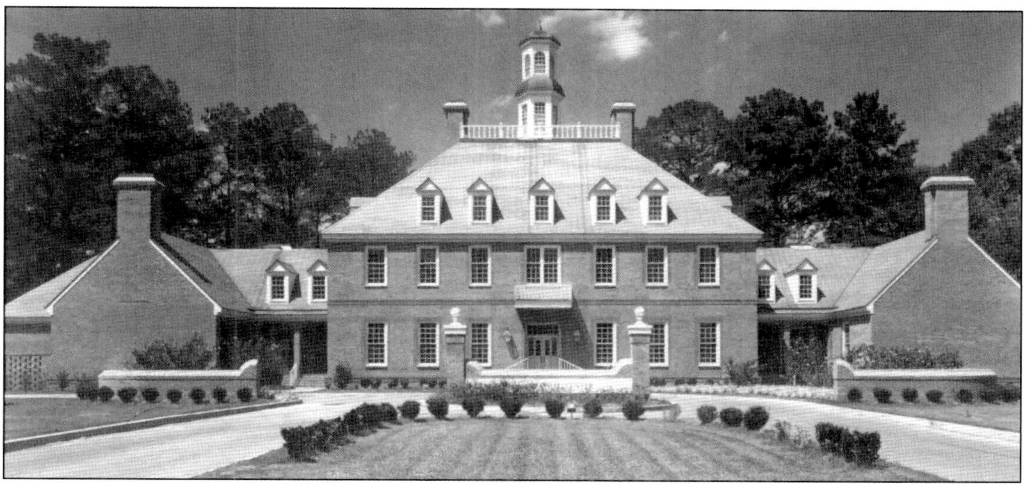

Neal Colonial Center at Jefferson Davis Community College, in the Alco section of Brewton, has a great reputation with its many available courses. At this time it is a two-year school, but it is possible to earn a degree in several subjects through its online program. This building houses the nursing program and the administrative offices of the college.

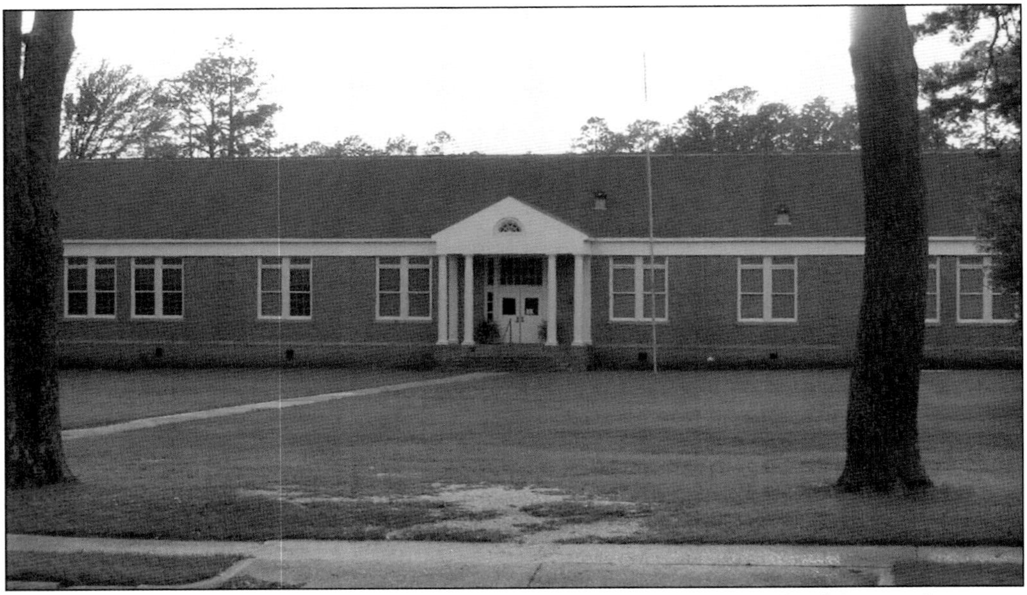

This building was constructed and used for many years as the elementary school. It is on the corner of Belleville Avenue and Underwood Street. It is now used as both the Brewton City Board of Education and the kindergarten classes.

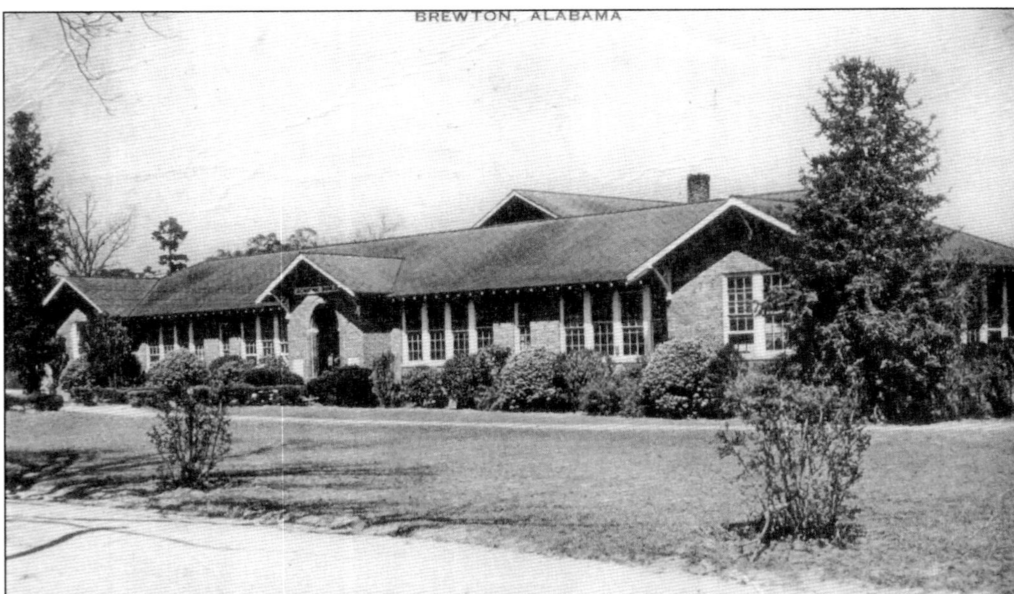

Van Vorst Hall is one of the buildings at Southern Normal High School. The school closed several years ago and was sold to Alabama State University. The campus is used for various programs. Southern Normal was built in 1911 to be a school for African American students before integration. When the school fell on hard times, it was subsidized by the Reformed Church in America. (Courtesy of Yancey Lovelace.)

A group of teachers gathers on the front lawn of Miller High School on Belleville Avenue. This school was torn down, and today, the Brewton Elementary School playground is where the old school once was. (Courtesy of Scott Hillman.)

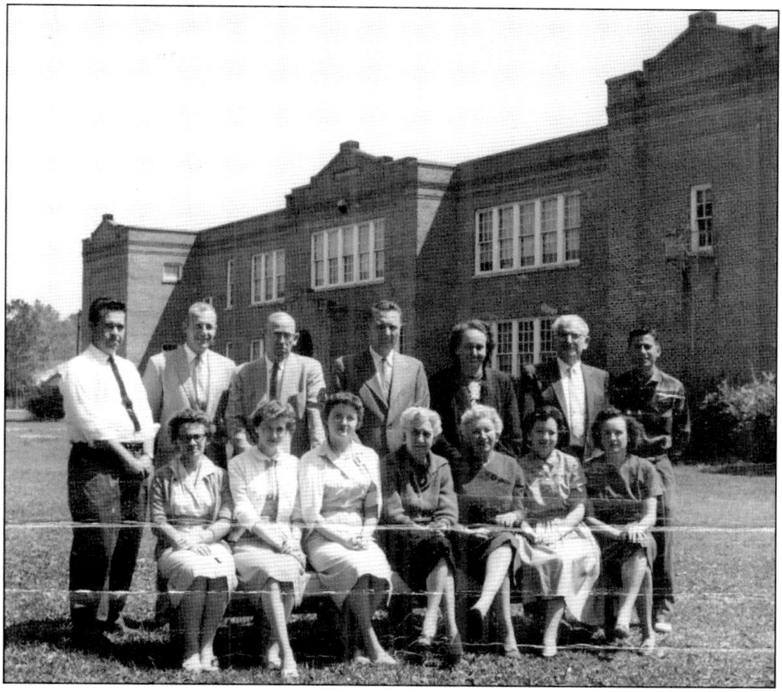

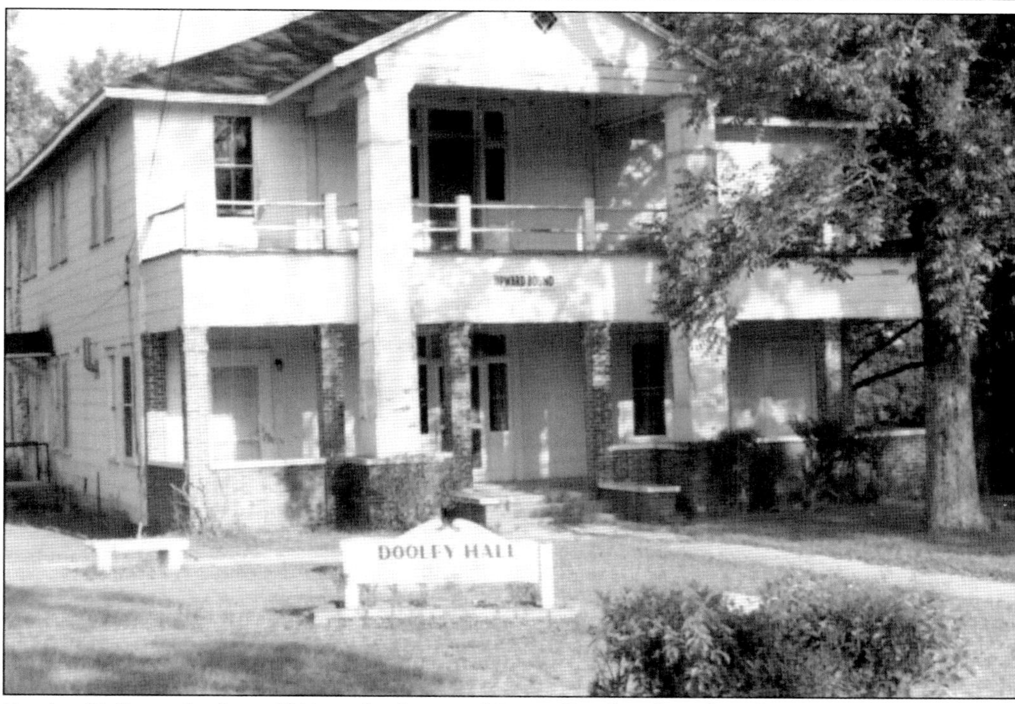

Dooley Hall was built in 1911 as the home of James Dooley, founder of Southern Normal High School. Dooley had the dream to open a school that would benefit the many African American students during the time of segregation. The building is still being used as part of the school, which is now owned by Alabama State University.

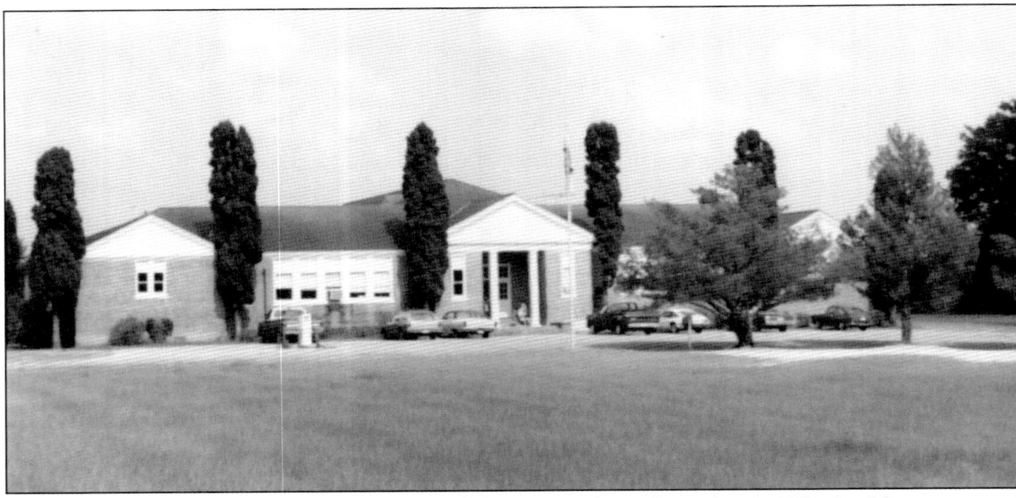

North Brewton was built in 1940 to consolidate several smaller schools. The building was used as a distribution area for water and supplies after Hurricane Ivan struck the area in 2004. There was much damage done by the storm, but true to their nature, Brewton and East Brewton worked together, along with many outsiders who came to the rescue of a devastated area. This building has since been torn down, and students are bussed to the county schools in East Brewton. (Courtesy of Barbara Carden.)

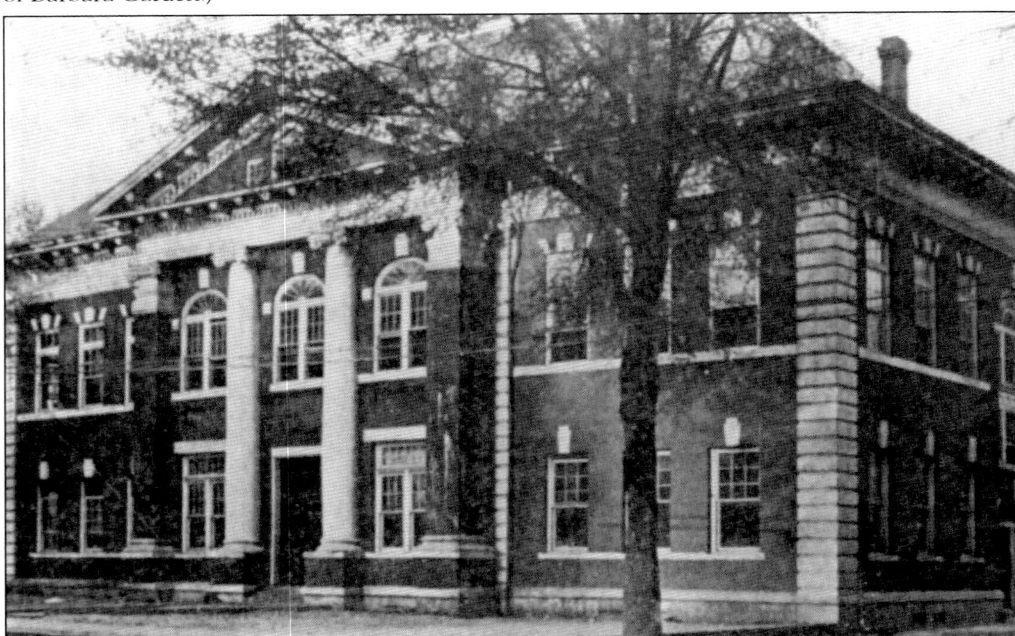

Brewton Collegiate Institute was the first school of any size in Brewton. It was located next to the Escambia County Courthouse. It was built in 1886 and was the home of all the grades until 1925, when a new high school was built farther up Belleville Avenue. The school was used for elementary classes until a new school was built in 1941 near the high school. After that, the building was used as office and storage for the courthouse. It was torn down, and today the site is part of Brewton First Baptist Church and the present courthouse. (Courtesy of WilEllen Elliott.)

Five

Flood Zone Scenes

Early settlers usually established townsites along streams and creeks. In the case of Brewton and East Brewton, the townsfolk probably never thought that the site on which they built their new towns were flood zones.

If they had known, the towns could very well have been moved, but that didn't happen. Brewton is located near where Murder Creek and Burnt Corn Creek joined together to flow into Conecuh River. East Brewton is on the other side of Murder Creek, and most of its damage during a flood is spread between a few stores. However, one of those stores is Magnolia Super Foods, the only grocery store in East Brewton. Problems really arise when people or workplaces are cut off during floods. Somehow, the two towns survived each flood and learned something from each one.

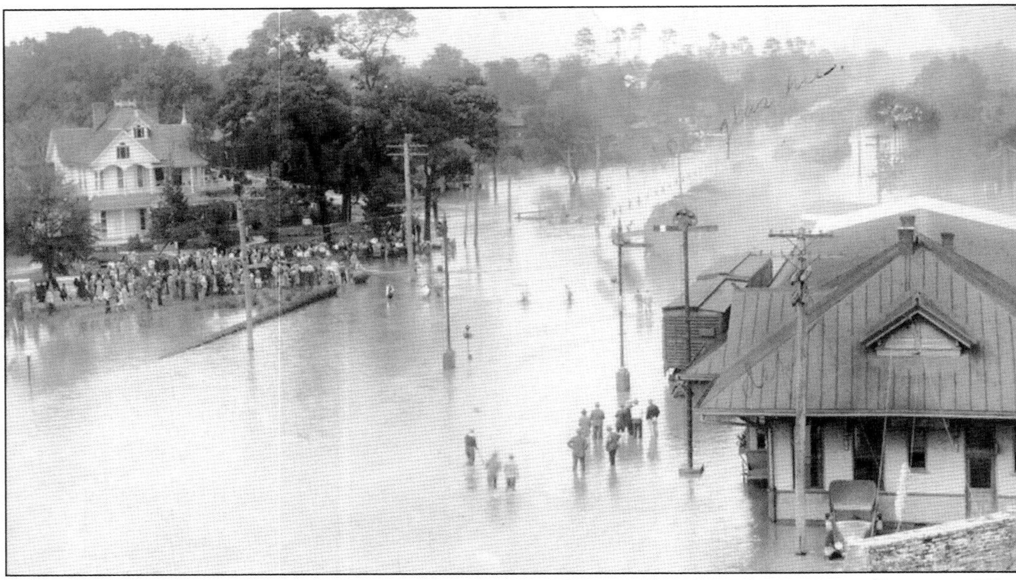

Brewton and East Brewton have experienced several major floods and many smaller ones. This photograph was made during one of those floods, and people can be seen standing in the park just beyond the water. A train at the depot seems to be a little closer than safety would allow. These floods always bring out the spectators to see the damage and wonder, yet again, if businesses will be rebuilt or not. The people of Brewton and East Brewton have learned to cope with Mother Nature, and most of them begin all over again.

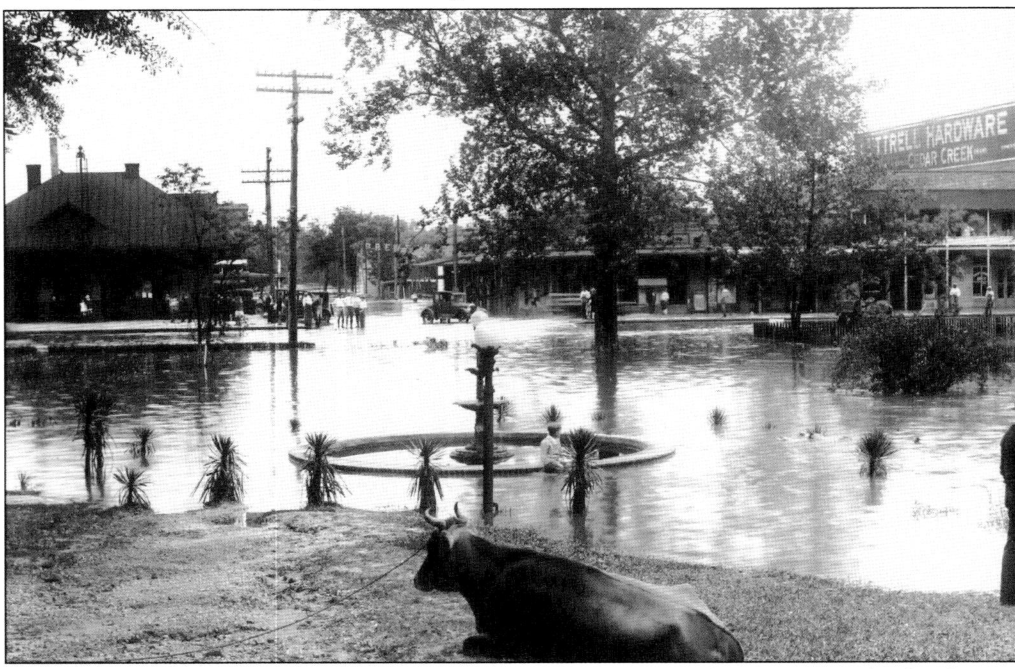

Taken during the 1929 flood, this photograph shows a lot of attention being given to the floodwaters, but the cow is not impressed by all that is going on. There was a time when livestock was allowed to run free, until the citizens of Brewton decided it was not the thing to do.

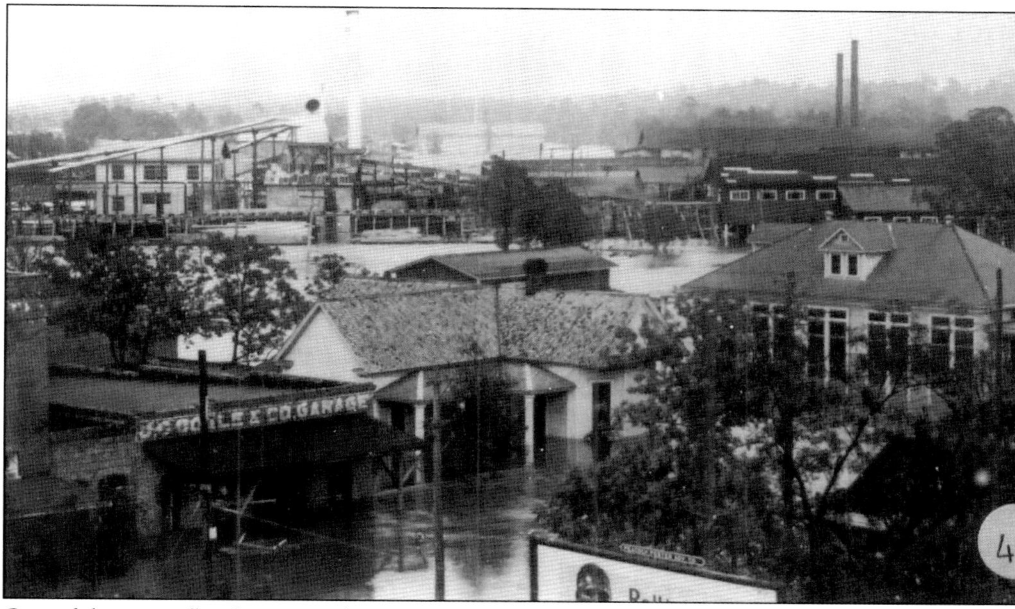

One of the worst floods occurred in 1929. It affected Brewton and many other towns and cities in south Alabama. The T.R. Miller Mill was hit very badly, which was hard on everyone, as many of the people in the area were employed at the mill.

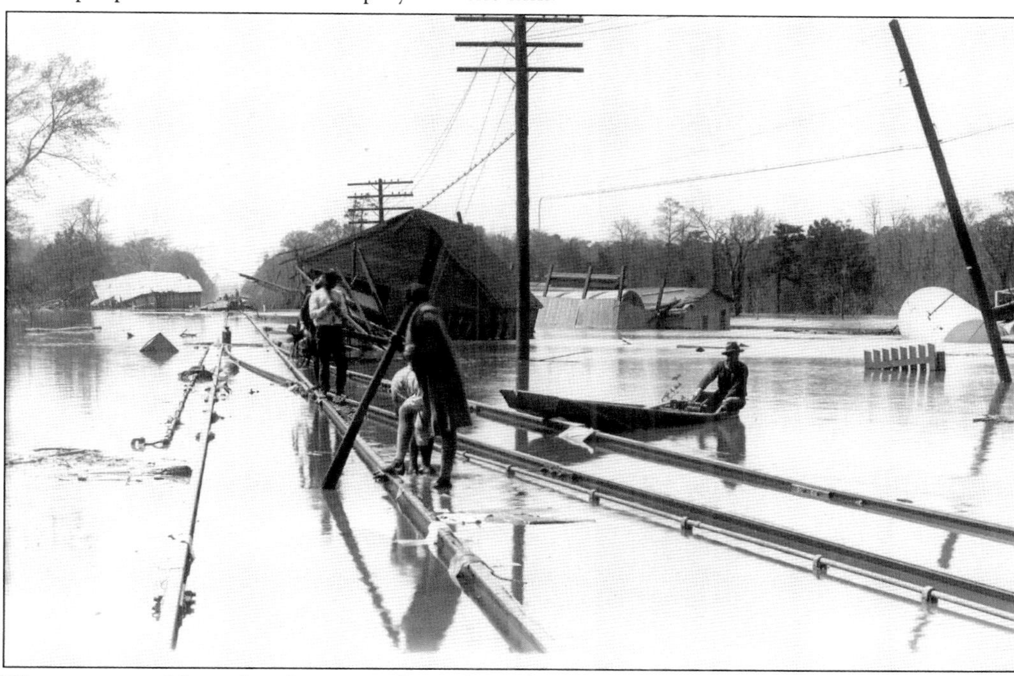

This was one of the sights that greeted people in the Sunday, March 17, 1929, flood. The building to the left of the railroad is the Gulf refining warehouse that stood by Lovelace Lumber Company's old office. The two to the right were the two residences on either side of the road by the Alco Bridge. The one by the man is Robie Potter's. Note the Texas and Standard Oil tanks and more houses floating. Other tanks were found below the ballpark.

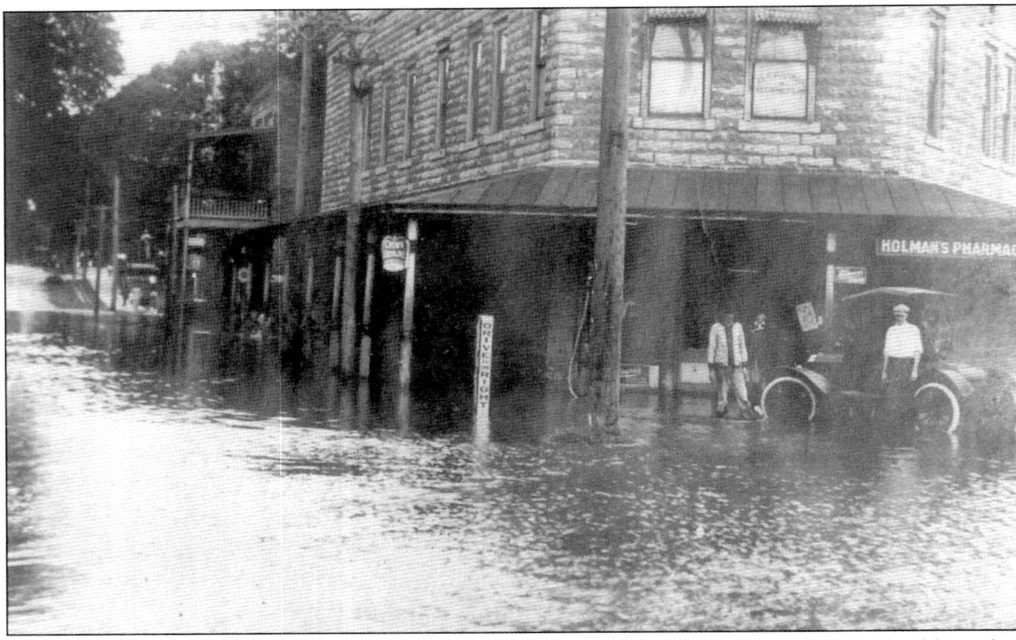

During one of the floods in downtown Brewton, Holman's Pharmacy occupied the building that has been called the "flatiron building." It is the same as what is now called Old Willie's.

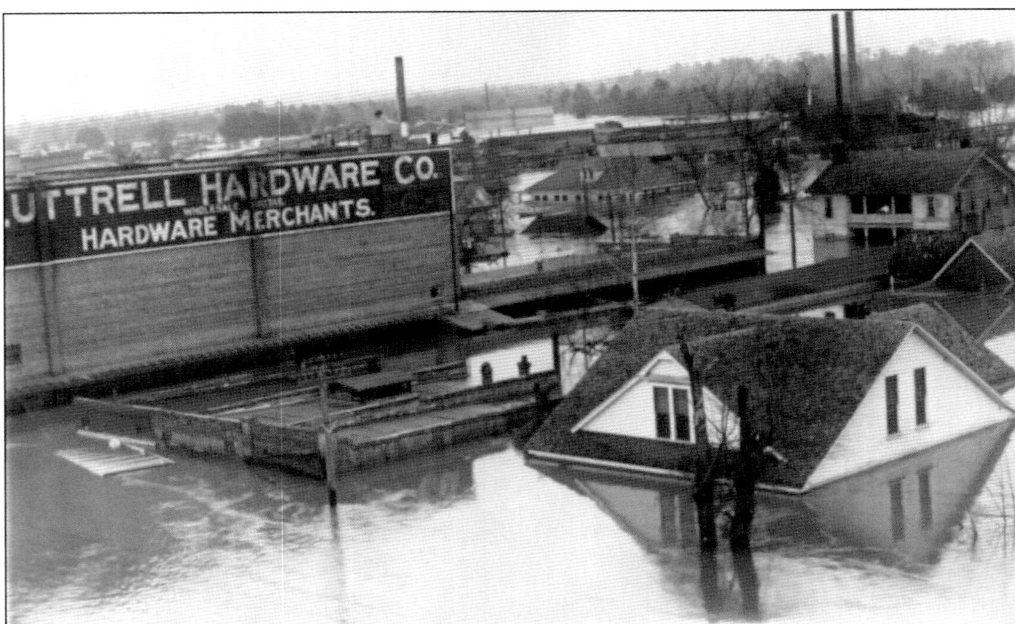

This is another view of the flooded area in downtown Brewton. With all the problems that go along with flooding, local citizens always pull up their bootstraps, clean everything up, and go on with business. When prospects of flooding are known, neighbors who are out of the flood zone offer their help to put things up and out of the way of the water.

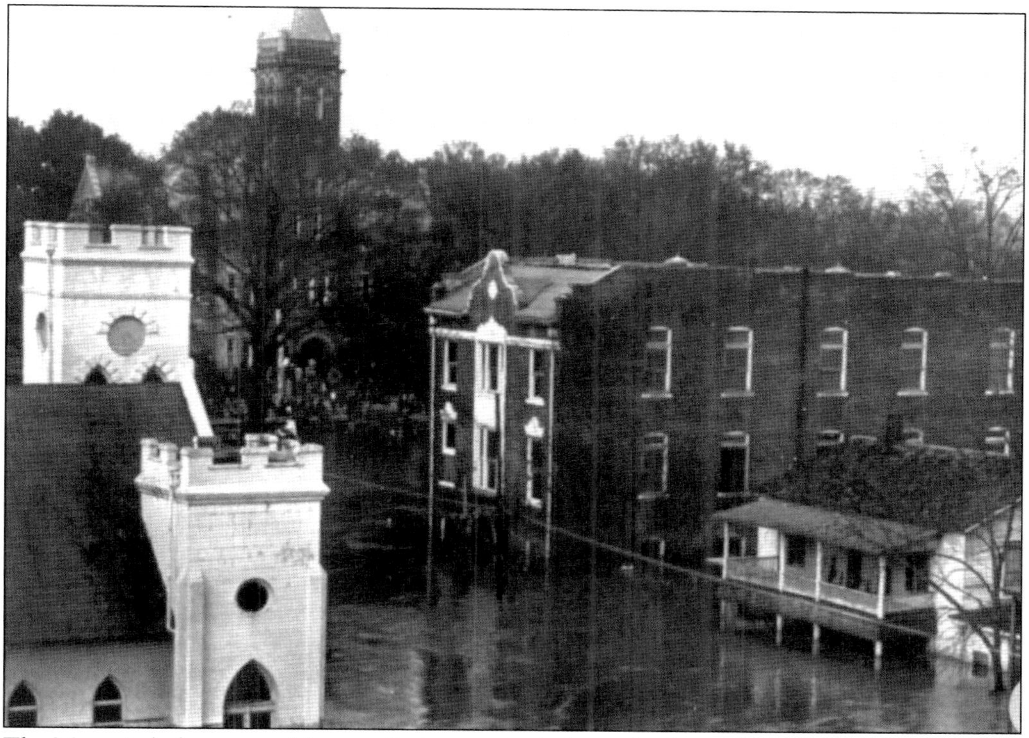

The Masonic lodge was architecturally interesting before a fire burned one floor and caused a lot of damage. The building left does not fit into the list of those 27 that have been named in the Alabama Historical Registry. (Courtesy of Yancey Lovelace.)

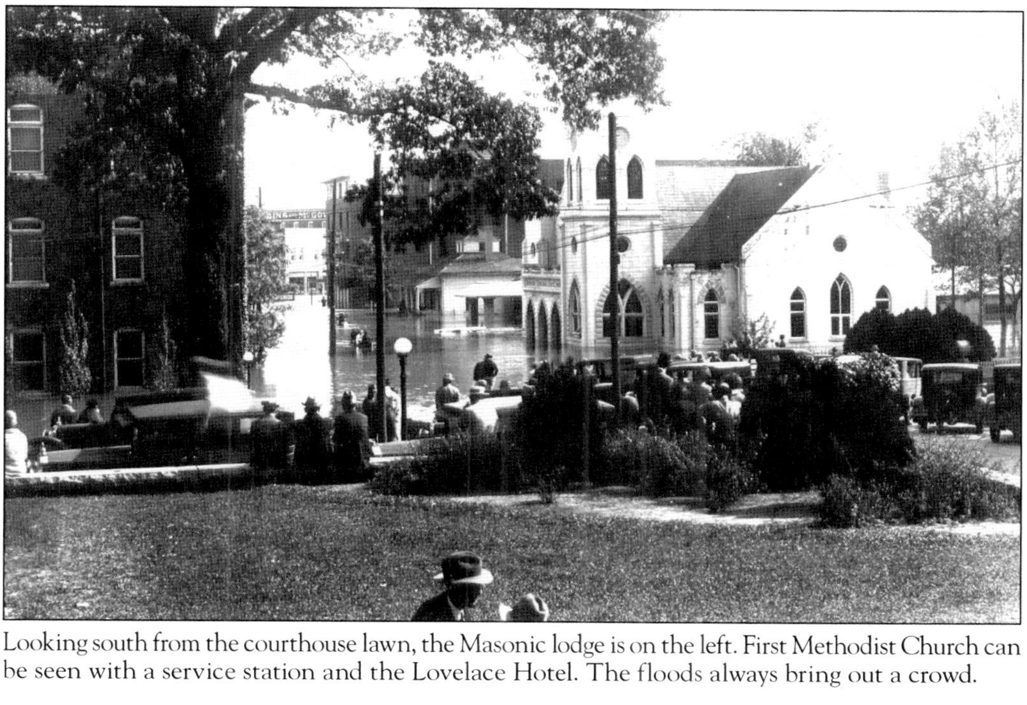

Looking south from the courthouse lawn, the Masonic lodge is on the left. First Methodist Church can be seen with a service station and the Lovelace Hotel. The floods always bring out a crowd.

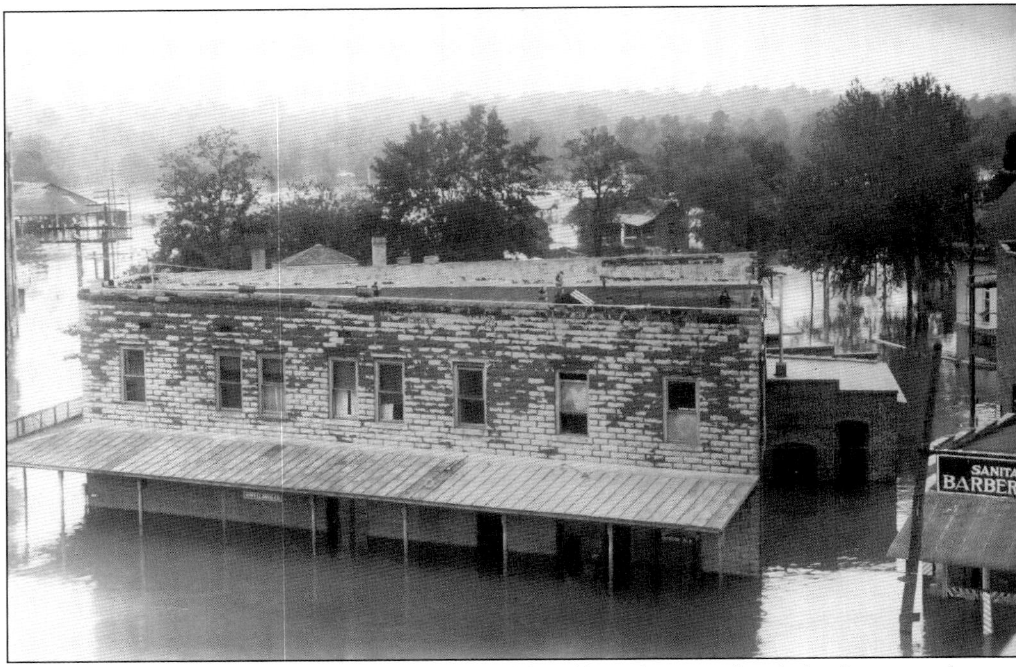

This is a view of the building, best known as Old Willie's, during a flood. At the time, the post office was located in the building. The building next door was a barbershop named Sanitary Barber Shop.

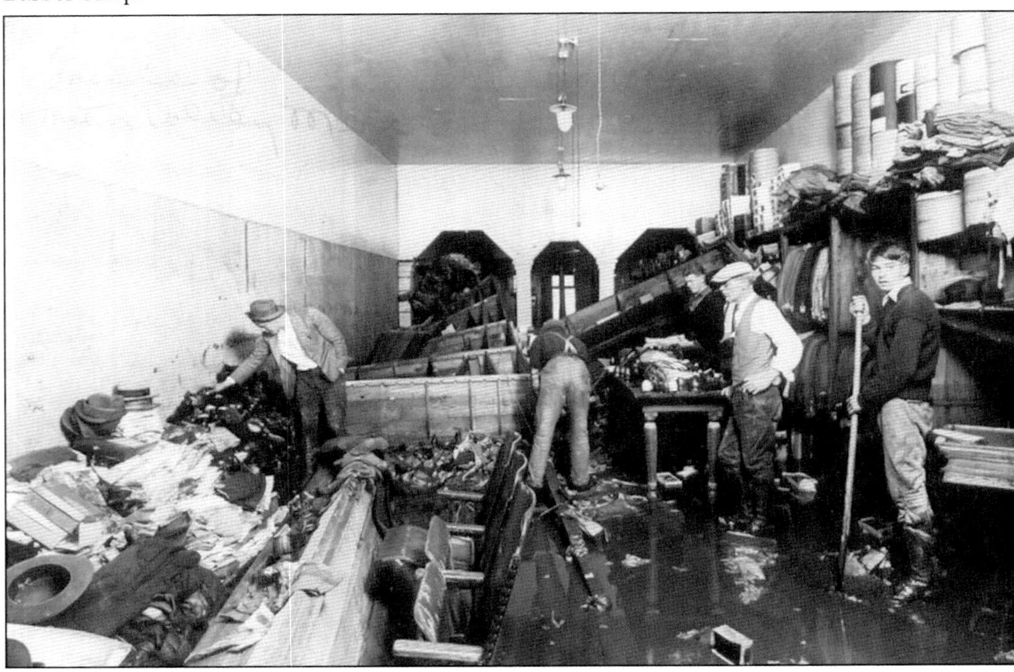

This is what Smith Colley Mercantile looked like after the flood of 1929. The merchants downtown have learned a lot of ways to combat the dangers of floods. There are several that have large elevators to be able to move merchandise to higher floors. (Courtesy of Barbara Carden.)

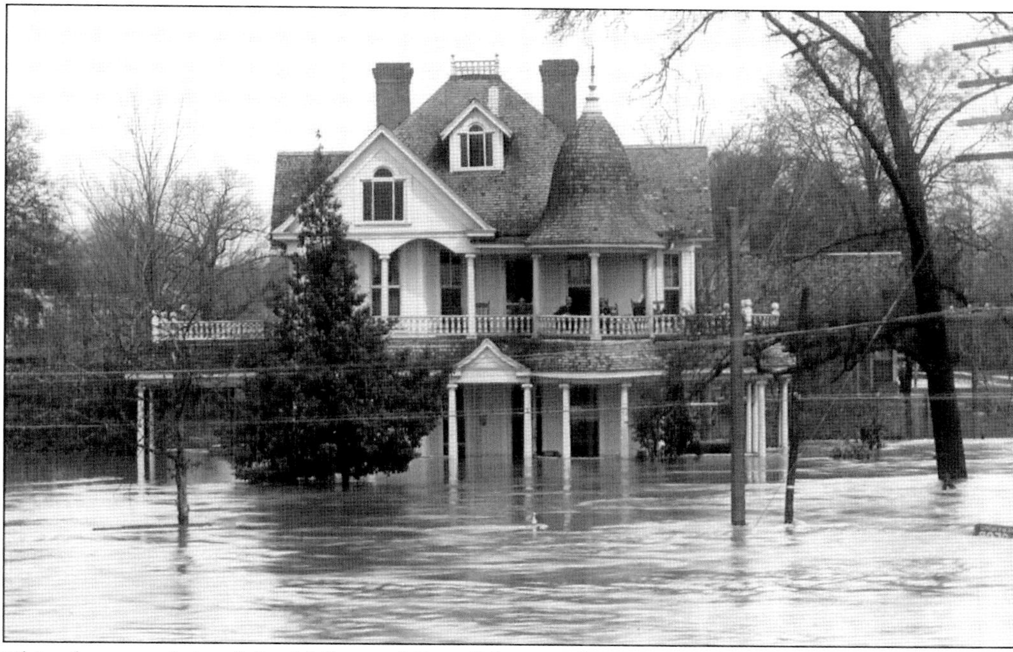

This photograph is of the Miller and Sowell homes during one of the disastrous floods to hit Brewton. This is where City Park would later be.

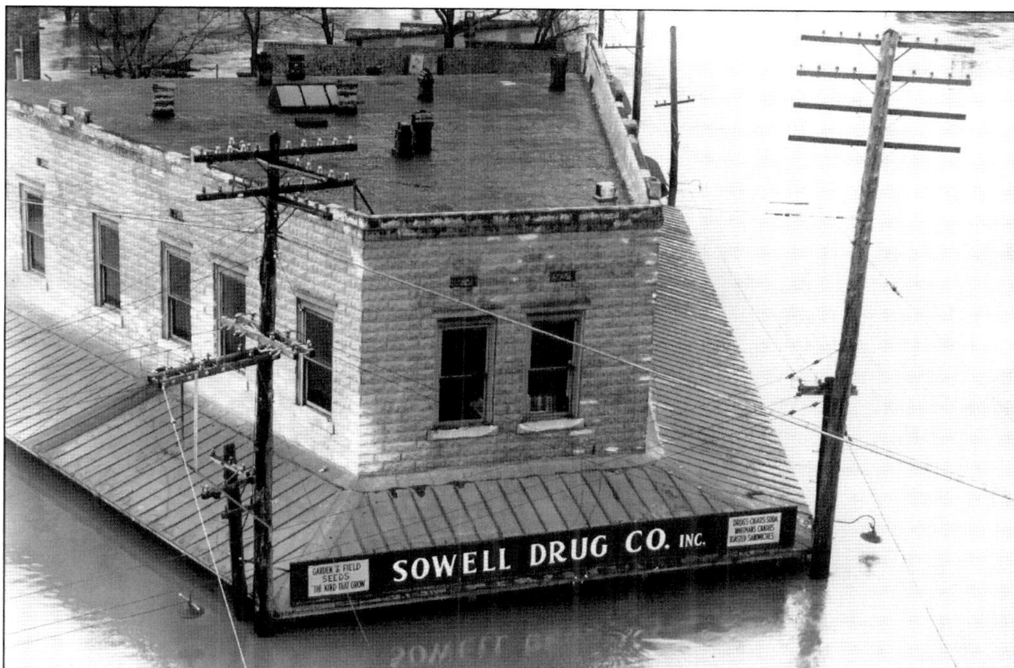

Sowell Drug Co. is pictured with floodwaters up to the bottom of the overhang. This photograph was taken from the roof of the Lovelace Hotel, probably during the flood of 1929. During that flood, Brewton was cut off from the rest of the world. As the people waited, supplies were flown in from Whiting Field near Milton, Florida.

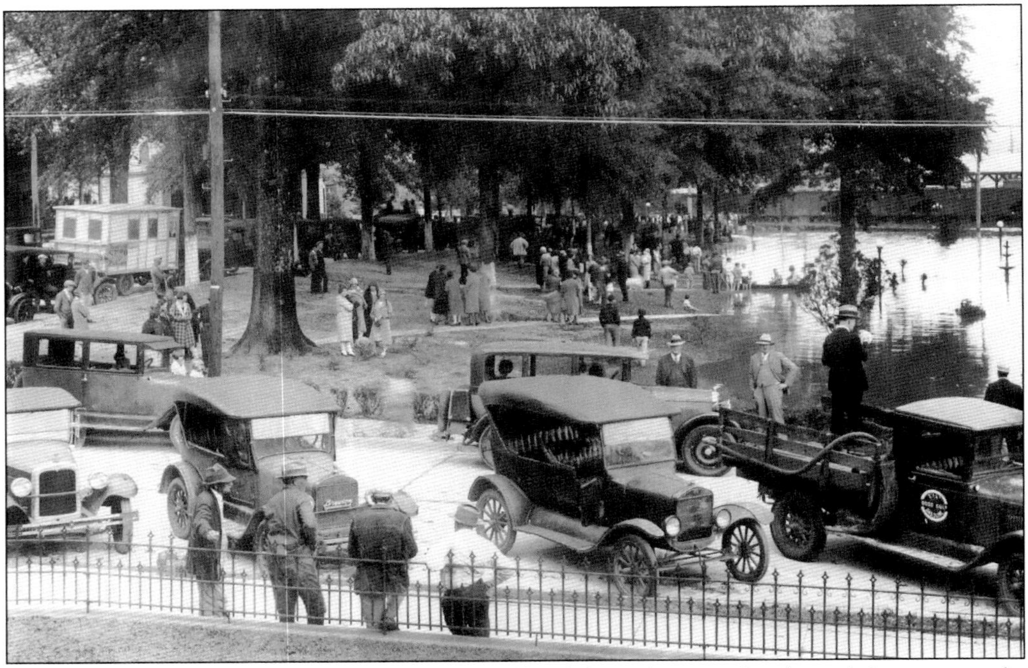

City Park and the rest of the downtown area suffered through many floods, and this one caught some cars that got left to the rising waters. This section of the downtown area has been a meeting place for many events that happen in Brewton.

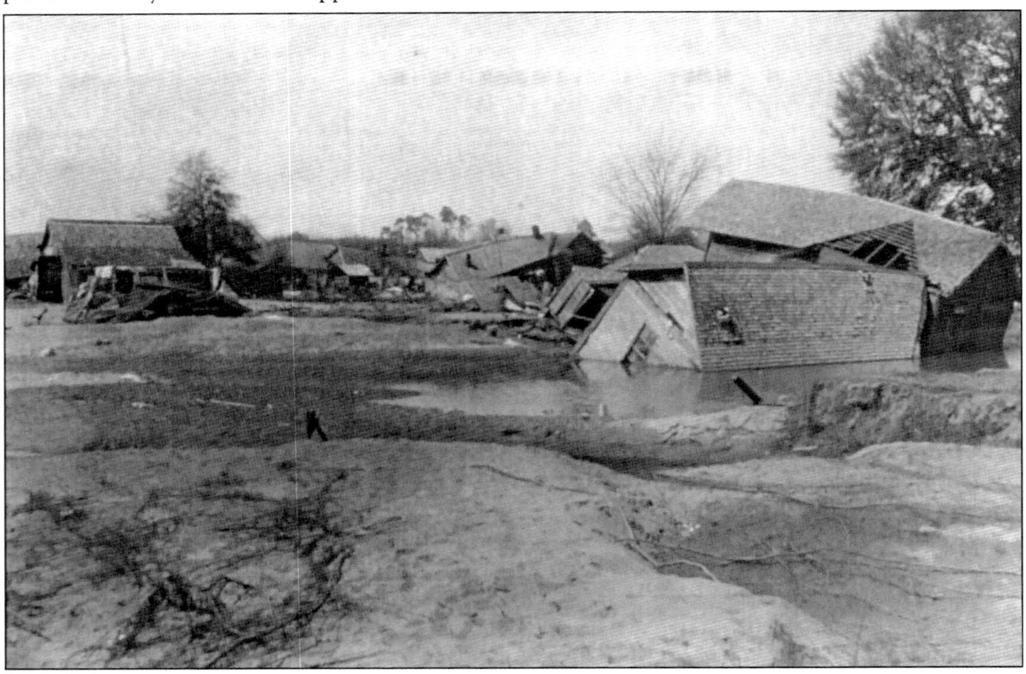

This was identified on the back of the photograph as Shiloh. Note how the water washed out in some places and piled up in others. The hole in the roof is where people were taken out after the water reached the loft. Tom Neal's cook lived here during the 1929 flood.

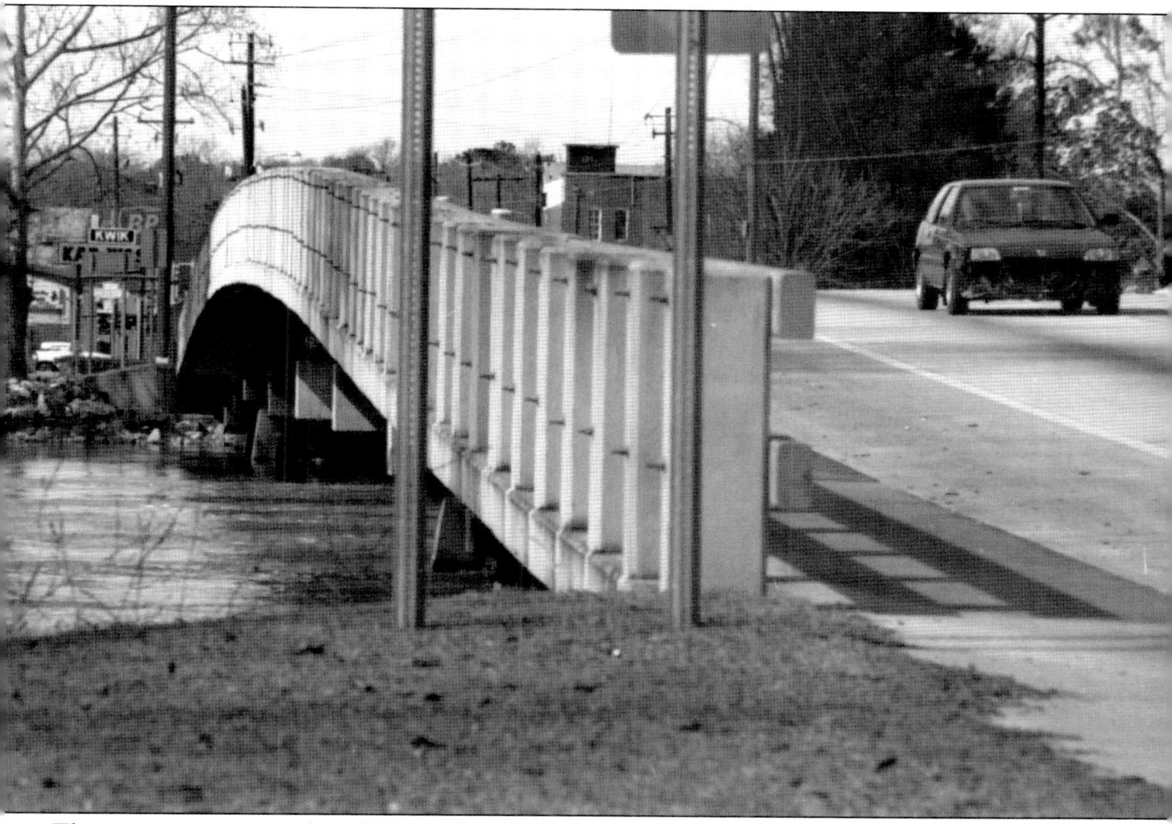

The water is rising in this photograph of Murder Creek. In addition to the many floods that Brewton has had to endure, there have been many times when the water would almost get to flood stage. With the water getting this high, business owners would have been working hard to get everything out of harm's way. At a time like this, friends and neighbors offer their services to help either put things up higher or move them to a safe location. A couple of businesses downtown have freight elevators only for use during times of flooding or potential flooding. (Courtesy of Robert Crenshaw.)

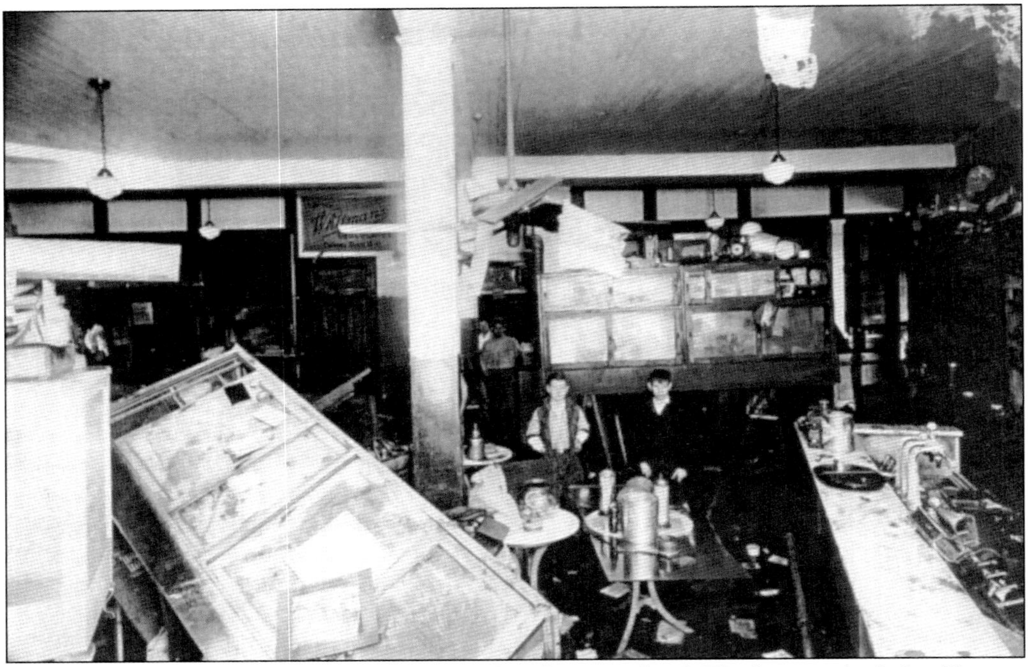

This was taken inside of Sowell Drug Store after the 1929 flood. The boy on the left is Tommy Liles. In the midst of all the destruction, the soda fountain can be seen on the right. It was one of the only things left standing as the water rushed in and out.

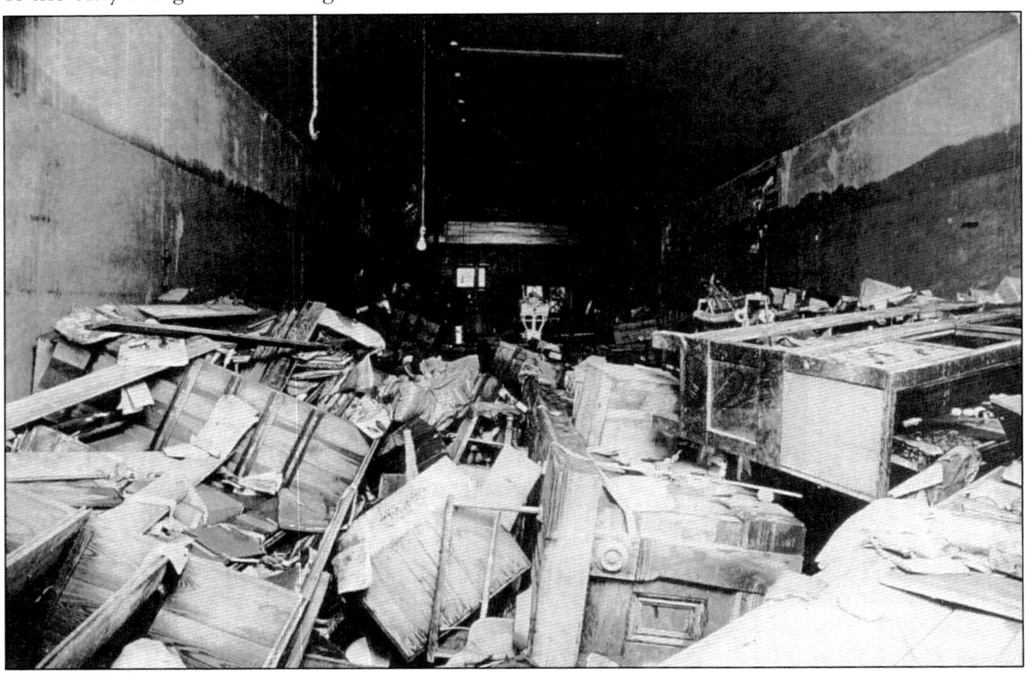

This is the inside of another business after the flood of 1929. There was not much spared by the wrath of the rushing waters. Owners were forced to do a lot more remodeling than they wanted to, as the waters usually caused a lot of damage to everything inside.

Six

LUMBER, THE MAJOR INDUSTRY

Lumber and timber are what put Brewton on the map. Most of the major businesses here have something to do with lumber. The eastern part of Escambia County is covered in pine trees, just as it was when the settlers came into the area. Those who wanted to do some farming had to travel a few more miles to the western end of the county, where the land is flat and built for farming. There are only three major towns in the county. Brewton is in the east, Flomaton is in the middle, and Amore to the west. The county is not very wide, but is long. Thus the terrain is very different. Most of the first people into the Brewton and East Brewton area who decided to stay were those who had the vision to recognize the future in all those trees. The two major employers in this area are the T.R. Miller Mill and Georgia-Pacific. One deals with the trees directly, while the other concentrates on the products to be made from the natural resource of timber. The many fine homes in town were built by those who made their fortunes in the business of cutting and planting trees.

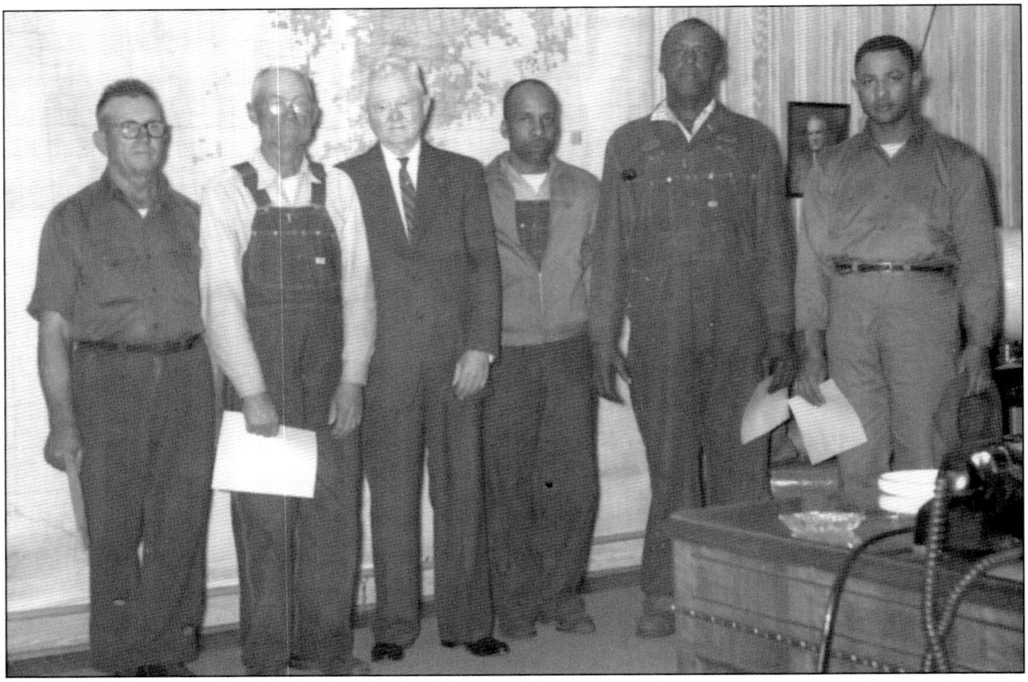

This group of employees from the T. R. Miller Mill includes, from left to right, Miles G. Rowell, Aubrey Chavers, Ed Leigh McMillan, Judge Lee Payne, Roosevelt Hall, and Burl Hall. (Courtesy of Robert Crenshaw.)

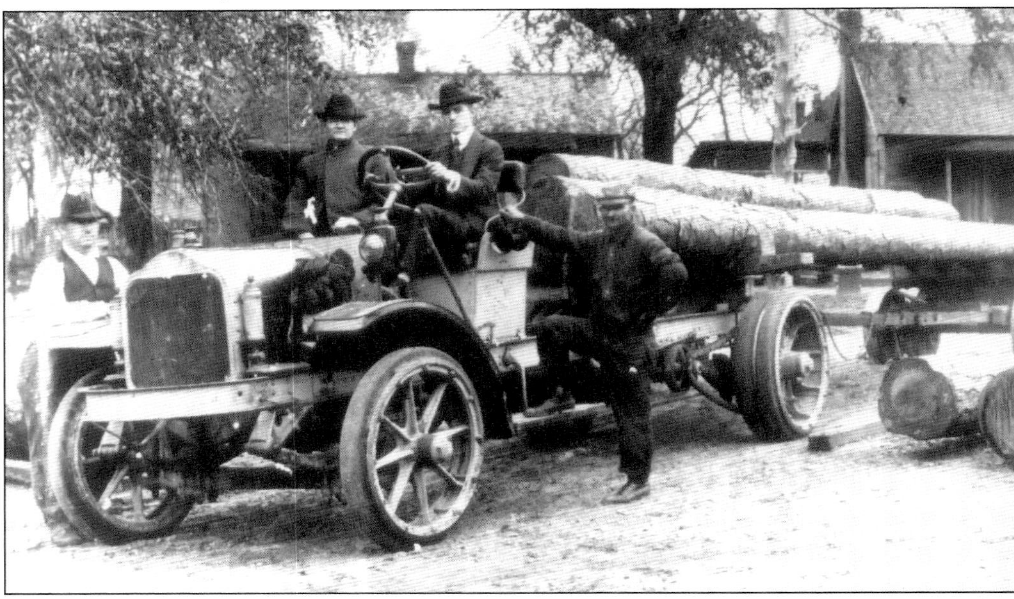

This is the first logging truck in Brewton in 1915. Pictured are, from left to right, Charlie Stokes, W.Y. Lovelace, John R. Miller, and an unidentified man standing by the driver. Modern equipment and innovative thinking have kept T.R. Miller in the thick of the lumber and timber business. Those who entered the timber business found it to be very profitable, and the homes along Belleville and Evergreen Avenues reflect this.

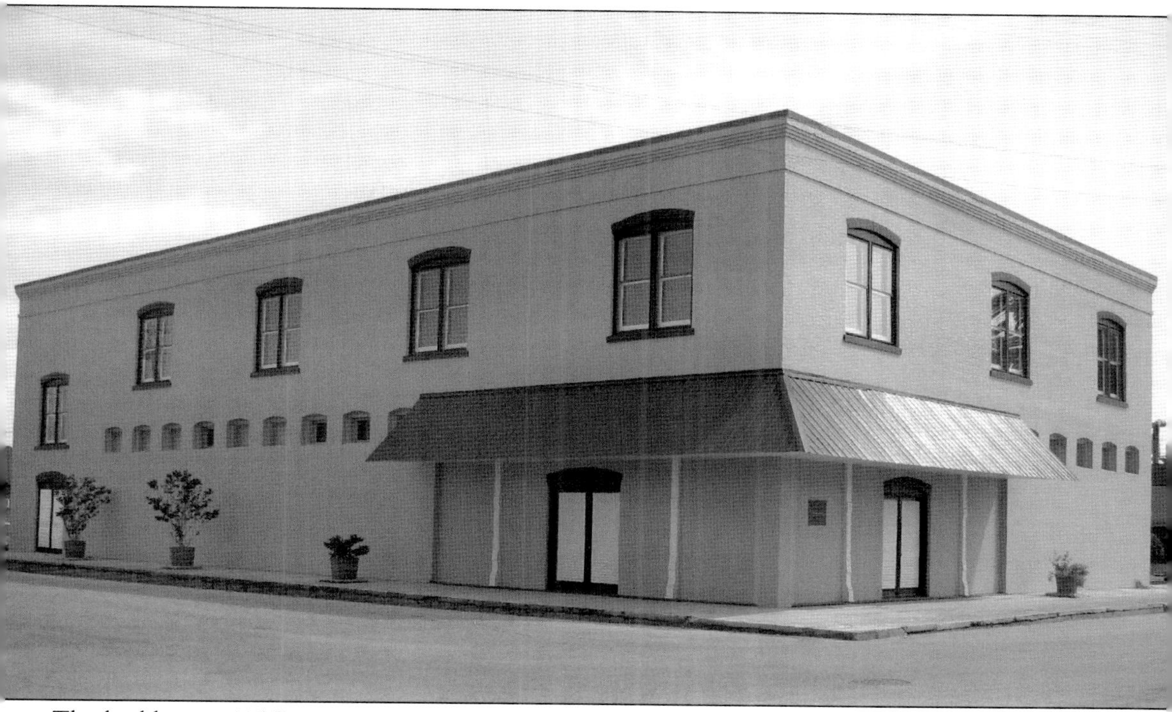

The building at 115 Deer Street, the commissary for the people working at the mill, was built about 1911. After its use as a commissary, Sherrer Brothers ran a department store there for some years. It is now used for office space for the Miller family and Miller Investments.

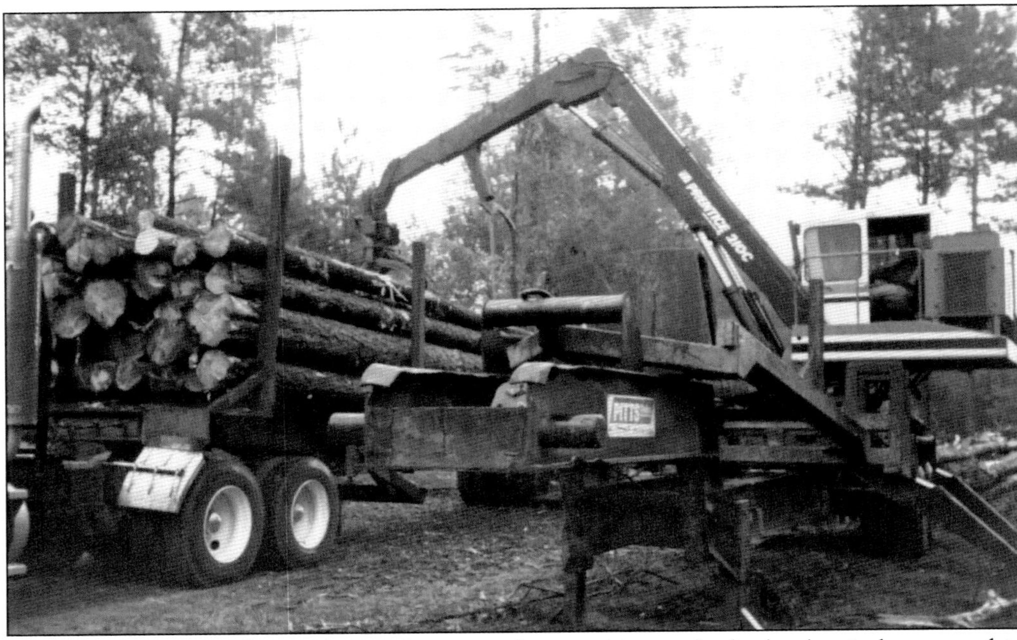

Large trucks and machinery have taken over the primitive tools the lumber industry used in the early days of settlement. T.R. Miller was one of the first who realized the value of replanting the forests to make sure they continue to be the source of some of the best timber in the world. (Courtesy of Robert Crenshaw.)

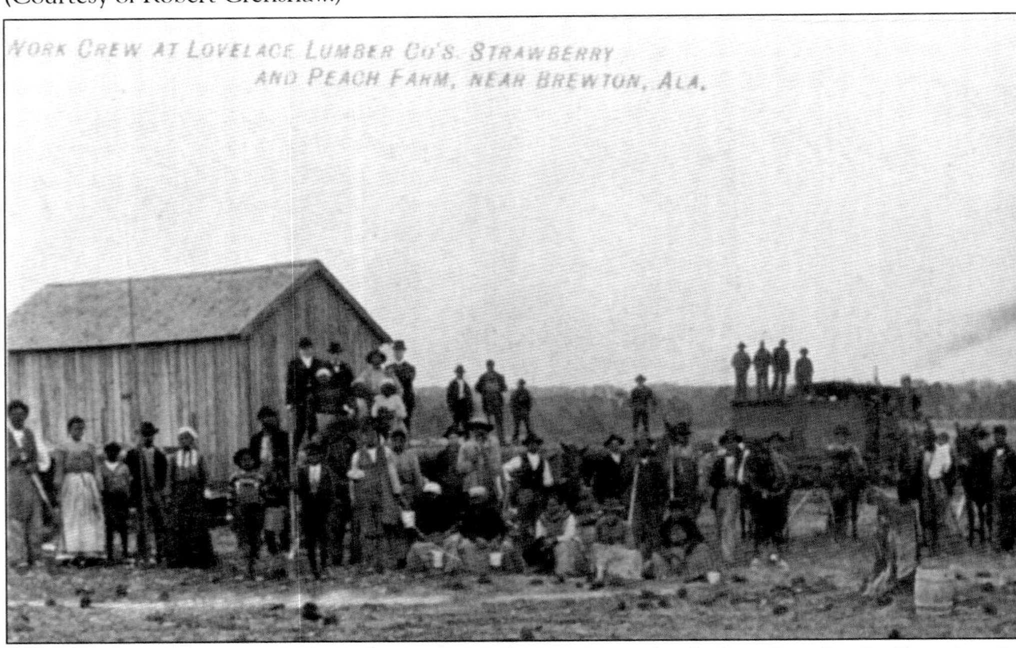

These are workers who picked peaches and strawberries grown by the Lovelace family. Strawberries remained a shipping crop well into the 1960s. Many strawberries were picked and shipped to the northern states to grace someone's table. Today, the main fruit crop grown in this area is blueberries. (Courtesy of Robert Crenshaw.)

Seven

HOMES OF DISTINCTION

Although most homes in Brewton and East Brewton are for normal-sized families, there was a time when the word "house" meant the biggest and the most modern. During the immediate boom of the big lumber mills, the people connected to the mills built some of the most magnificent homes in the state. The name "lumber barons" was given to a handful of men who made their fortunes in the forests surrounding Brewton. The Downing, Lovelace, T.R. Miller, McGowin, and other families wanted to let their wealth show in the homes they built. Most of them are located on Belleville Avenue, and many are still owned by descendants of the original owners. Their owners were able to travel and see what the rest of the world looked like, and they wanted their homes to incorporate some of what they had seen on their trips. Today, many of the modern houses are being built in locations outside of the city limits. The Country Club of Brewton has been relocated there, and many home sites have been bought in that area.

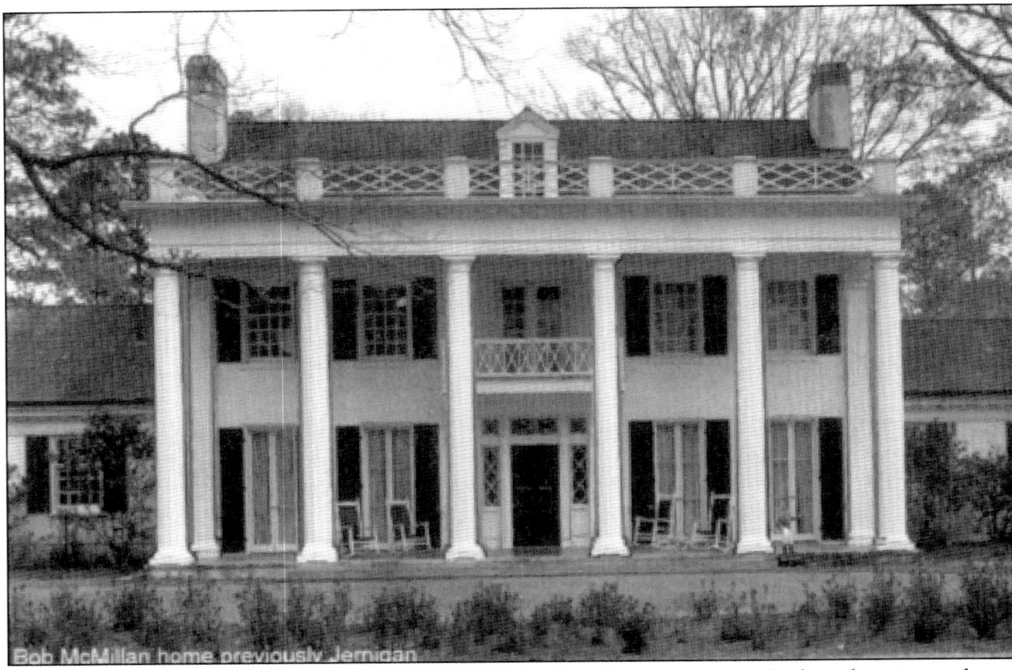

This stately mansion has been owned by Bob McMillan for many years. Before that, it was better known as the Jernigan home. Bob McMillan is one of three sons of Thomas E. and Elvira McMillan. The Fine Arts Center at Jefferson Davis Community College houses the Thomas E. McMillan Museum, the repository of the materials of the Escambia County Historical Society.

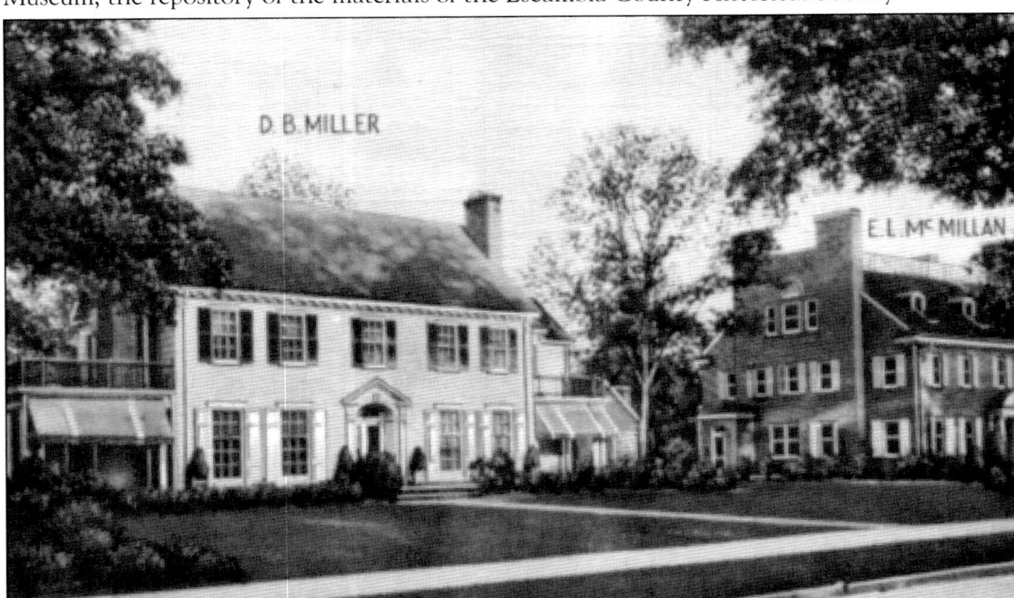

An early postcard shows the Belleville Avenue homes of David Brent Miller and Ed Leigh McMillan. They were both from wealthy lumber families. The fortunes of several families were based in the lumber business, and many of the homes on Belleville Avenue were built during the early 1900s. They were built with the latest materials and styles of the time.

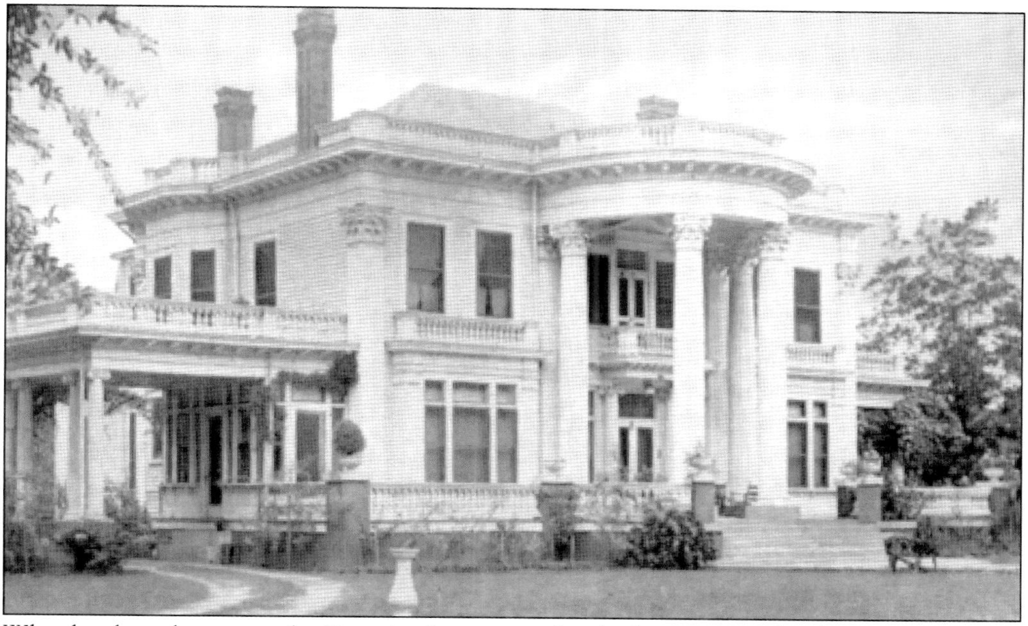

What has been known as the Downing home was also the home of another lumber family. The Downings were in the lumber business, and this home reflects that it was indeed a lucrative business. The last of the Downings to live in the house was the late Marie Downing, the widow of Adrian Downing. At her death, her niece inherited the property. It stands on the corner of Belleville Avenue and Rankin Street, almost a replica of the Lovelace house that once stood across Rankin Street.

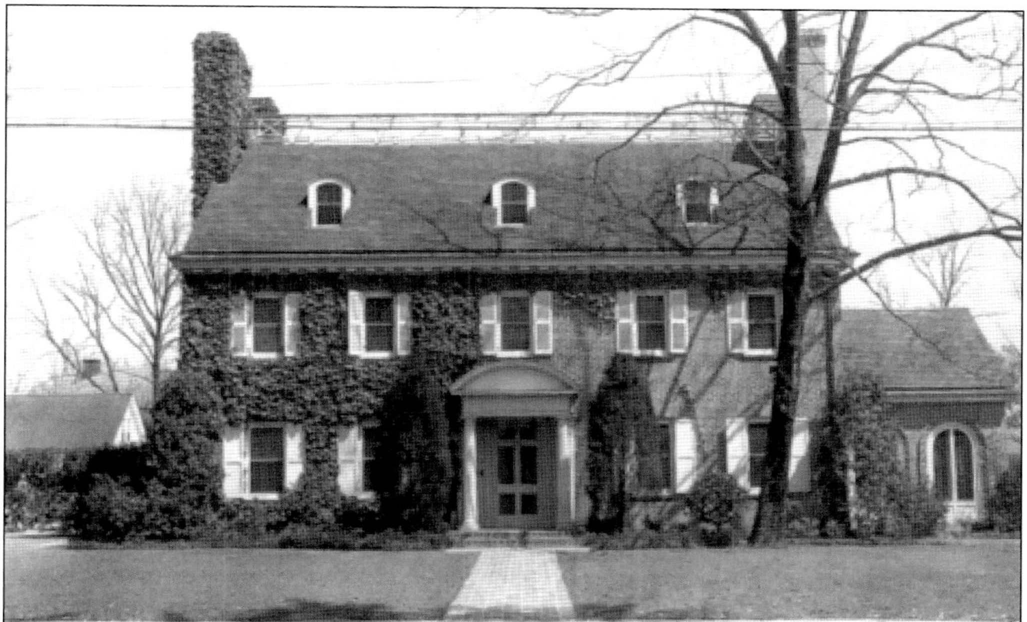

This was the home of Ed Leigh McMillan I and his wife, Iva Lee McMillan. The home still belongs in the McMillan family. This is one of the homes that was paid for with lumber and timber.

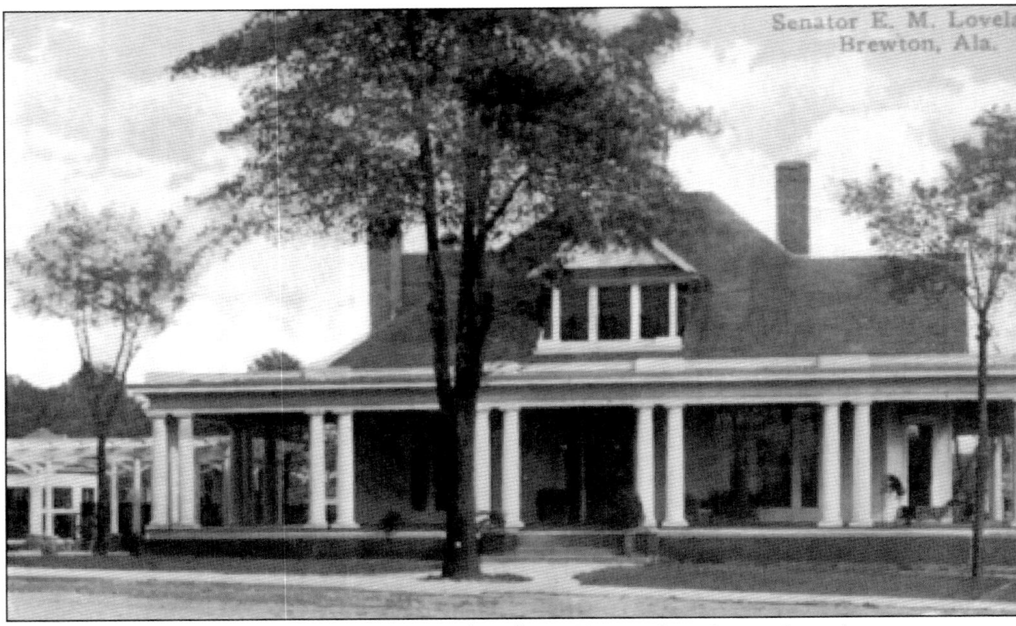

Edwin Marshall Lovelace was the father of William Yancey Lovelace, whose home was one of the showplaces on Belleville Avenue until it burned in 1929. E.M. Lovelace was president of the Lovelace Brothers Lumber Mill, which was in downtown Brewton on the banks of Burnt Corn Creek. (Courtesy of Yancey Lovelace.)

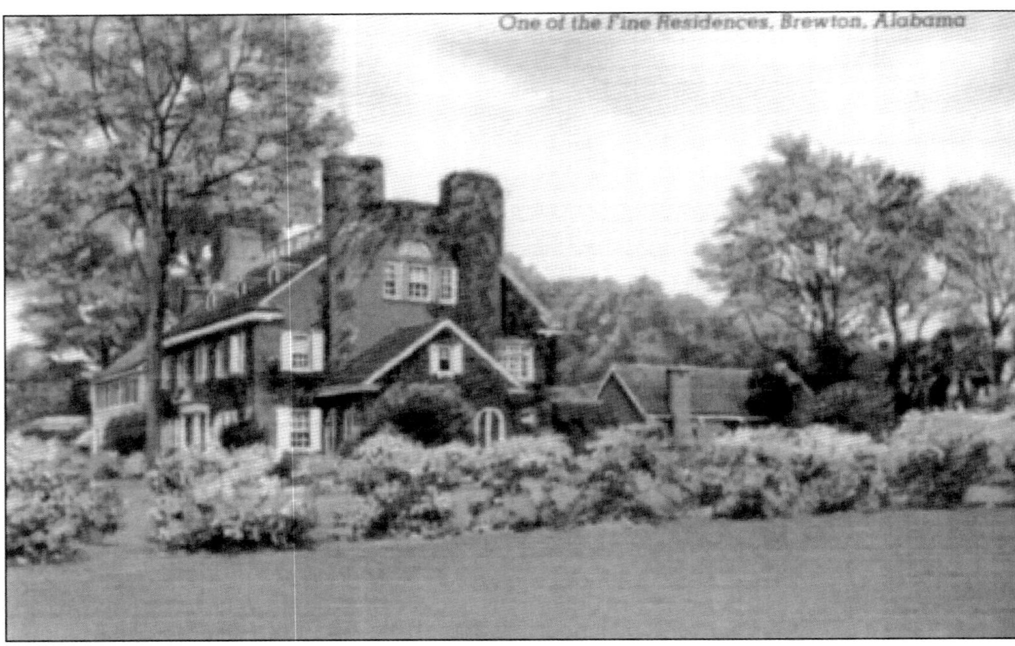

This was the home of Ed Leigh McMillan II, viewed from the south, on an old postcard. Not only was the home stylish and beautiful, but it also had gardens of flowers that bloomed to the south of the house.

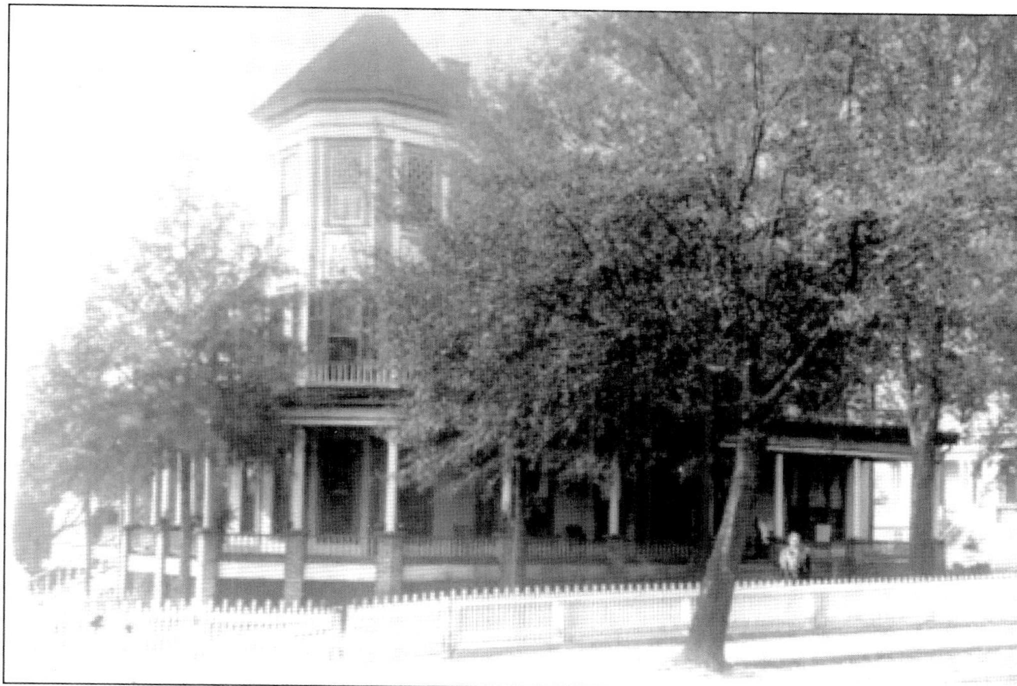

When the McMillan and Finlay families merged, they lived in this house on Belleville Avenue. The widow of Edward Sylvester McMillan brought her children to a new marriage with John David Finlay after the death of her husband, who was shot in 1895 by the bandit Railroad Bill. McMillan and a posse were looking for the man, who was named so because he liked to rob trains. (Courtesy of Katherine Finlay Fountain.)

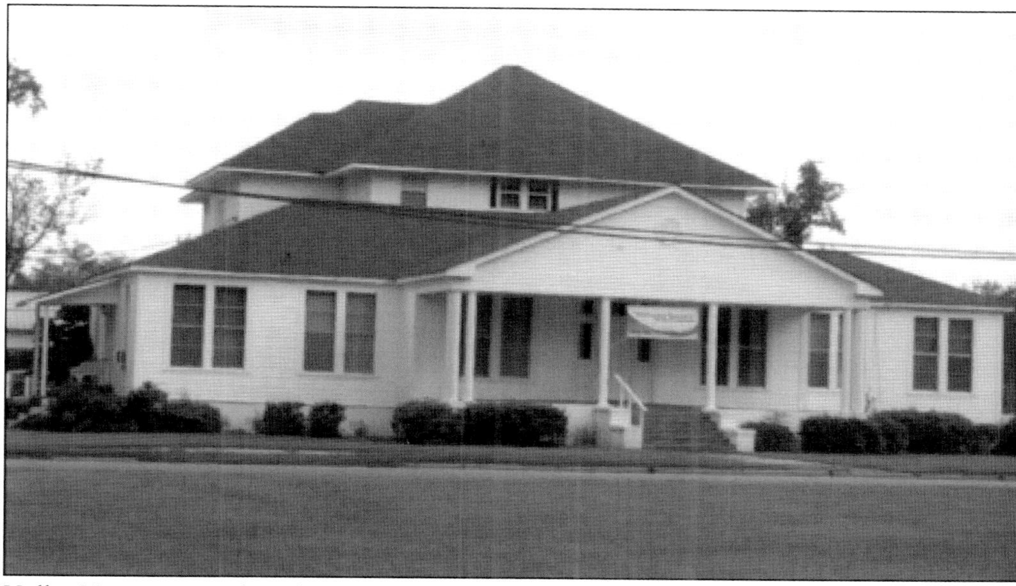

Holley House operated as a hospital in the Brewton–East Brewton area for many years. Dr. W.R. Holley was one of the local doctors working there. His wife later owned the house and ran an assisted living home. It has now been sold but continues to be an assisted living home.

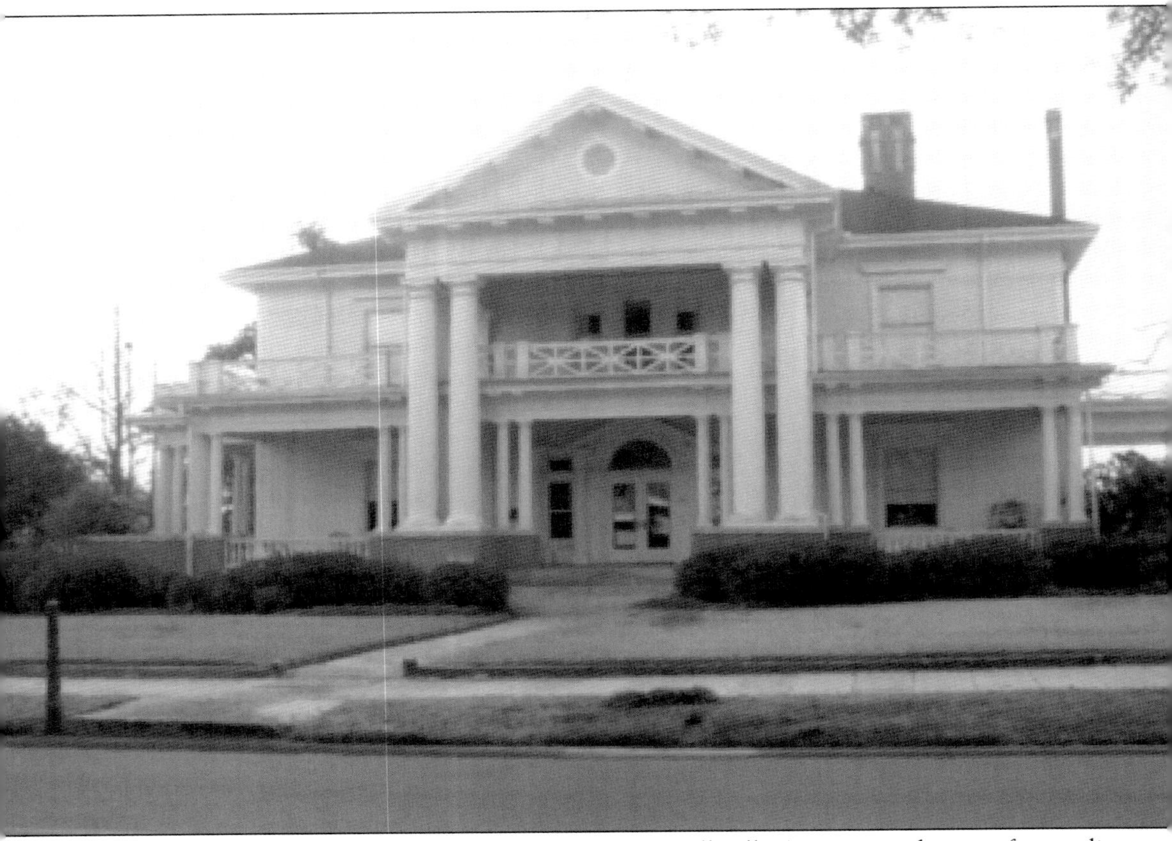

T.R. Miller constructed his home at what is now 212 Belleville Avenue, on the site of an earlier home built in 1887. He and his family lived in it for many years. Jim and Trisha Hart bought it in the 1980s, and their son, James Hart III, now lives in it with his family. Jim is an attorney in Brewton.

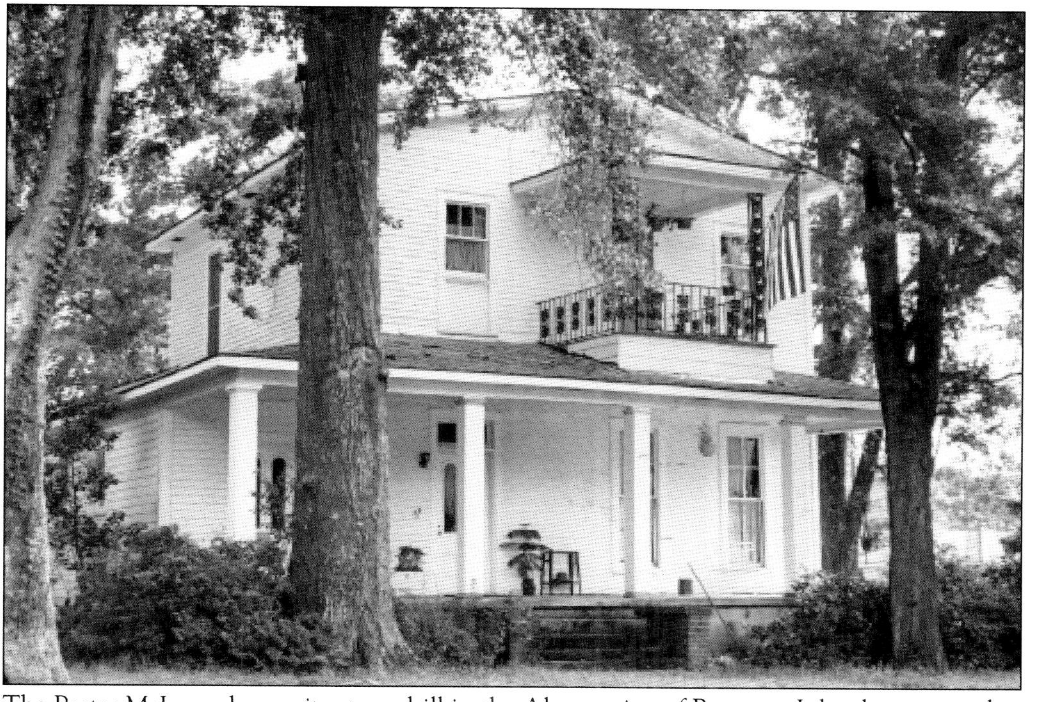

The Porter McLaren home sits atop a hill in the Alco section of Brewton. It has been named to the Alabama Historical Register. (Courtesy of Barbara Carden.)

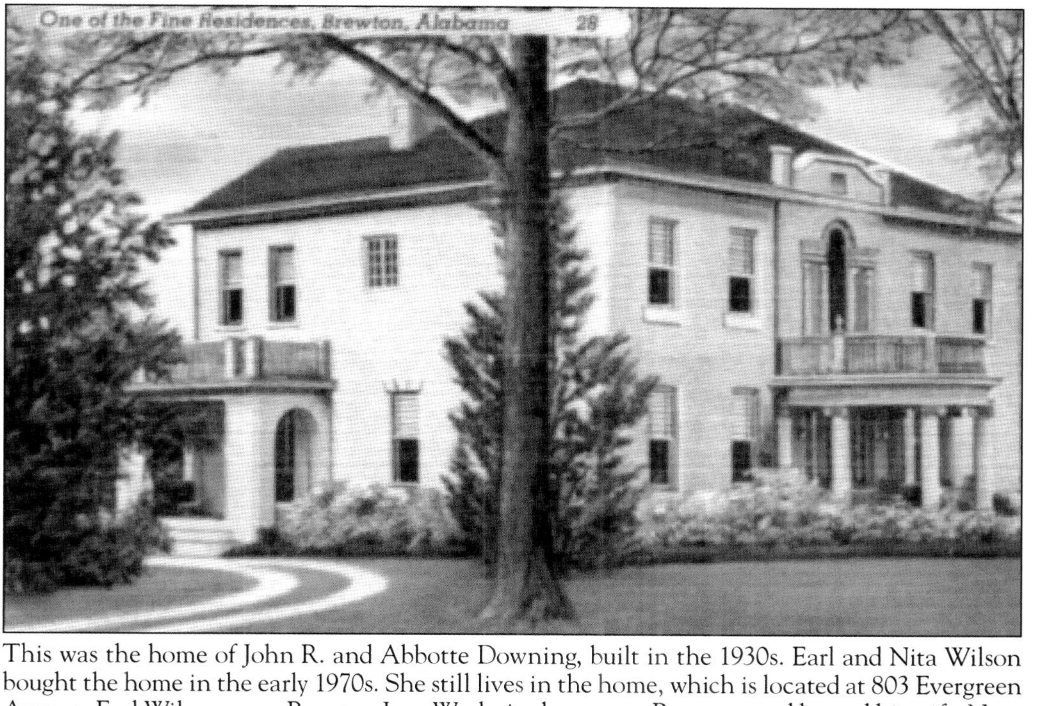

This was the home of John R. and Abbotte Downing, built in the 1930s. Earl and Nita Wilson bought the home in the early 1970s. She still lives in the home, which is located at 803 Evergreen Avenue. Earl Wilson owns Brewton Iron Works in downtown Brewton, and he and his wife, Nan, live on Wilson Street.

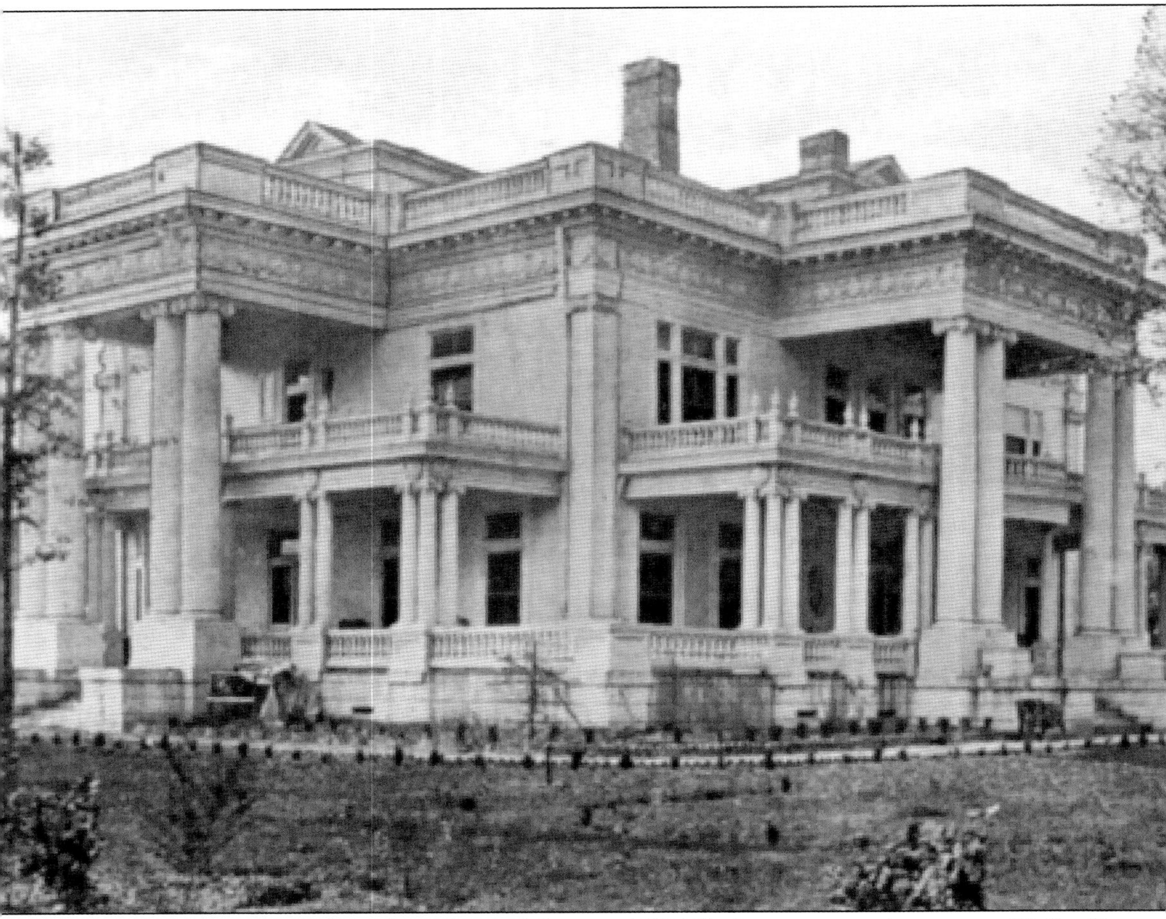

William Yancey Lovelace's home burned down in 1929. The home was on the corner of Belleville Avenue and Rankin Street. William Yancey Lovelace was the son of Edwin Marshall Lovelace, who was president of the Lovelace Lumber Company. The fire that destroyed this house burned it down to the foundation. Later, another house was built on the foundation. Today, the home belongs to the Thompson family. Dr. Marina Thompson is a pediatrician in the Brewton Medical Center. The Lovelace family would suffer the loss by fire of another home, which was on the corner of Belleville Avenue and Blacksher Street. (Courtesy of Yancey Lovelace.)

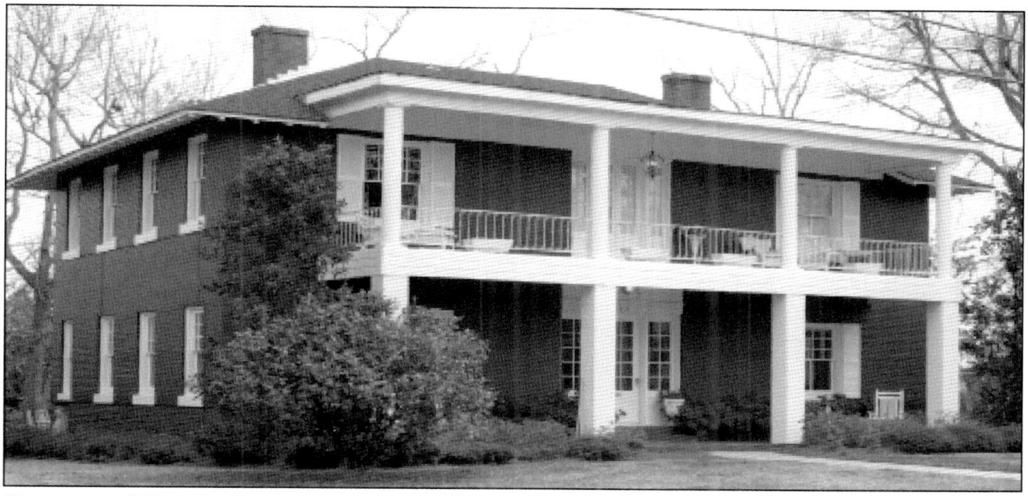

Gerome and Donna Brackin own this home located at 414 Belleville Avenue. The house was built in 1914 for Oscar Forney Luttrell and his wife, Mollie. He came to Brewton to help Charles P. Sowell open the Bank of Brewton. The Brackins bought the home in 2004. It was designed by architect Frank Lockwood of Montgomery.

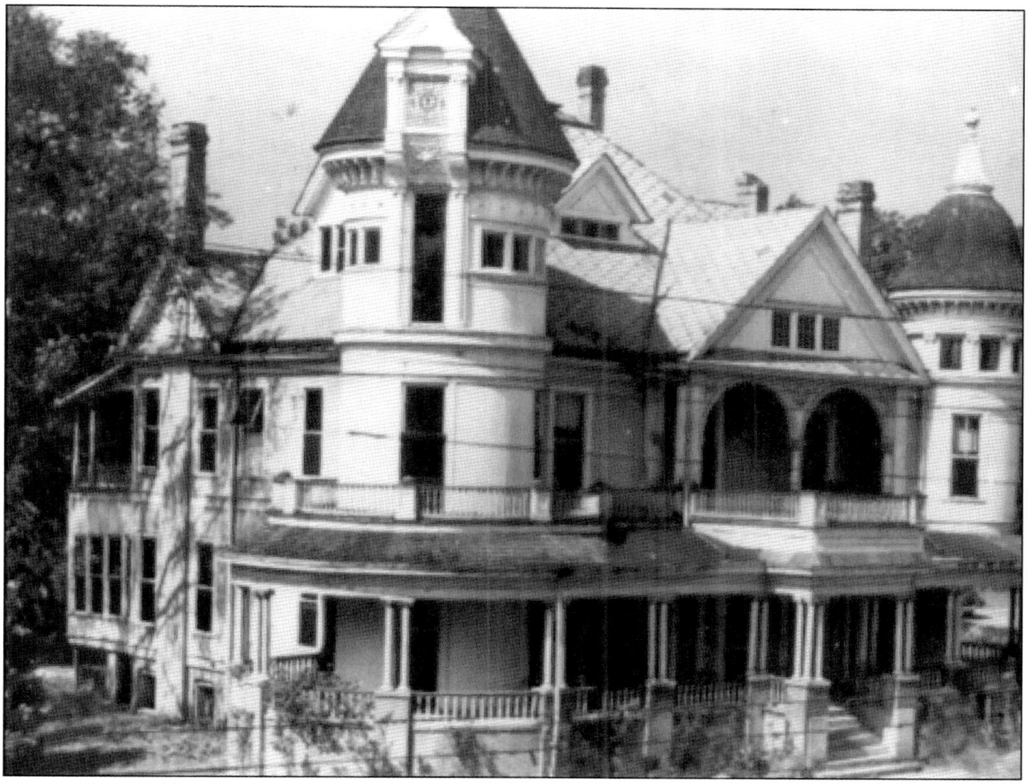

Alexander McGowin built this home across the street from City Park in Brewton, about where BankTrust sits today. The home used all the best materials and modern equipment of the time. It is said to have been centrally heated before anyone else's house in town.

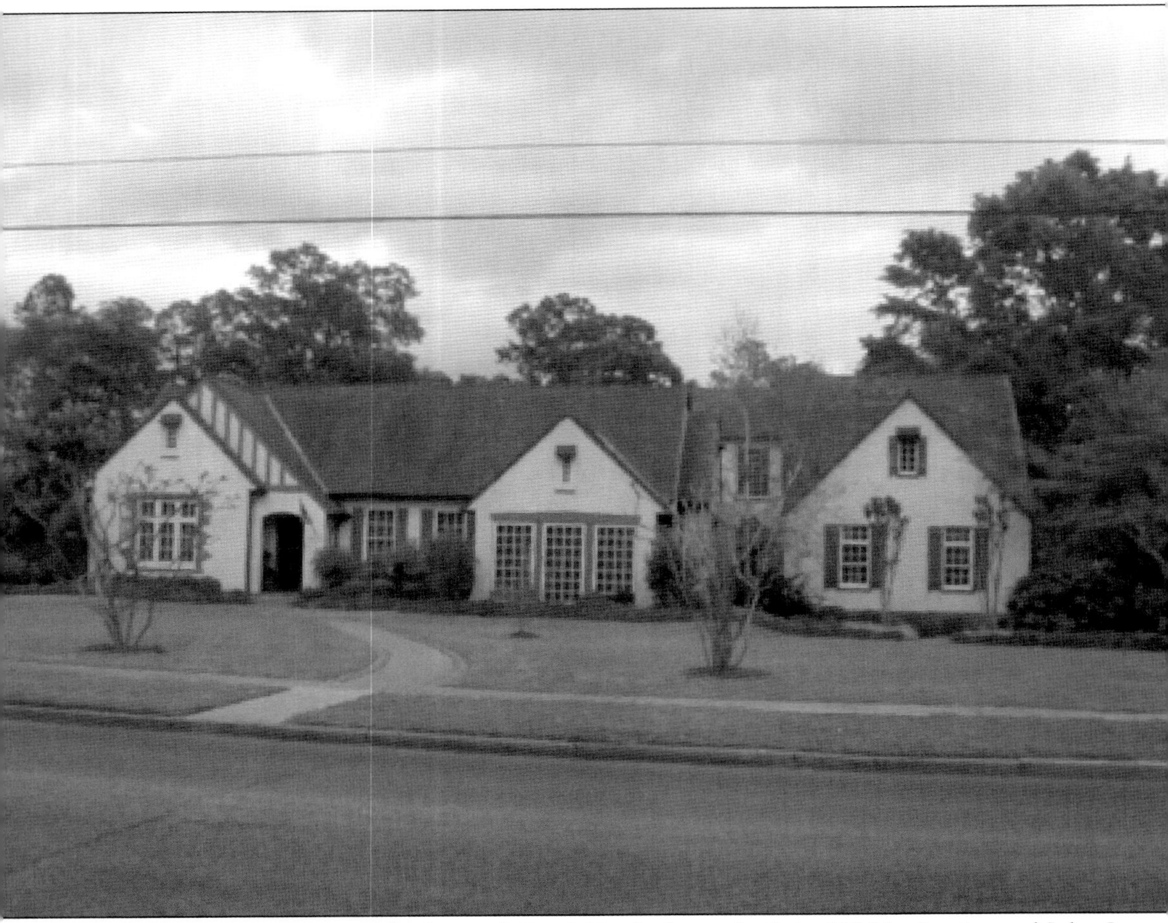

This house is now owned by Joe and Carol Gordy. It was built in 1926 by Louise and John J. Jernigan Sr. In 1965, Clarence and Dorothy Turnipseed bought the house, and they lived there for three years. Jerry Kelly bought the house in 1970, and his family lived there until 1992. The Gordys bought the house in 1992, and they are the current owners. In 2000, a south wing was added, keeping true to the Norman style. It is so well done that it looks as if it was always there. The grounds now include a garden house and greenhouse to accommodate Joe Gordy's hobby of growing orchids.

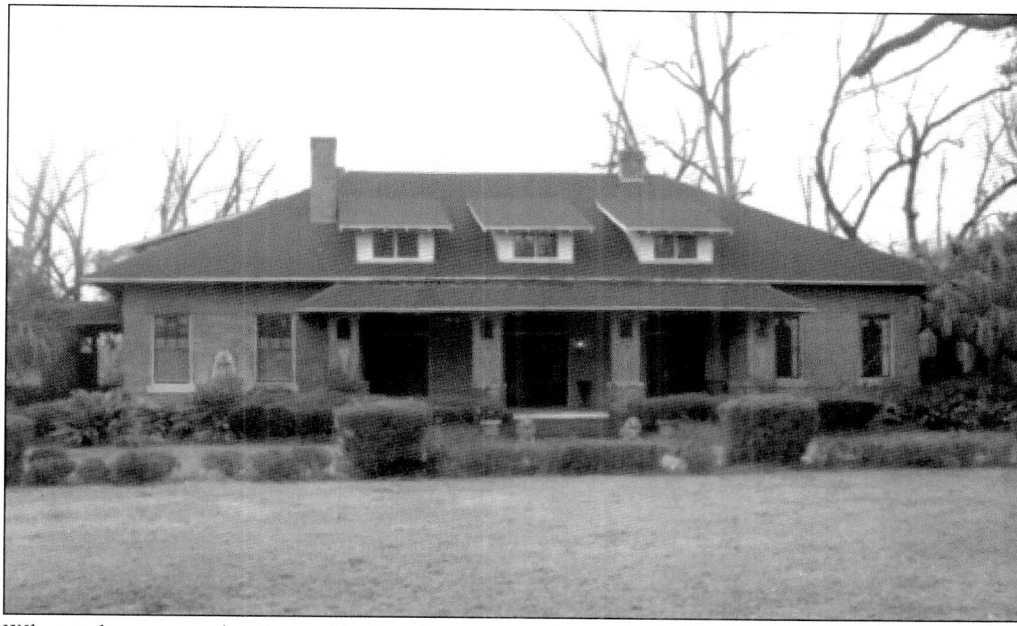

What is known as the Oscar Gordon home occupies a whole block. Gordon was at one time president of the Bank of Brewton. The home was always a showplace, and several years ago, the old place was refurbished and a lot of landscaping was done to prepare it to become a bed and breakfast. Due to zoning problems, the new business never opened.

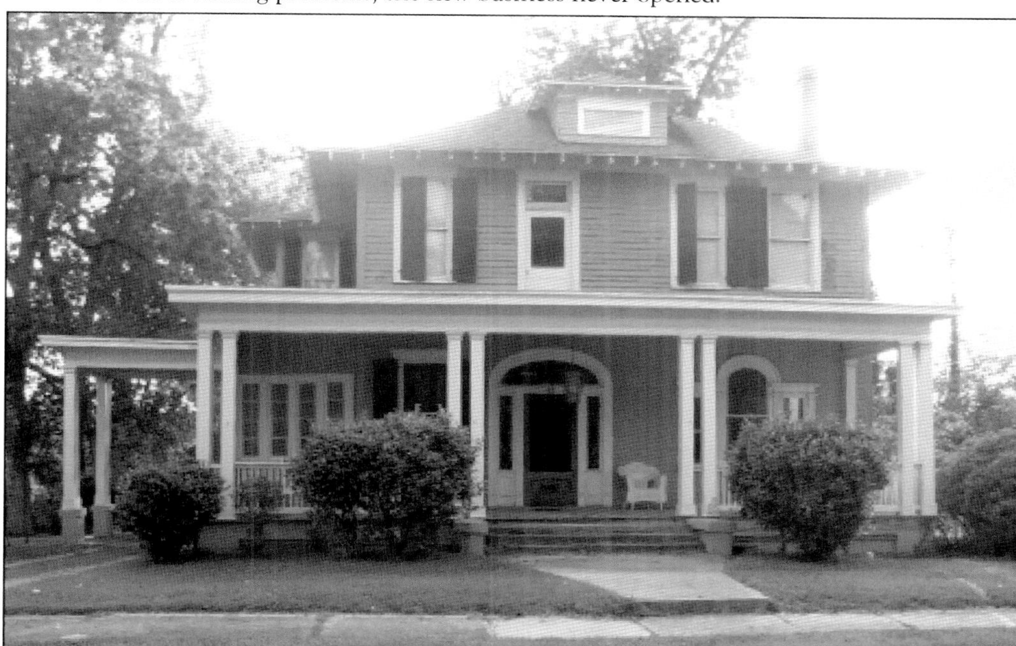

This house, which sits on Belleville Avenue next to the ivy-covered church, was the G.W.L. Smith home. It is at least 100 years old. A photograph taken in 1911 shows the house looking much as it does today. Changes did take place, but the one architectural detail that did not change was the roofline.

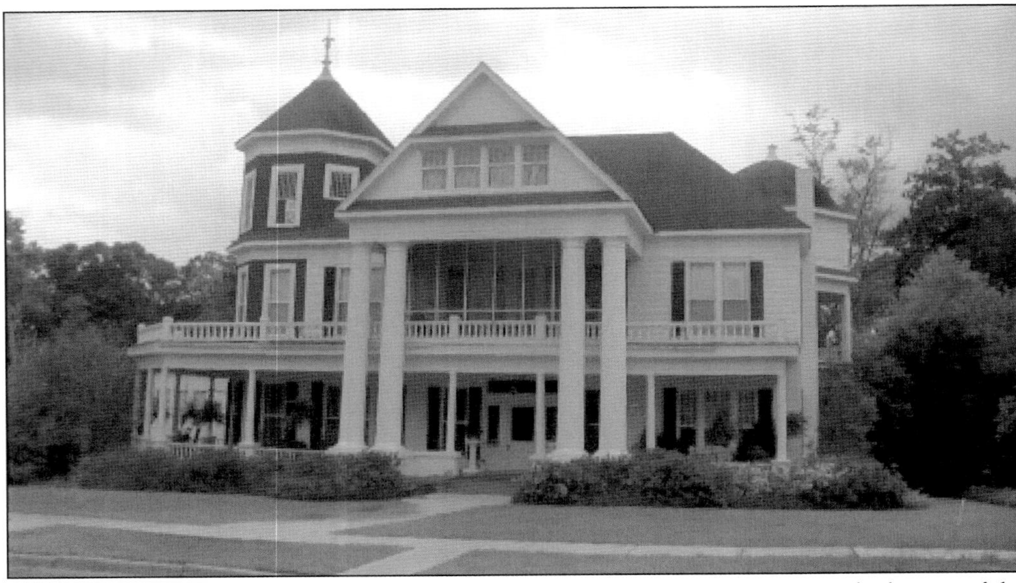

This more modern photograph of the Finlay home on Belleville Avenue shows the beauty of the building. Donnie Fountain and his wife, Catherine Finlay Fountain, are the present owners. The Finlay family, including the McMillan children of the murdered sheriff of Escambia County and their Finlay half-siblings, lived in this house for a while. It was actually built as the home of the Foshee family.

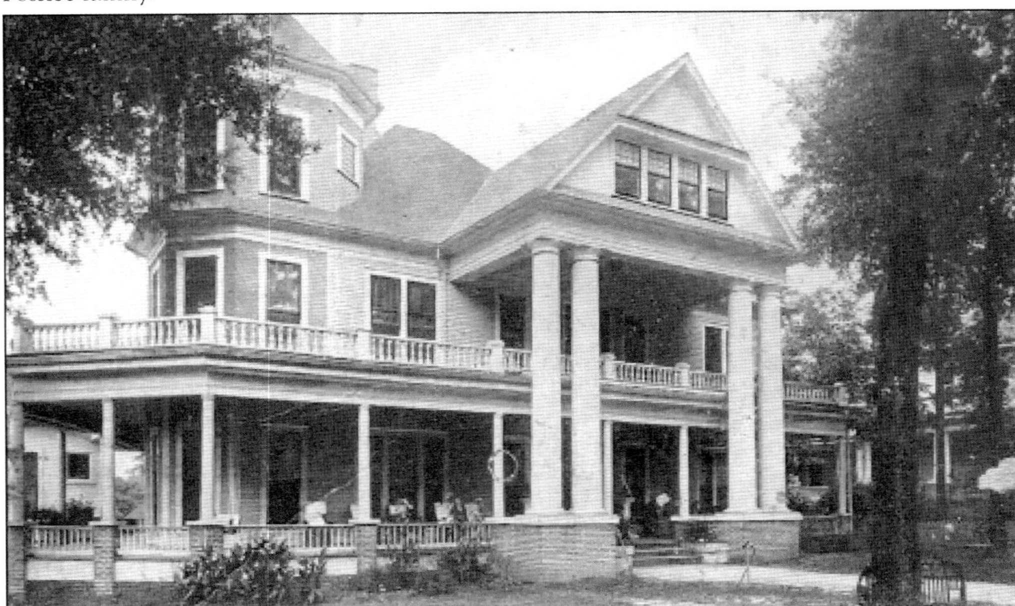

This is a photograph taken after the remodeling of the Finlay house. The story goes that Kate Finlay was not happy about the house next door—the T.R. Miller home—having such imposing columns. She decided to make some changes, and not only did the renovated house have columns, it also has a sleeping porch on the second floor. It still retains the beauty it had 100 years ago. (Courtesy of Katherine Finlay Fountain.)

Eight

Businesses of the Area

From the very beginning, Brewton has been fortunate to keep most of the downtown stores in business for most of its 126 years. That is not to say there have not been times when things looked bad, but because many downtown businesses are family-owned, they have managed to hang on when things were tough. Even the Great Depression did not do them in.

To begin with, almost all of the business was done in the downtown area, but as time has passed, several shopping centers have sprung up, taking some of the business away from downtown. Business owners have responded by organizing and focusing on keeping business alive and urging shoppers to shop at home.

Some of the oldest businesses have managed to not only stay afloat but to thrive. The T.R. Miller Mill has been a part of the community for more than 100 years and is still one of the major employers in Brewton. The forward thinking of T.R. Miller led the company to practice good cutting and replanting.

Georgia-Pacific (GP), the former Jefferson Smurfit and Container Corporation, is perhaps the largest employer in this area. It has been in business since the late 1950s, making and processing paper products. They are not only employers, but they contribute funds and time to the community as well. Natural Decorations, Inc., (NDI) is situated in the industrial park to the south of Brewton, along with several other businesses.

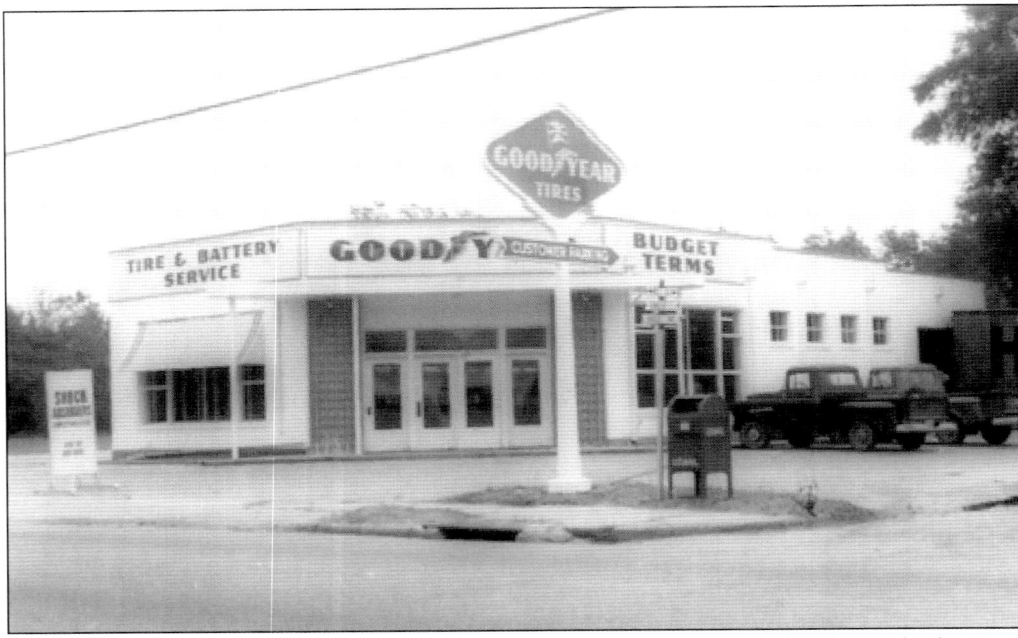

The building on the corner of Granberry Street and Douglas Avenue has been the home of several businesses. The Brackin family had a grocery store there at one time, and it has also been a sporting goods store. At the time of this photograph, it was a Goodyear Tires store. (Courtesy of Robert Crenshaw.)

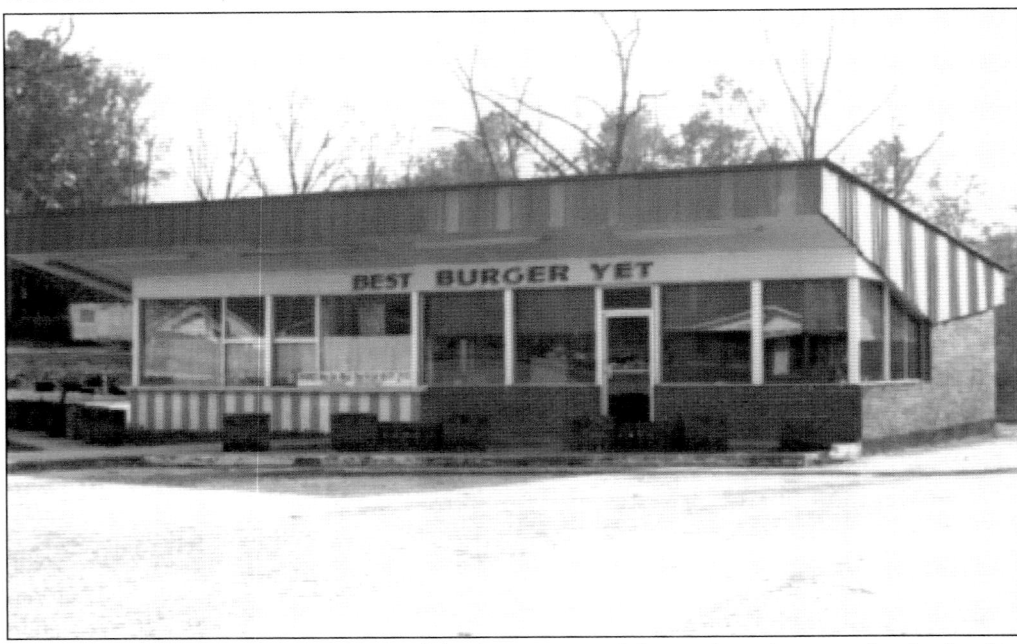

Best Burger in East Brewton was one of the forerunners of the modern-day stops for the familiar burgers and fries. The building is still on Forrest Avenue next to the Shell Oil station. It has been many things since the last burger was cooked there, including a restaurant, a seafood retailer, and a tattoo parlor. (Courtesy of the *Brewton Standard*.)

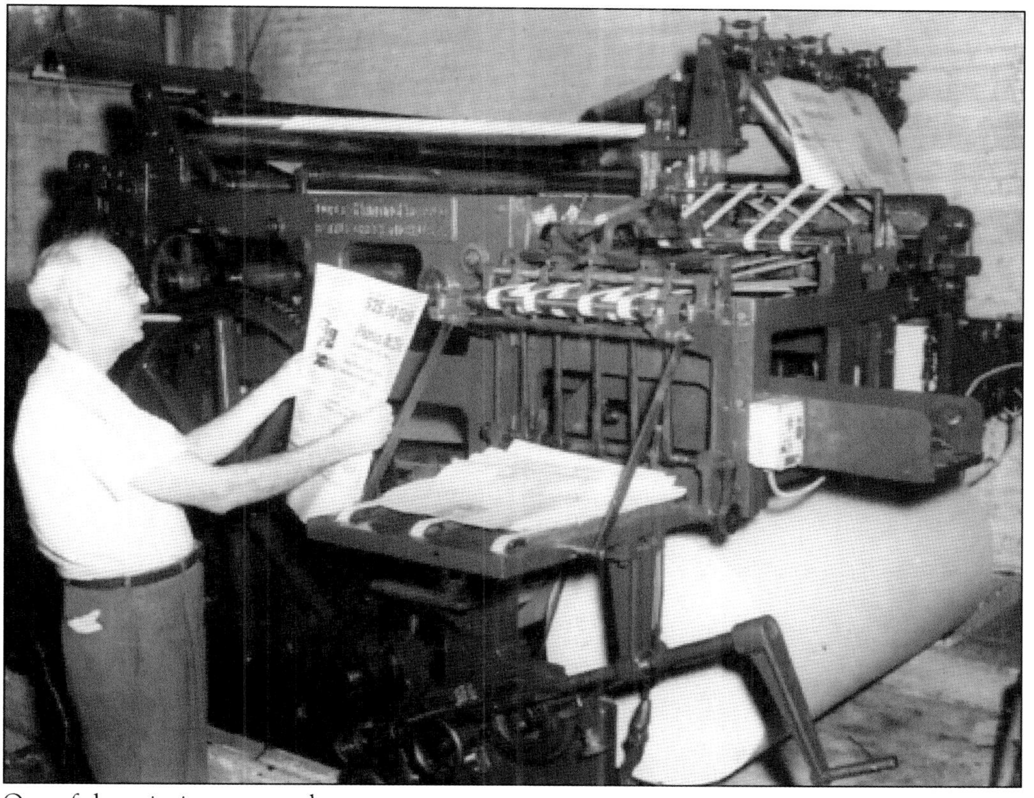

One of the printing presses that was once used by the *Brewton Standard* is pictured. The man who operated the machine was Steve Morton, and it is said that he was a very smart man who knew the right way to spell just about anything. The printing is no longer done on-site at the newspaper; it is done in Andalusia. The *Brewton Standard* was the result of the merging of several newspapers over the years. The *Standard Gauge* published its last issue in December 1905, and it printed the first issue of 1906 as the *Brewton Standard*. (Courtesy of Robert Crenshaw.)

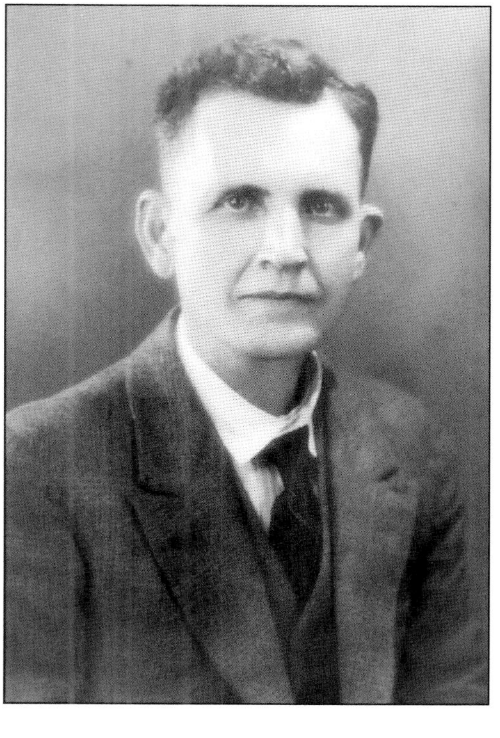

Eugene Morton Neal was the son of W.S. Neal. He ran a store in downtown Brewton on St. Joseph Avenue for many years. The store carried a variety of items for sale. (Courtesy of the Escambia County Historical Society.)

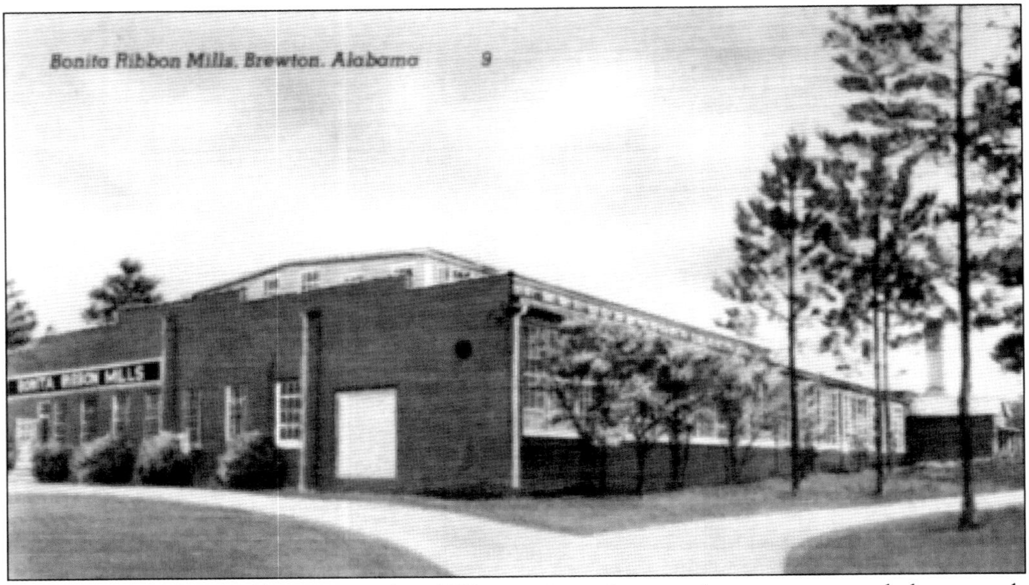

The Bonita Ribbon Mill was opened in 1929, at a time when employment was needed as a result of the Depression. The owners, who were from New York, constructed a building that still stands today on St. Nicholas Avenue. The owners of the business were also instrumental in getting a recreation area called Bonnie Beach south of Brewton at Franklin Mill. The water was dammed up, creating a place to swim. Bathhouses were added, as well as dressing rooms and a concession stand. This is a postcard that circulated in the 1940s.

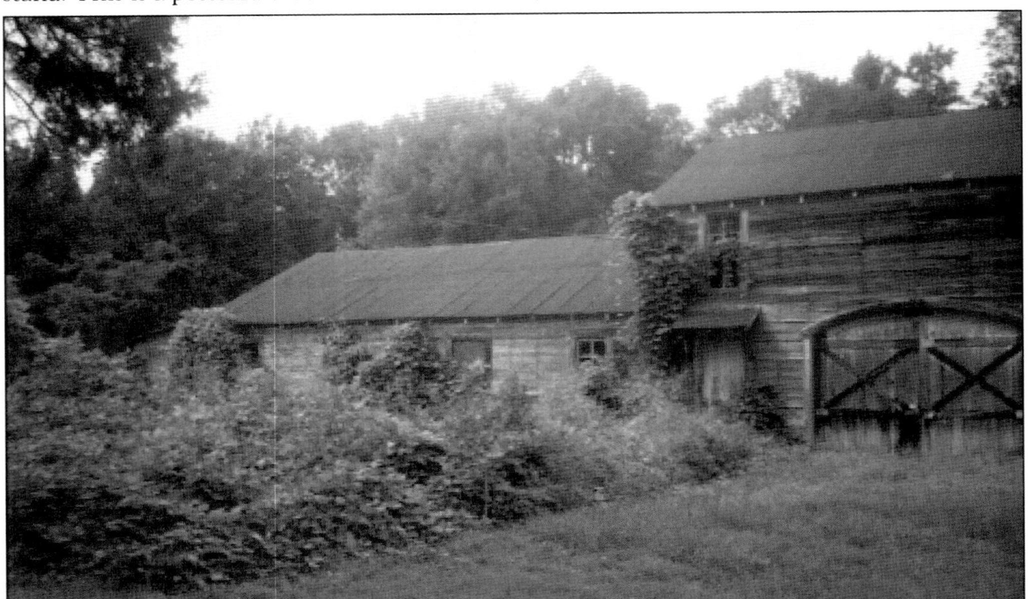

This strange building looks like it could have served several purposes. It was actually the home of Crenshaw Cabinets and is located on Snowden Street in East Brewton. The current owner, Billy Harris, a descendant of the Crenshaw family, said the building is strangely rounded and shaped like a boat's hull—the result of Mr. Crenshaw working in the ship-building business in Mobile during World War II.

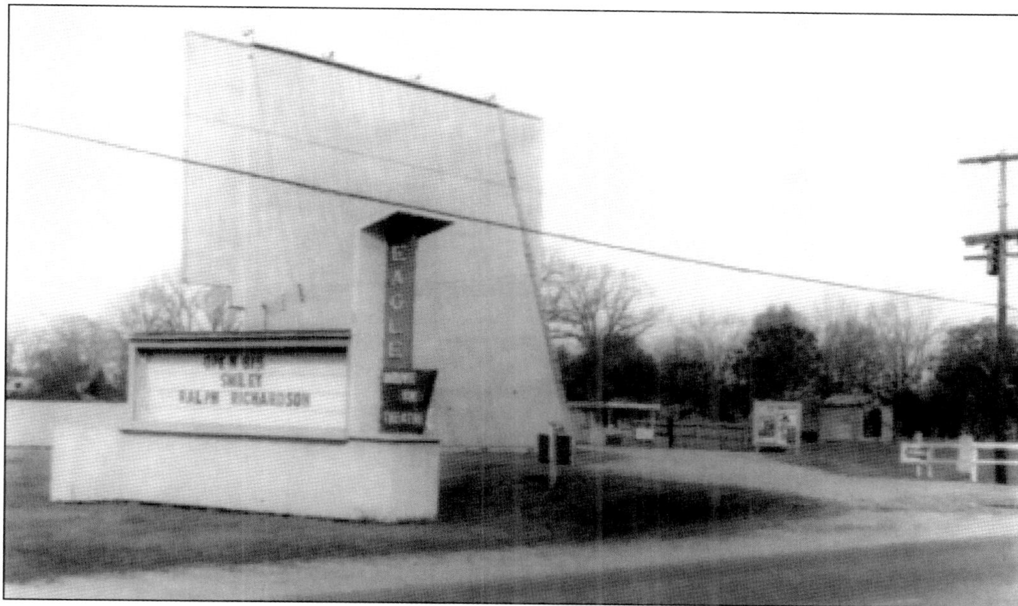

There are those who still remember the days (or nights) when people drove to the drive-in movie. The Eagle Drive-in was a popular spot for many years for families who wore their pajamas and carried their own snacks and young couples out for a night of spooning. It was located in East Brewton on Florida Street. The theater was eventually torn down, and today, this is the site of a church. (Courtesy of Robert Crenshaw.)

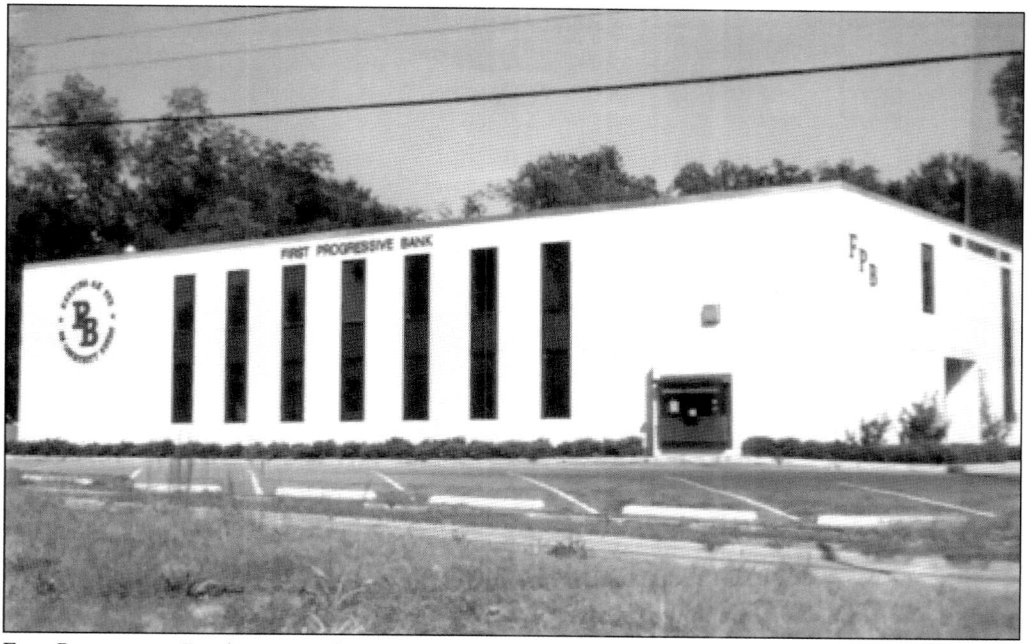

First Progressive Bank is owned and operated by the Finlay family. Sally Finlay and her brother Doug are the current Finlays associated with the bank. Sally tends to the family business as well as devoting her time and energy to several philanthropic community events. The bank sits on the corner of St. Nicholas Avenue and Sowell Street. (Courtesy of Escambia County Commission.)

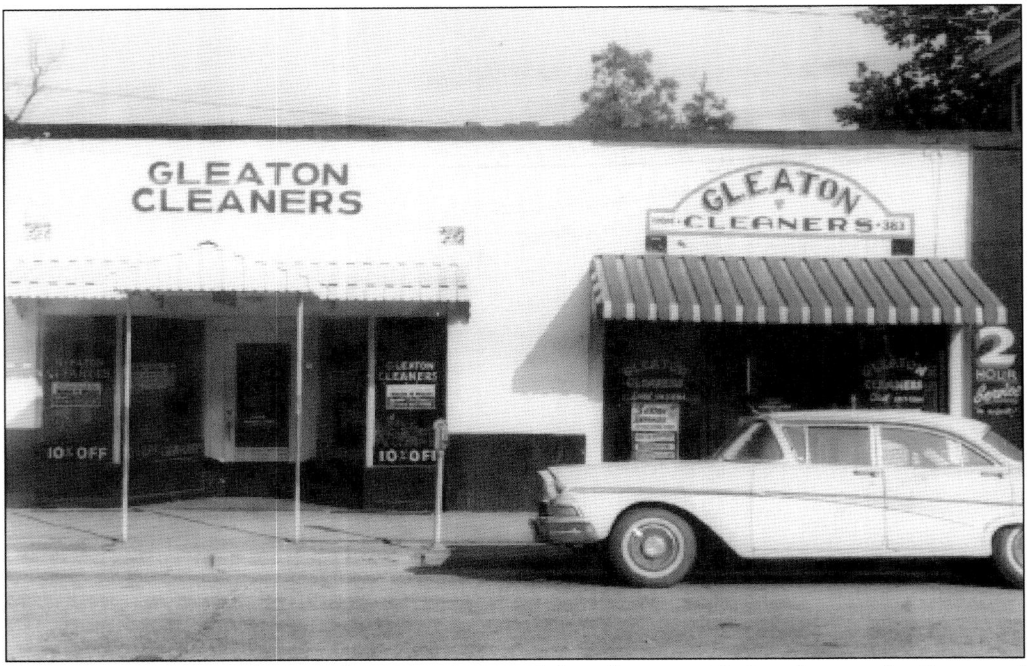

Gleaton Cleaners is only one of two dry cleaners left in Brewton. Today, this is a family-owned business run by John Gleaton. It is located on Rankin Street east of Douglas Avenue.

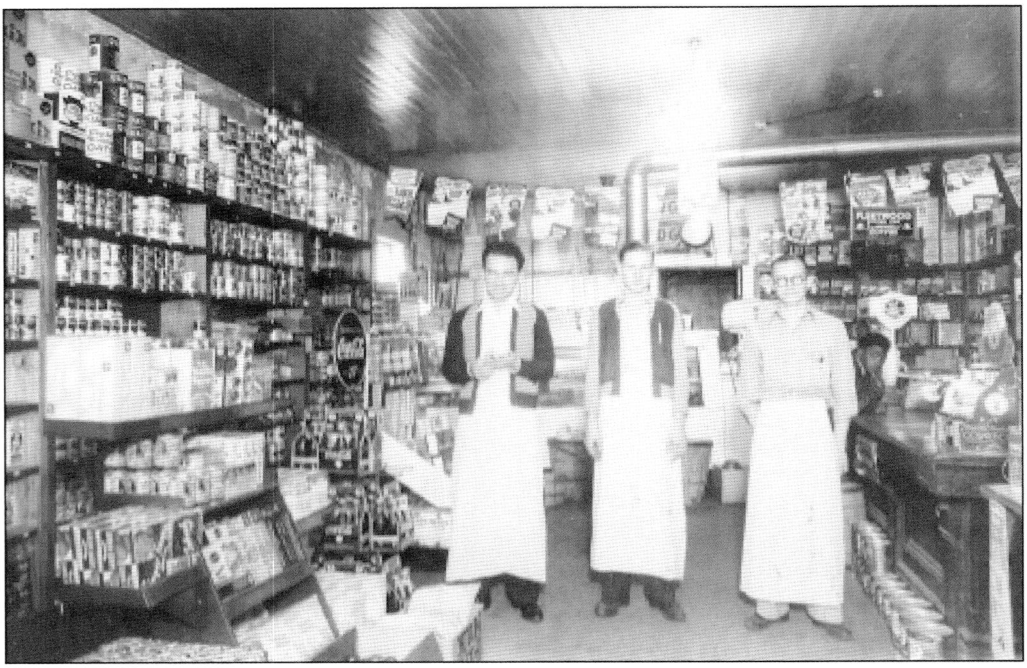

James Knox owned and operated Knox Grocery and Market on the corner of Granberry Street and Douglas Avenue. Shoppers could buy on credit and have their groceries delivered. In this 1939 photograph, Knox is standing on the left. The man in the middle is John R. Sowell. (Courtesy of Betty Knox Clark.)

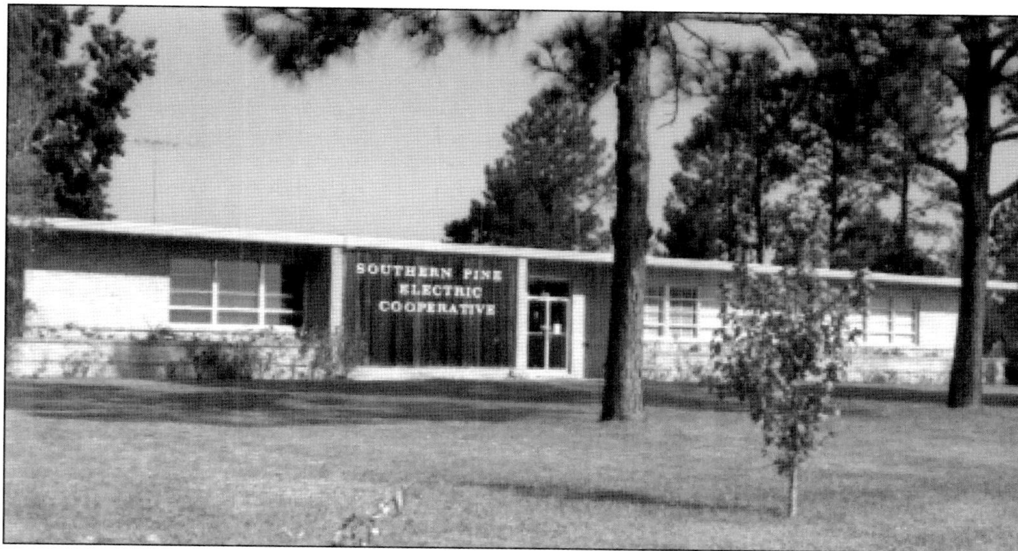

Southern Pine Electric Company is pictured before it was updated. It furnishes power to the rural areas of Escambia County. Since this photograph was taken, the building has undergone tremendous changes. It is located on the four-lane highway south of Brewton. (Courtesy of Escambia County Commission.)

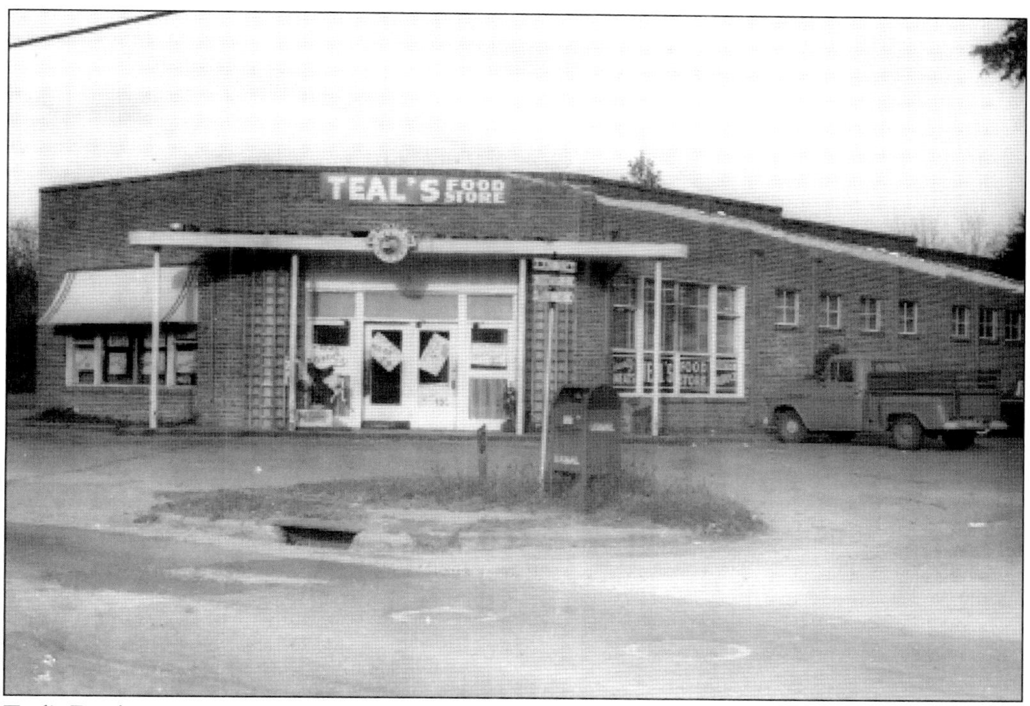

Teal's Food Store is only one of the businesses that have been located in this building. It is on the corner of Douglas Avenue and Granberry Street and at one time was a grocery store owned by the Brackin family. (Courtesy of Robert Crenshaw.)

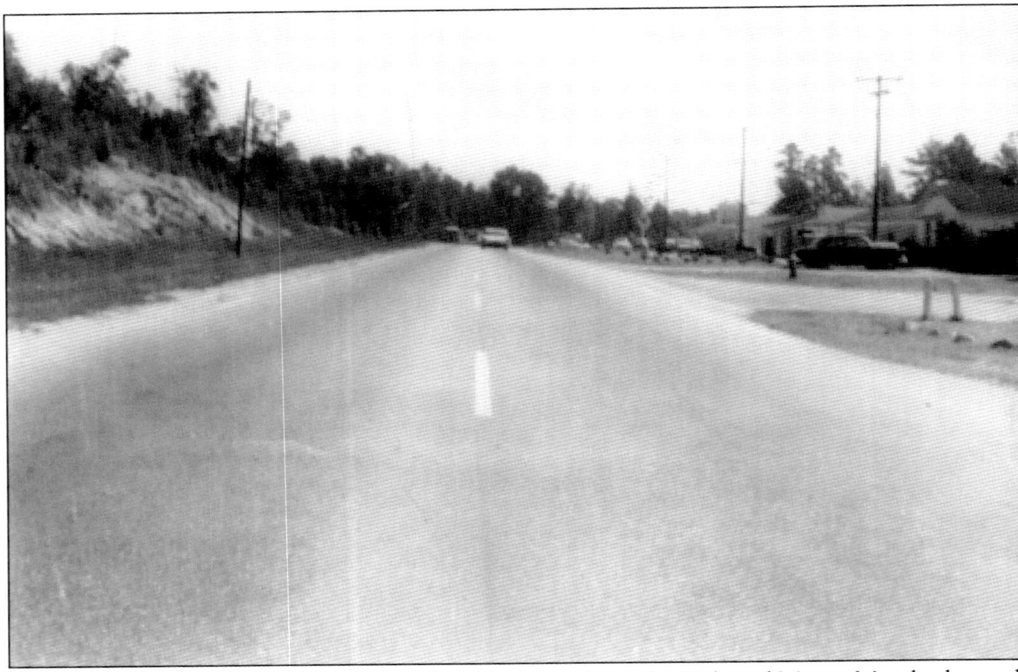

This photograph was taken looking north from about where the Colonial Manor Motel is located. It was taken before the other businesses were located there. Now on the left are Peach Motors and McDonald's, while the Days Inn is on the right. (Courtesy of Robert Crenshaw.)

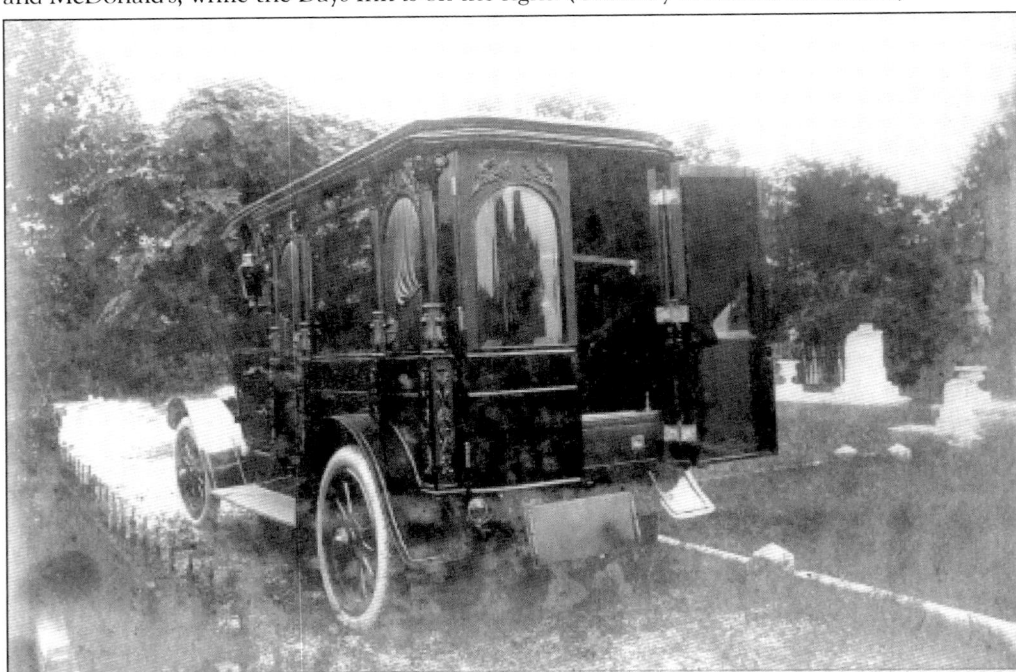

This hearse was the first in the area that was motorized. It was owned by J.W. Adkisson and offered a beautiful way to be delivered to the cemetery.

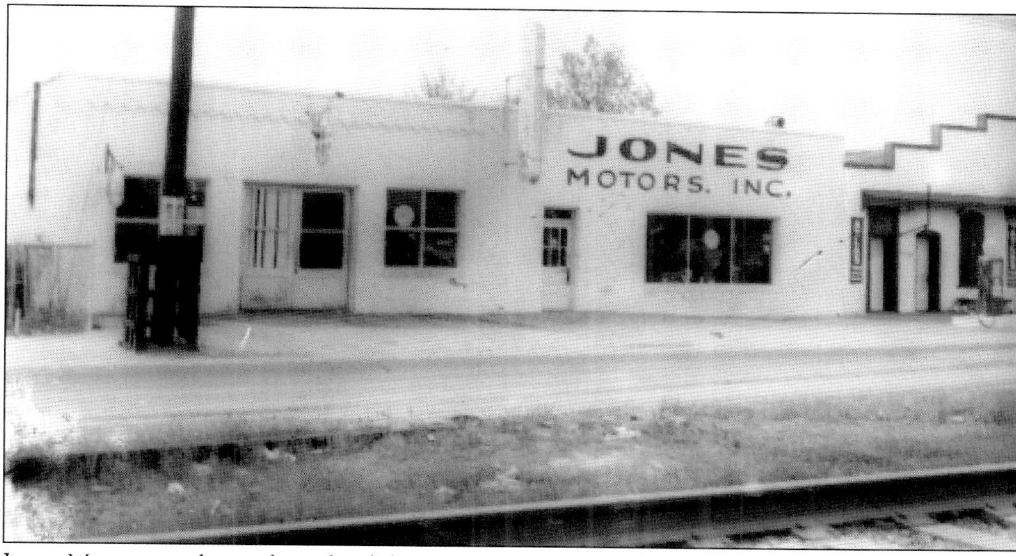

Jones Motors was located south of the main intersection of St. Nicholas Avenue, U.S. 31, and Mildred Street. This was an area that once had a spur off the railroad tracks that came behind the Ritz Theater by the old farmers exchange. (Courtesy of Frank Scott.)

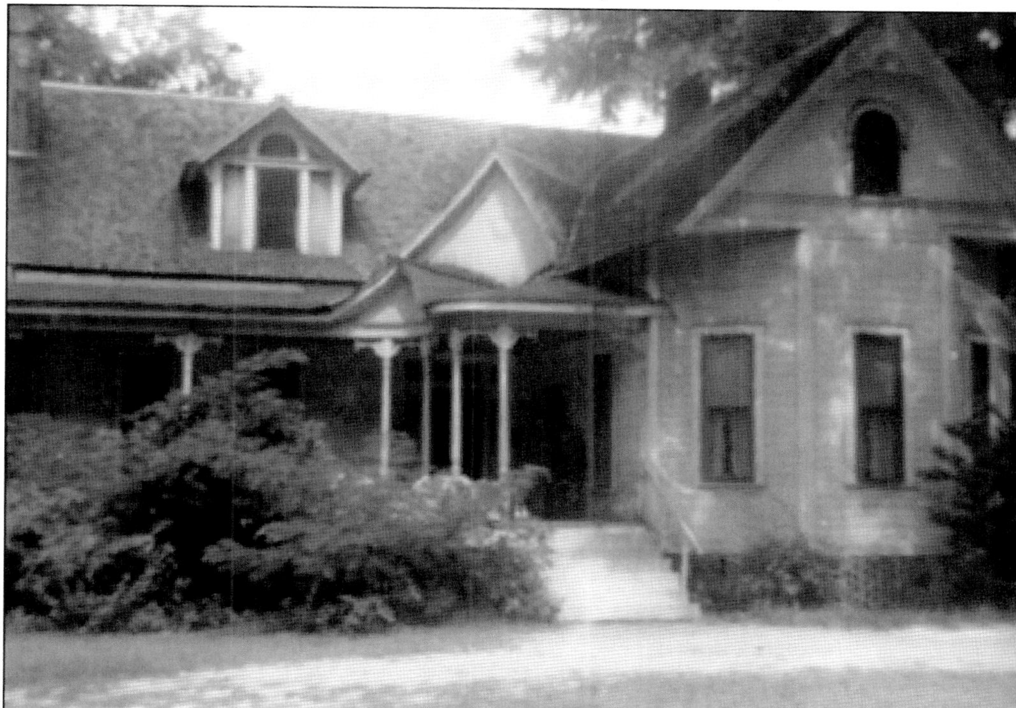

This was the Strain home, located between the T.R. Miller home and the W.Y. Lovelace home on the corner of Belleville Avenue and Rankin Street. Ann Strain operated the family home as a boardinghouse for a number of years in the 1940s and 1950s. Her daughter Barbara Strain Miller Carden told of the boardinghouse being one of the places where visiting teams of the Alabama-Florida AAA Baseball League stayed while in town. (Courtesy of Barbara Carden.)

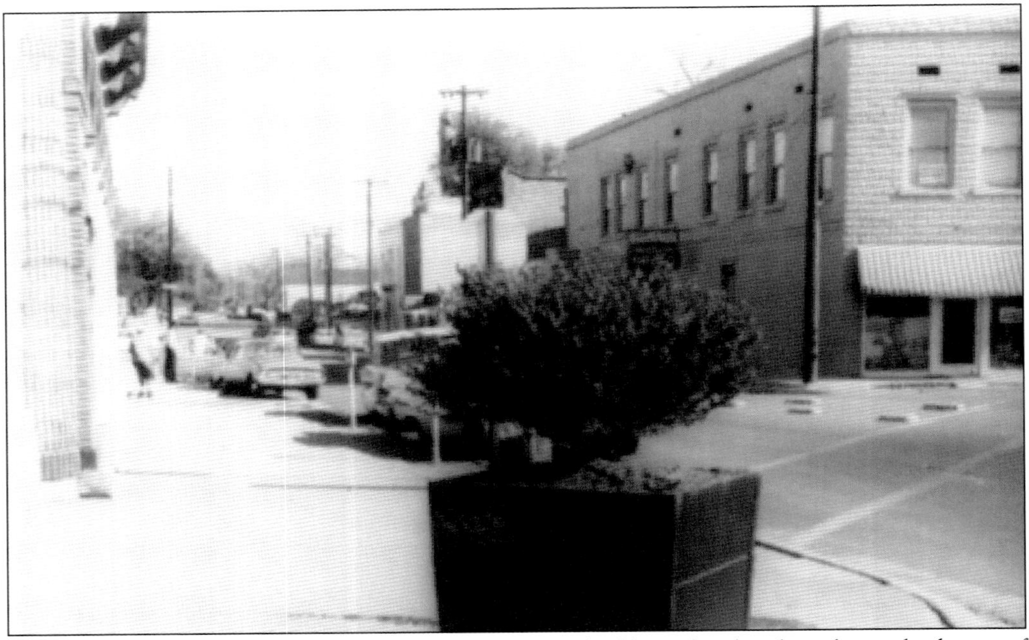

To the side of the large flower box is the distinctive building that has long been the home of several drugstores and restaurants in the downtown area. It is considered part of the downtown historic district. The flower boxes were put in to decorate and bring some color to the area. (Courtesy of Robert Crenshaw.)

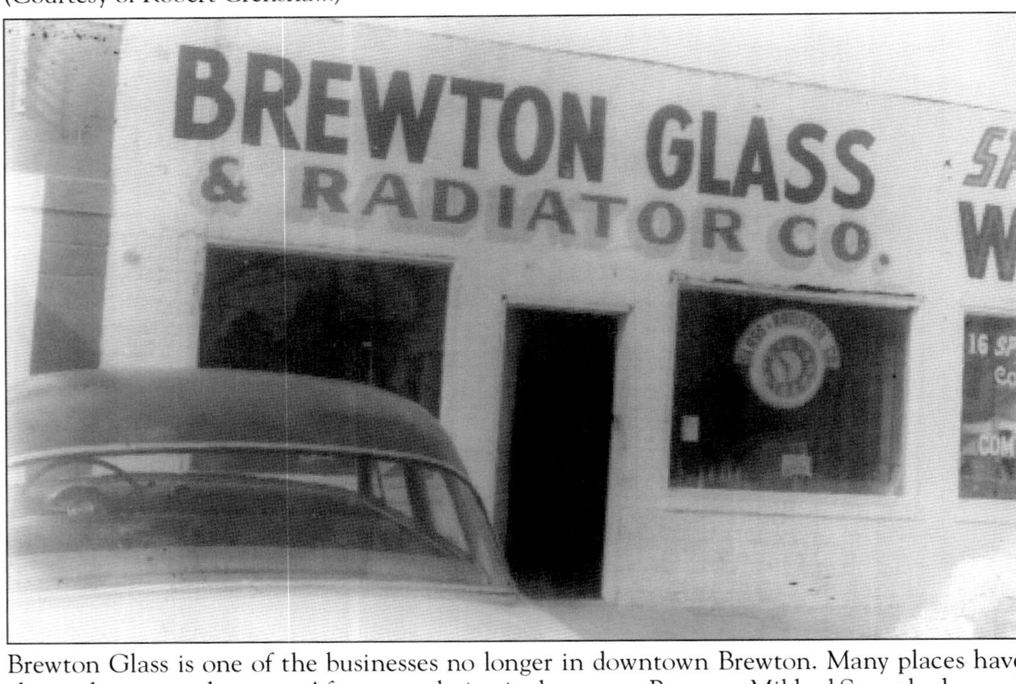

Brewton Glass is one of the businesses no longer in downtown Brewton. Many places have changed names and owners. After an explosion in downtown Brewton, Mildred Street had several businesses that never reopened. Moye's Office and School Supplies was one of the exceptions. (Courtesy of Robert Crenshaw.)

Nine

Favorite Pastimes

Like most Southern towns, Brewton and East Brewton love their sporting events. School teams participate in everything from baseball and football to volleyball, softball, soccer, and tennis.

Sports are one area that pits the residents of Brewton and East Brewton against each other. Over the years, a rivalry has grown, and today, both participants and coaches put each other at the top of the list of teams to beat. One of the most famous games is the football game played between the two teams. Today, many don't even know how the rivalry began, but it all started in 1946. Equipment was needed for the local hospital, and the idea of playing a charity game to raise money was what started it all. At the time, both towns had football teams, but they didn't play each other in the season. After some arrangements were made, the teams met for the first time. Today, that annual game is known as the Battle of Murder Creek.

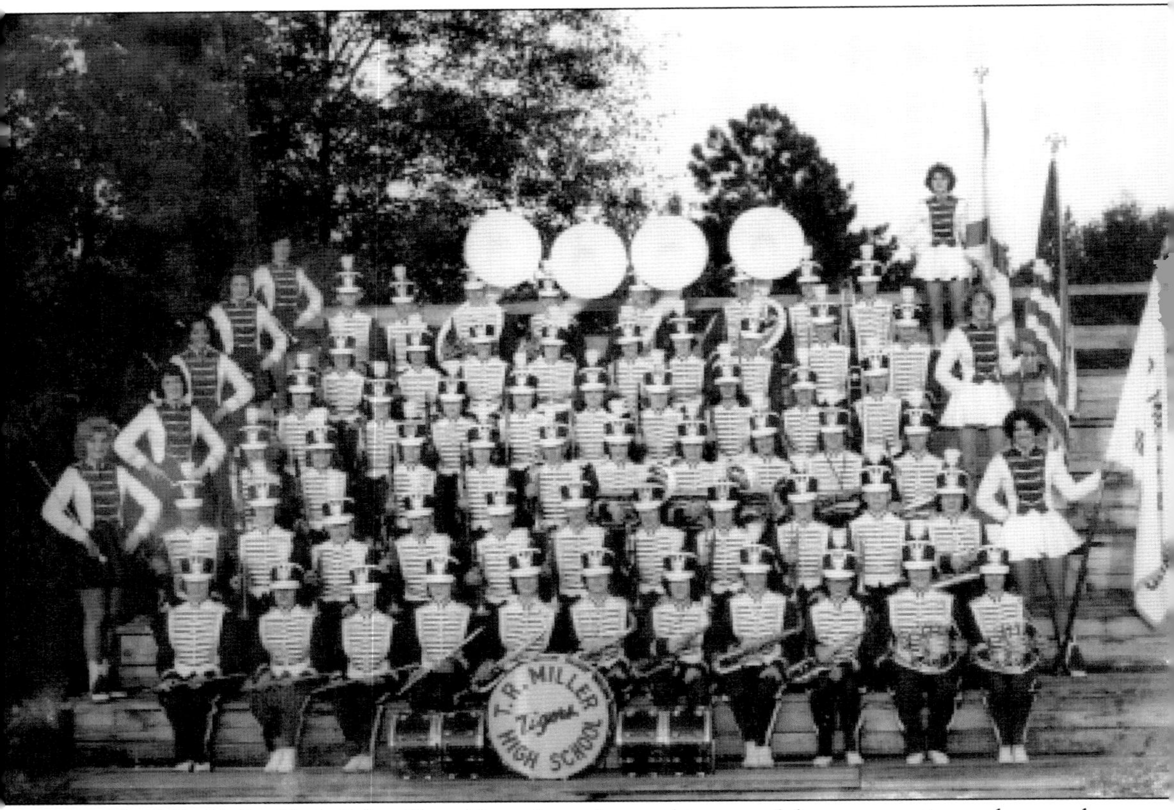

The T.R. Miller High School band has always been a big part of the community, and even when this photograph was made, it was large for the size of the school. This shows the band at old Rotary Field, which was where the Brewton Elementary School stands today. The photograph was taken around 1961. (Courtesy of Robert Crenshaw.)

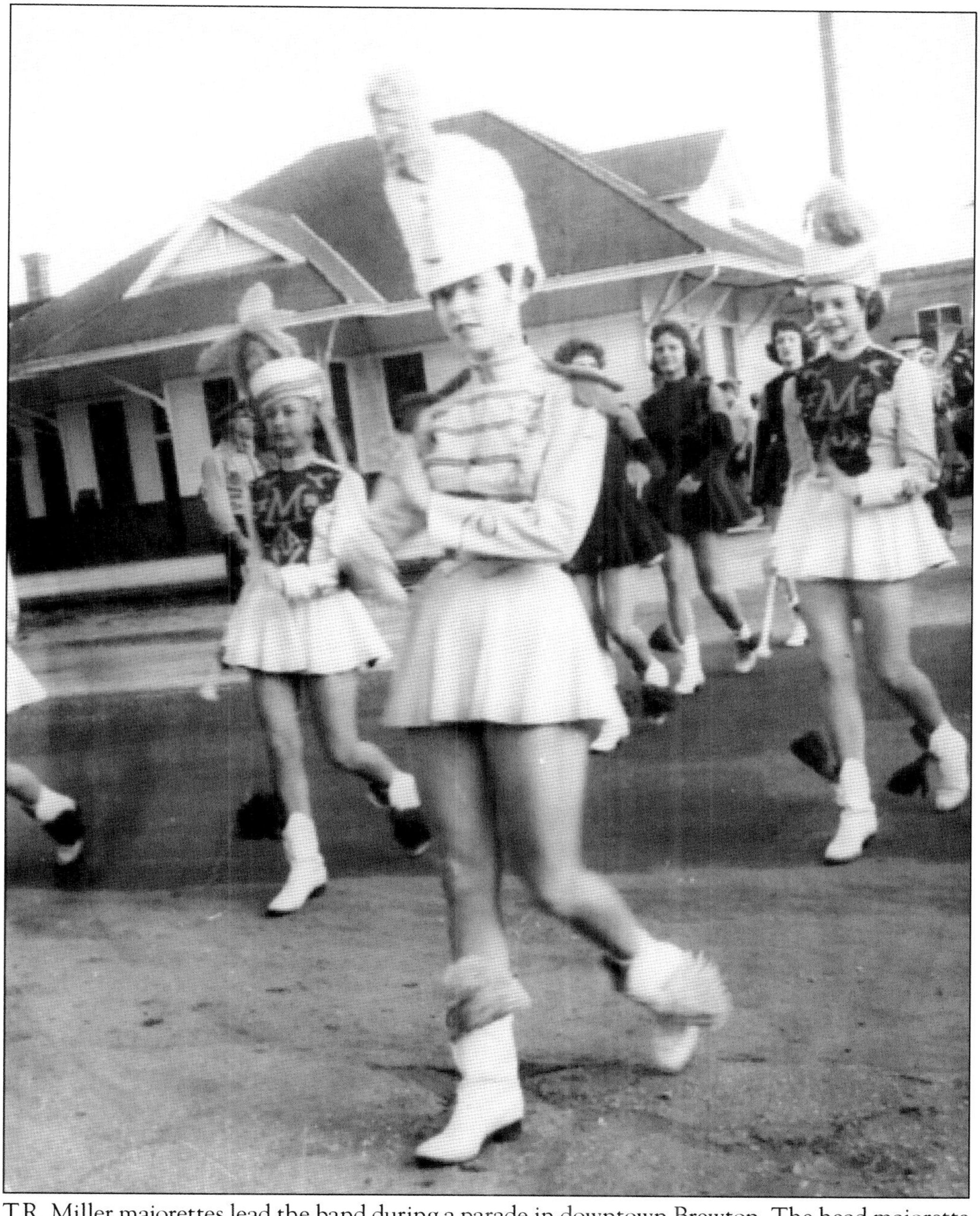

T.R. Miller majorettes lead the band during a parade in downtown Brewton. The head majorette is Diana Watson. The majorette to the right of her is Melanie Monk, and one of the girls behind her is Nancy Miller. The others are not identified. (Courtesy of Robert Crenshaw.)

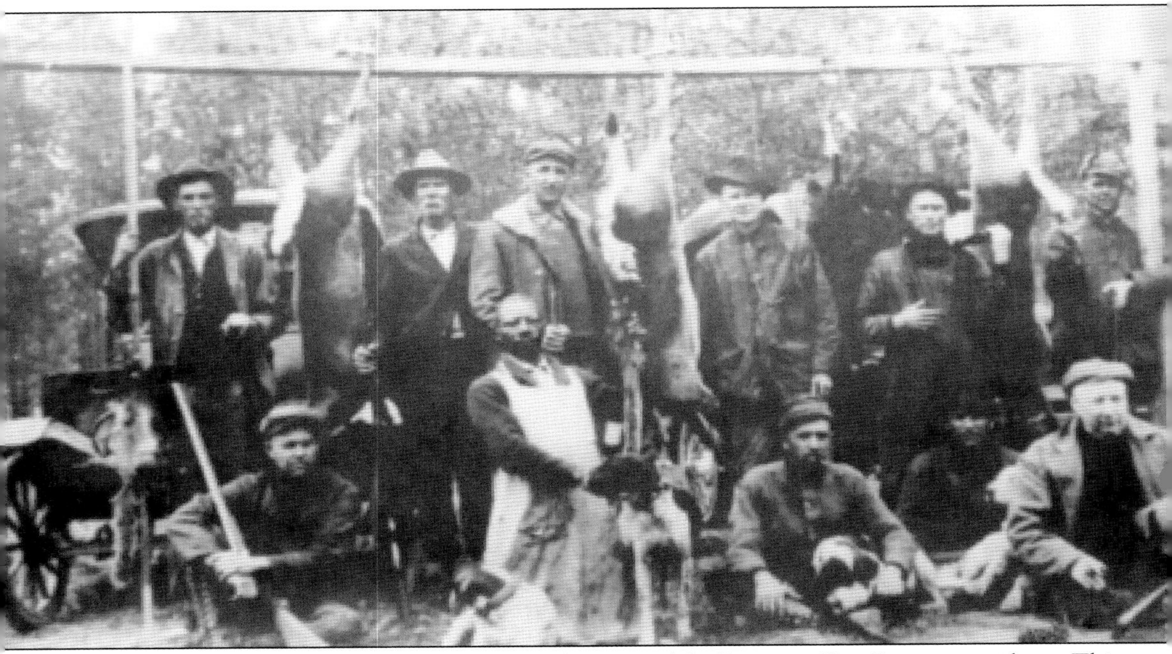

Hunting has always been a favorite pastime for many of the Brewton–East Brewton residents. This is a deer and turkey hunt in 1918 at Dozier Camp in Brooklyn. Those in the photograph standing are, from left to right, John Baggett, Ash Clark, D.P. Liles, Ed Leigh McMillan, ? Gibson, and Paul Till; seated from left to right are C.B. Garrett; Sam Taylor, the camp cook; Arthur Allen; and two unidentified.

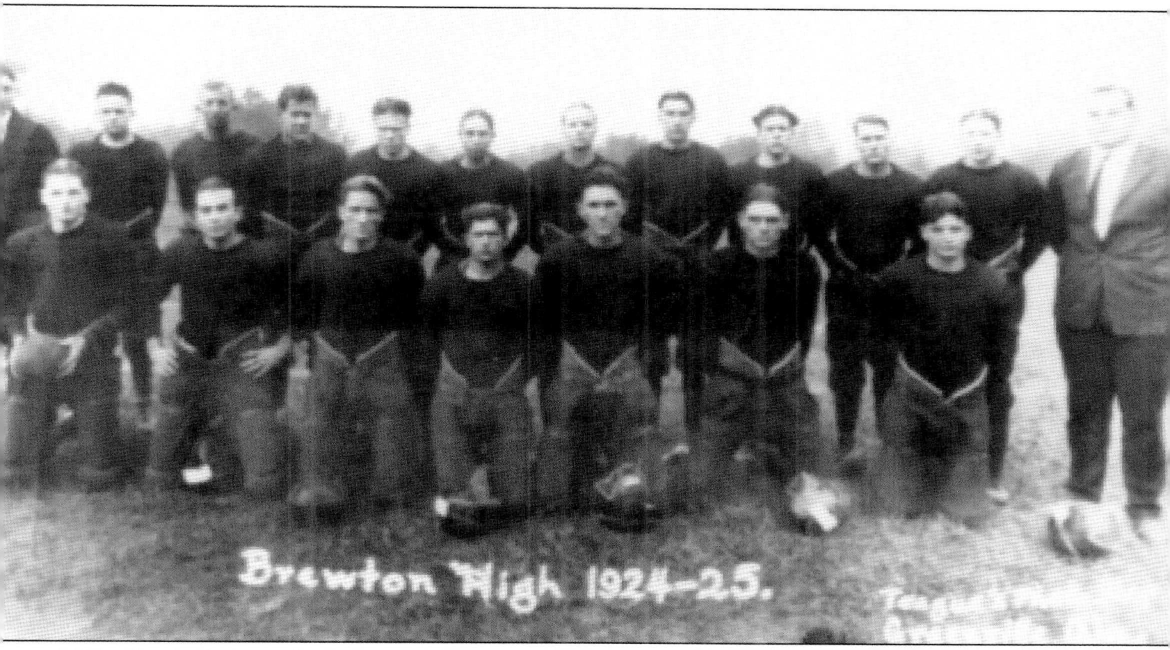

Miller Football players looked very different in 1924. One would think that there was no protection for the players at all. The uniforms do not have a lot of padding, and the helmets do not have the protection of today's football gear. Members of the team are, from left to right (first row) Durwood McPhall, Dick Jordan, Houston Odom, Tick Bedgood, Edwin Malone, Gus McPhall, and R.A. Srong; (second row) coach Chapman Curry, Curtis Finlay, Coleman Fuqua, Jim Lovelace, Ernest Hand, Boots Miller, Edgar "Red" Moore, Lawrence Holiday, Joe Cooper, J.C. "Country" Temple, Ned Grice, and coach Ike Rodgers. (Courtesy of James Wilson.)

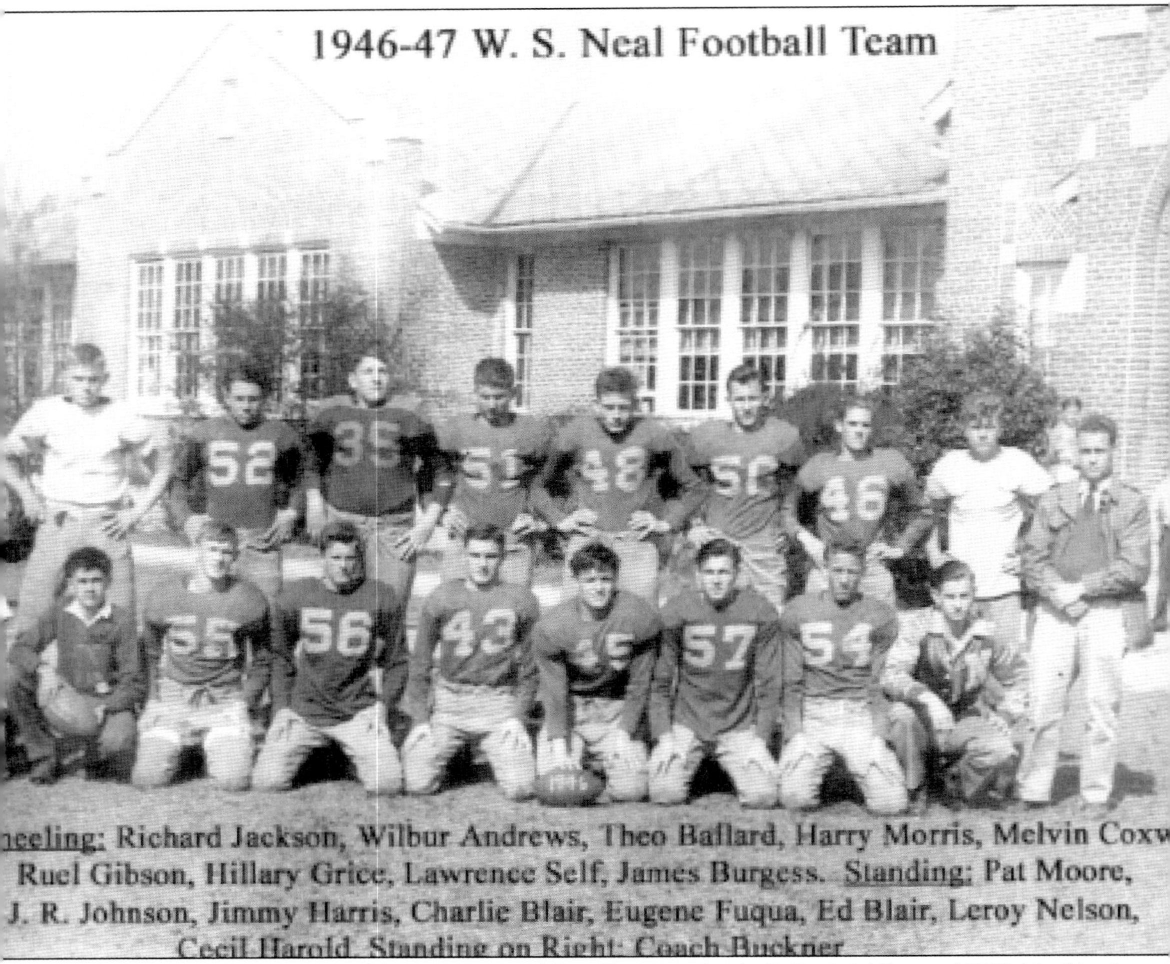

The year 1946 was pivotal for Brewton and East Brewton football. Both Miller and W.S. Neal had football teams, but they had never played each other. In 1946, Brewton was in need of hospital equipment. The Brewton Hospital was in Holley House on Douglas Avenue, and it was in dire need. Rotary club members came up with the idea of having the two football teams play against each other for charity. It called for some rearranging of the schedule, but after everything was worked out, the two teams gathered at Rotary Field, thus began one of the greatest rivalries in this area of south Alabama. This photograph is of the 1946–1947 W.S. Neal football team. They are, from left to right, (first row) Richard Jackson, Wilbur Andrews Theo Ballard, Harry Morris, Melvin Coxwell, Ruel Gibson, Hillary Grice, Lawrence Self, and James Burgess; (second row) Pat Moore, J.R. Johnson, Jimmy Harris, Charlie Blair, Eugene Fuqua, Ed Blair, Leroy Nelson, and Cecil Harold. Coach Buckner is standing at the right. (Courtesy of Charles Blair.)

1945 Football Team

Front Row , L to R: Bobby Long, Joe Petty Mason, Charles Jones, Frank Scott, Bill West, Floyd Jernigan, Stuart O'"Bannon, Ralph Smith, Pete Bryant, Ben Martin, Ray Langham.
Second Row: Claude Givan, Jack Long, Phillip Bradley, Robert Sellers, Charles Prestwood, Aaron Lazarus, Benny Stokes, Don Bryant, Roy Stokes, Ray Given.
Back Row:: Donald Ogletree, Mgr., W.T. Barron, Mgr., Scotty Byrne, Leon Martin, Frank Jones, Bernard Russell, Jack Martin, Theo Ballard, Earl Wilson, Arthur Jernigan, Chester Jernigan, Alfred Taylor, Coach Hal Wyatt.

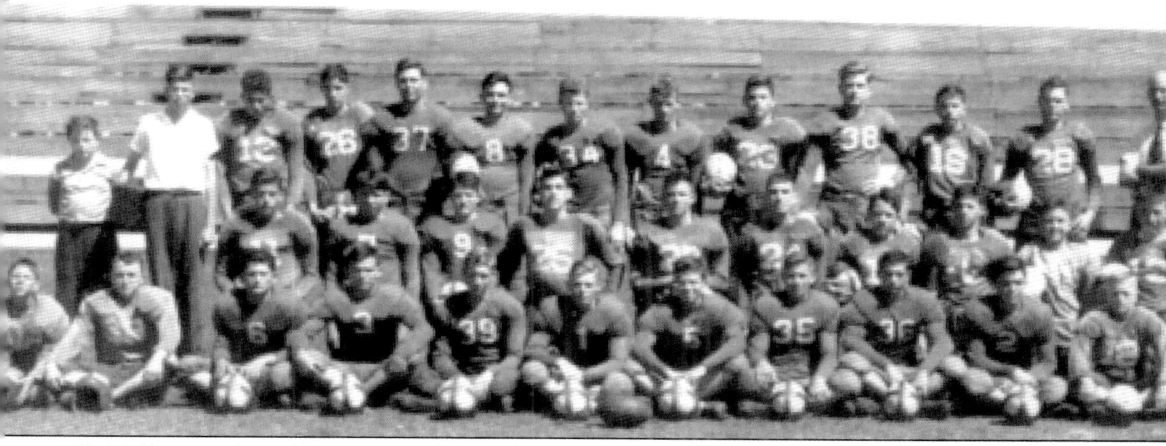

T.R. Miller was the other team to play in that notable football game that has gone down in the history of football in Brewton and East Brewton. Most of the players said they never thought of it in any way other than just another game. Sixty-four years later, in 2010, the first game has been almost lost in the excitement of today's game. Now, it is the game that players and residents look forward to. Most people would say that it is more important to win this game every year than any other game during the season. It brings to mind the rivalry between major football teams. Miller won that first game, and today, a trophy is awarded to the winning team to hold until next year. The players in this 1945 photograph are, from left to right (first row) Bobby Long, Joe Petty Mason, Charles Jones, Frank Scott, Bill West, Floyd Jernigan, Stuart O'Bannon, Ralph Smith, Pete Bryant, Ben Martin, and Ray Langham; (second row) Claude Givan, Jack Long, Phillip Bradley, Robert Sellers, Charles Prestwood, Aaron Lazarus, Benny Stokes, Don Bryant, Roy Stokes, and Ray Given; (third row) Donald Ogletree, manager W.T. Barron, manager Scotty Byrne, Leon Martin, Frank Jones, Bernard Russell, Jack Martin, Theo Ballard, Earl Wilson, Arthur Jernigan, Chester Jernigan, Alfred Taylor, and coach Hal Wyatt. (Courtesy of Ray Langham.)

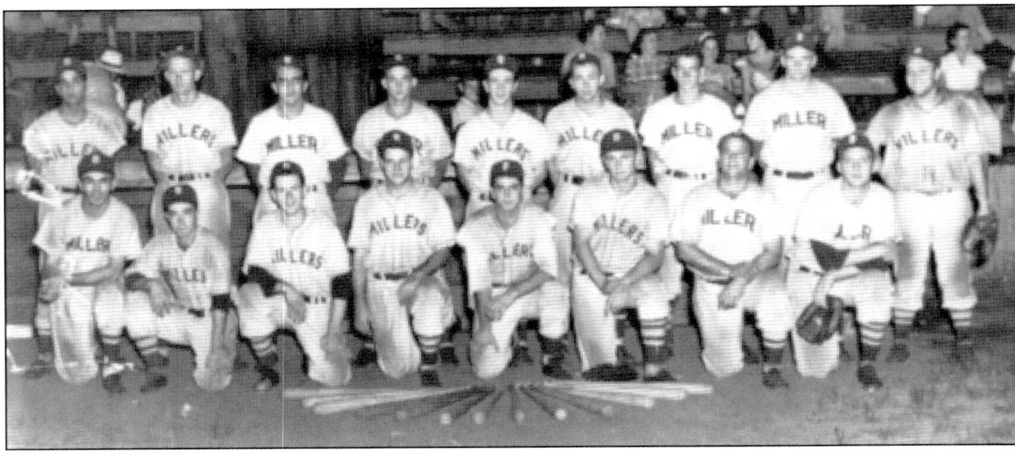

This is the 1950 Miller High School baseball team, the Brewton Millers. At the time of this photograph, the old Brewton High School on Belleville Avenue was still being used. The school had moved into the three-story school building in 1925.

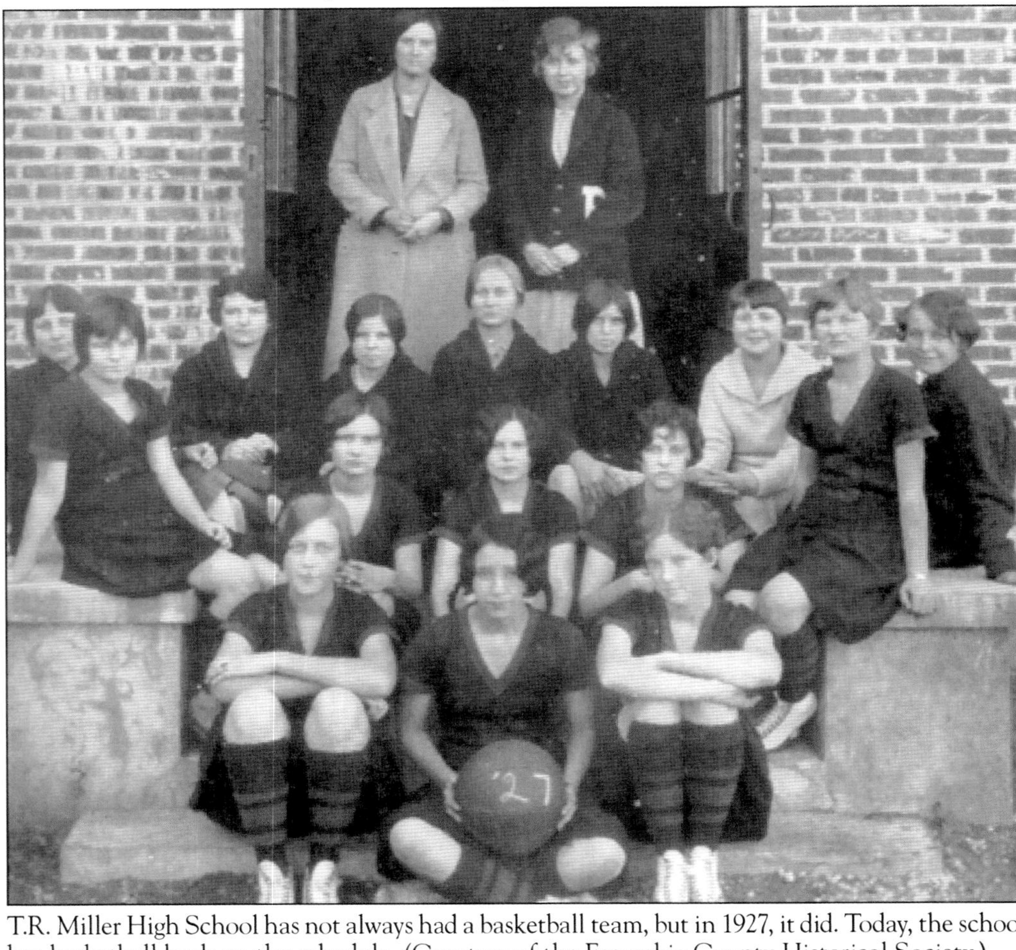

T.R. Miller High School has not always had a basketball team, but in 1927, it did. Today, the school has basketball back on the schedule. (Courtesy of the Escambia County Historical Society.)

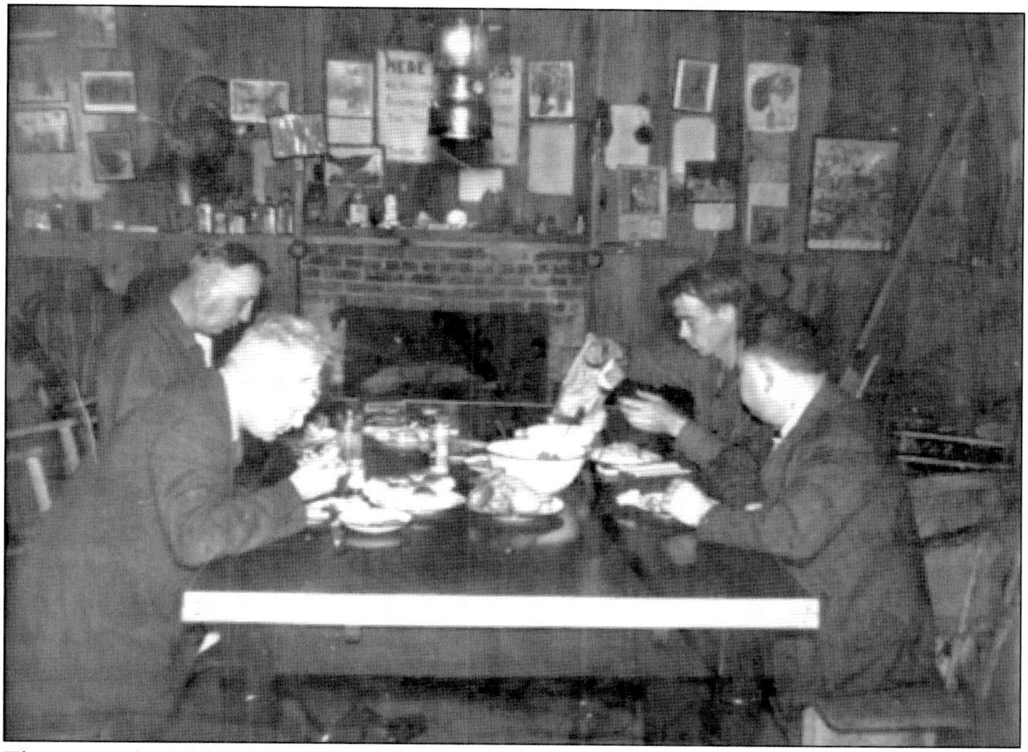

There is nothing like a good meal after a day of hunting. These men look as if they are enjoying their time together at a hunting lodge after a day in the woods.

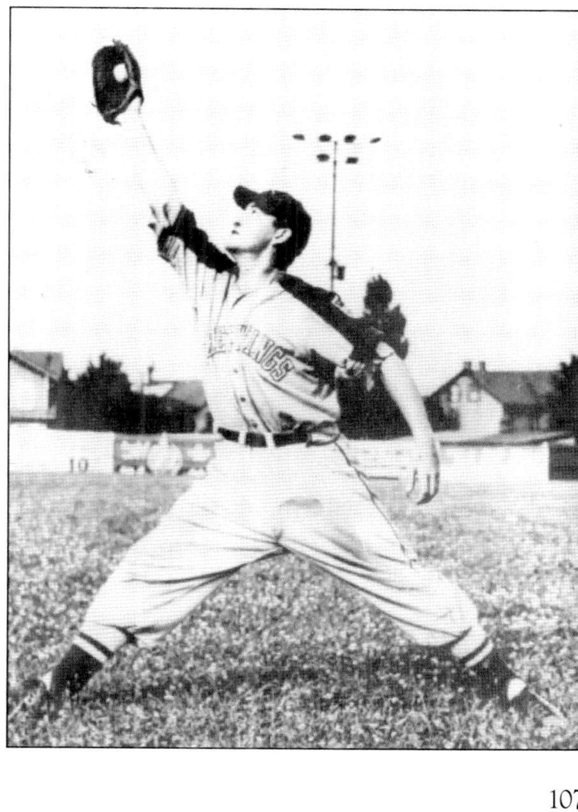

Tommy Liles was one of the boys who played baseball at Miller, and he carried his playing to new heights when he was signed by the St. Louis Cardinals. He played in the minor leagues but was injured before he could move up to the majors. (Courtesy of Tommy Liles.)

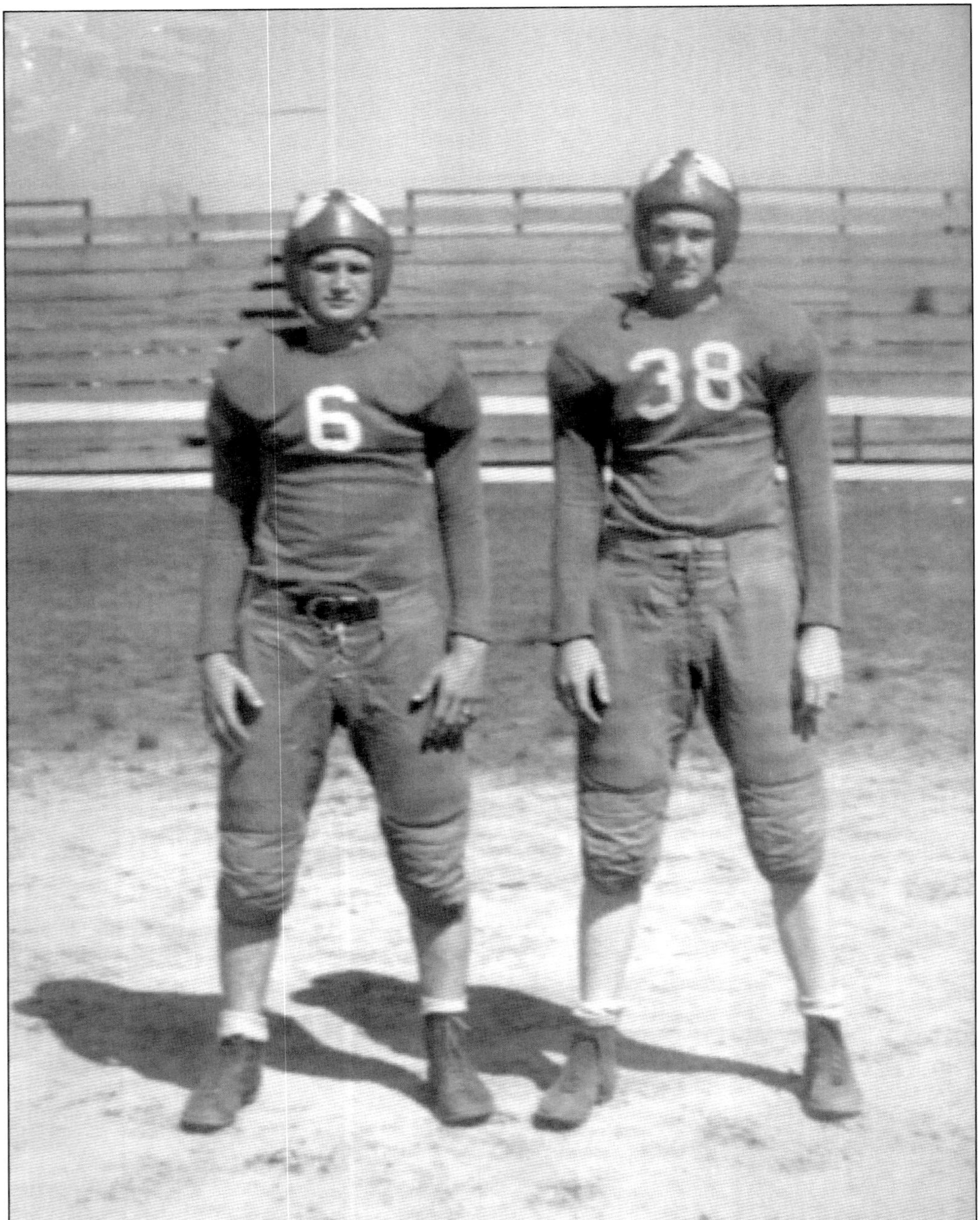

Charles Jones (left) and Arthur Jernigan were members of the T.R. Miller football team who met W.S. Neal on the field to raise money for the hospital. Some of the players from both schools left their education behind when they signed up to go to war during World War II. Most of them went back to the classroom and graduated after the war, which says a lot about the mentality of the young men.

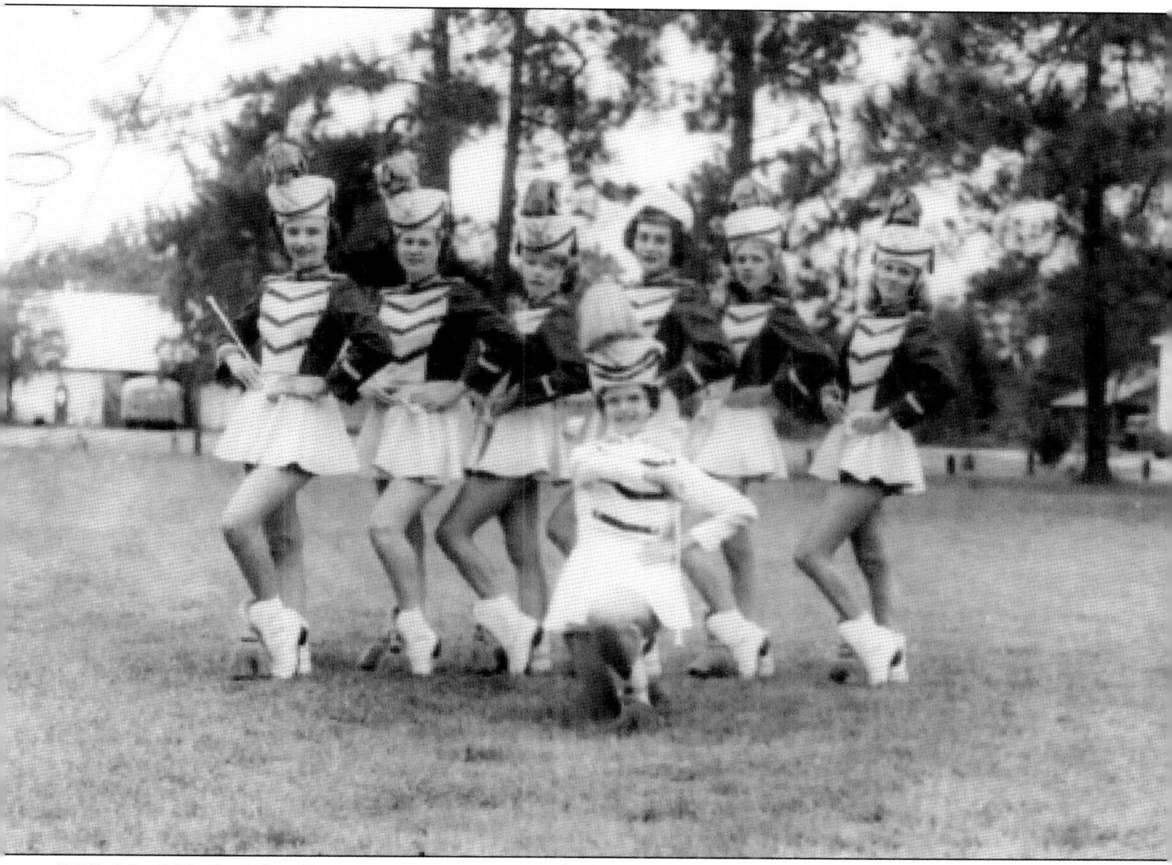

W.S. Neal High School majorettes are pictured about 1960. W.S. Neal, a part of the Escambia County School System, is situated in East Brewton. The girls are identified as Billie Jo Nolan (center) and, from left to right, are Juanita Beasley, Ann Mantel, Yvonne Lanier, Elana Sale, Mary Ann Johns, and Gilda Watson. (Courtesy of Robert Crenshaw.)

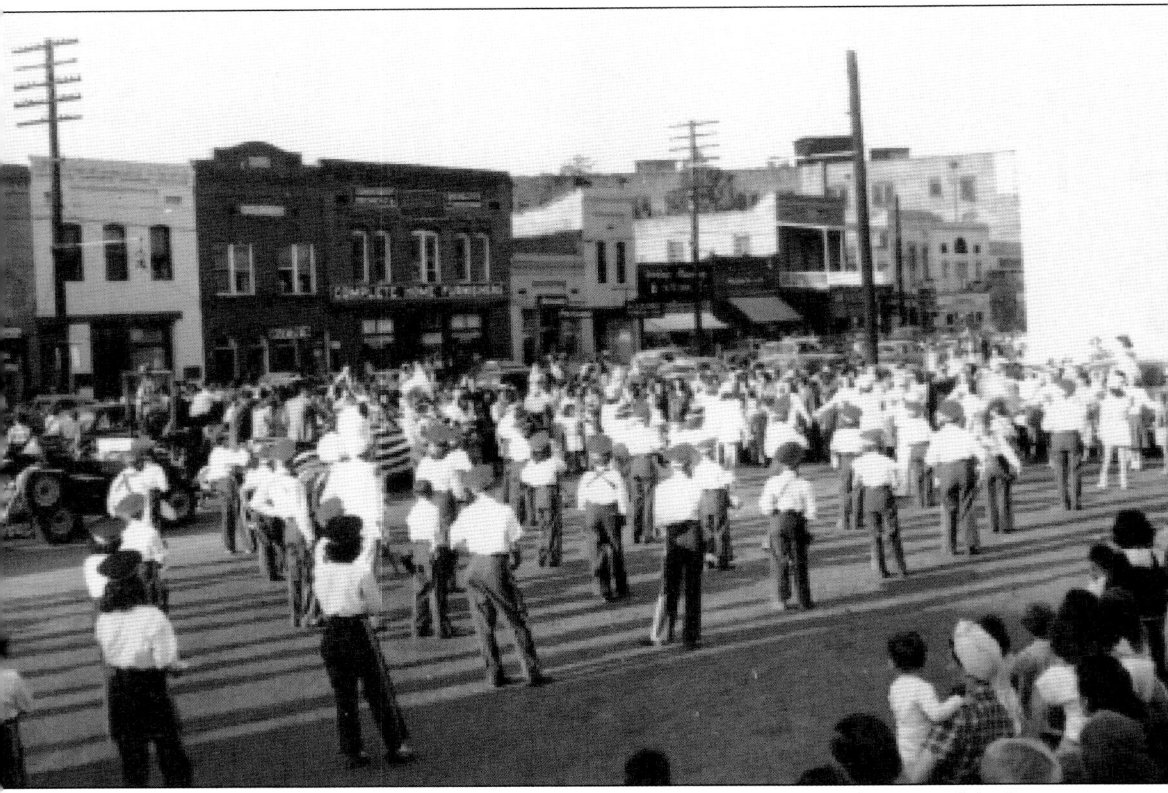

T.R. Miller is shown in the downtown area in 1948. In the background, some of the businesses along the west side of St. Joseph Avenue can be seen. Many of them look nearly the same today as they did then. Storefronts were changed sometimes, but the rooflines usually stayed the same. (Courtesy of Barbara Carden.)

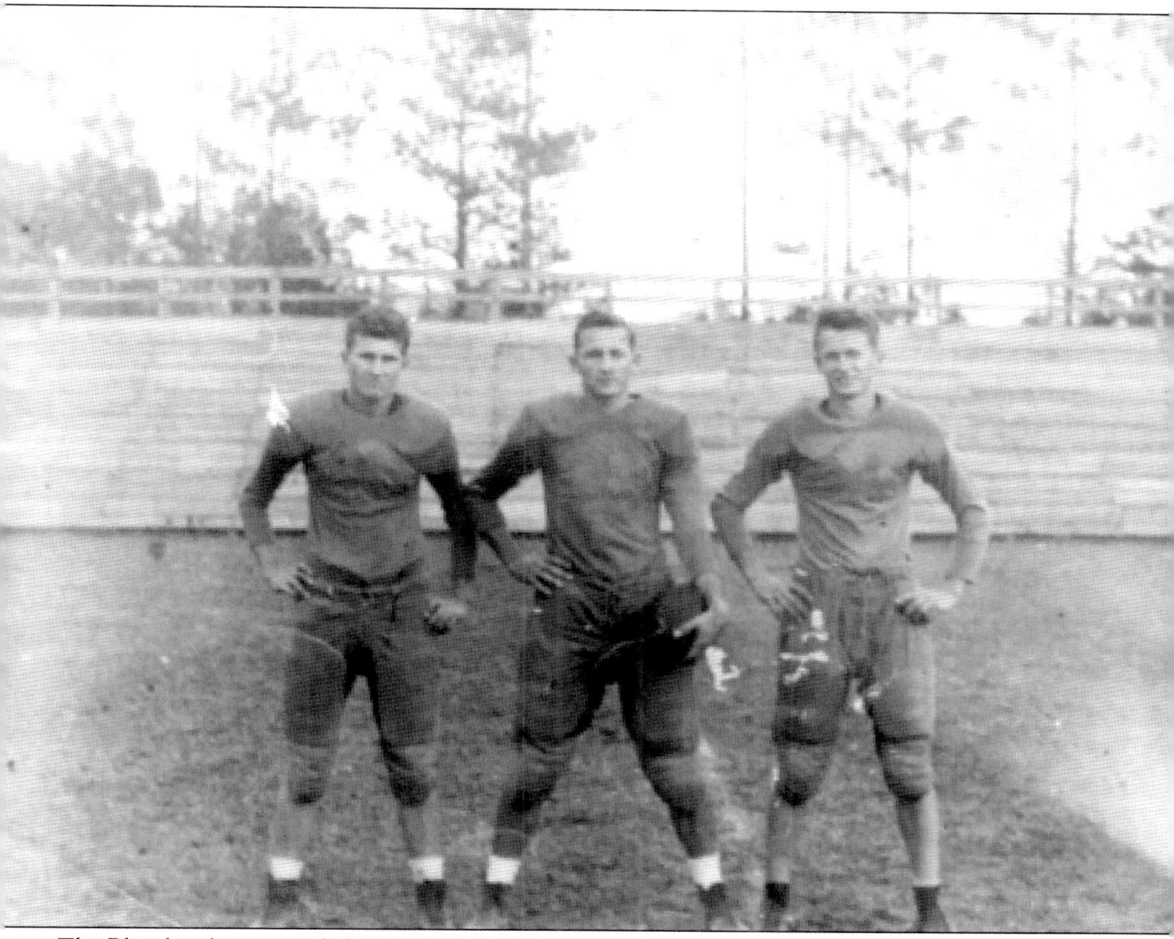

The Blair brothers attended W.S. Neal High School and were on the football team that met T.R. Miller High School in a charity game in 1946. Today the two schools would rather play and beat each other than any other team. The brothers shown, from left to right, are Ed Blair, Charles Blair, and Jack Blair. (Courtesy of Charles Blair.)

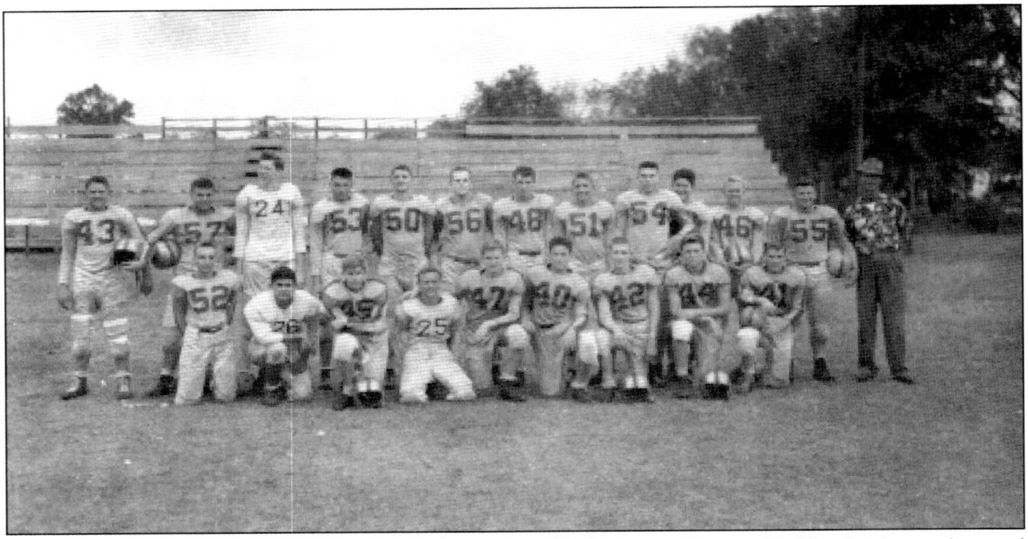

This is the T.R. Miller football team while it was still playing at Rotary Field, which was located where the present Brewton Elementary School is. (Courtesy of Charlie Blair)

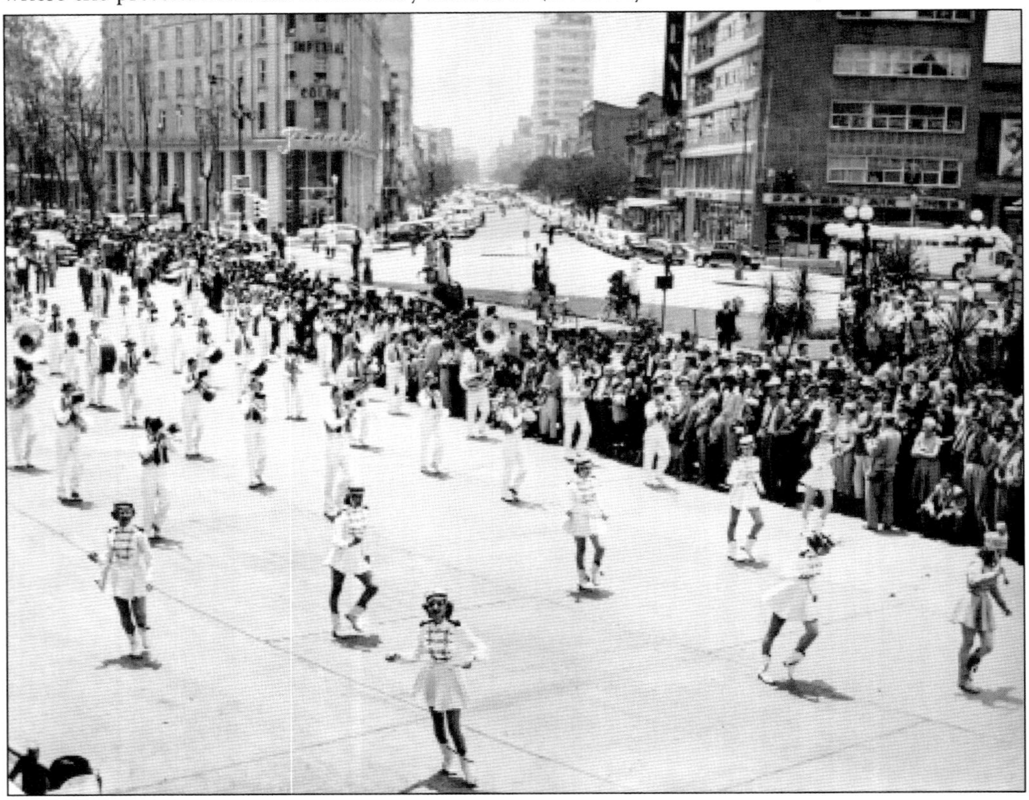

The T.R. Miller band has always been an award-winning band. It has been invited to march in many parades in many cities, both in the United States and south of the border. This is the band performing in Mexico City in 1952. With cuts in the education system of today, trips like this do not happen like they once did. (Courtesy of Barbara Carden.)

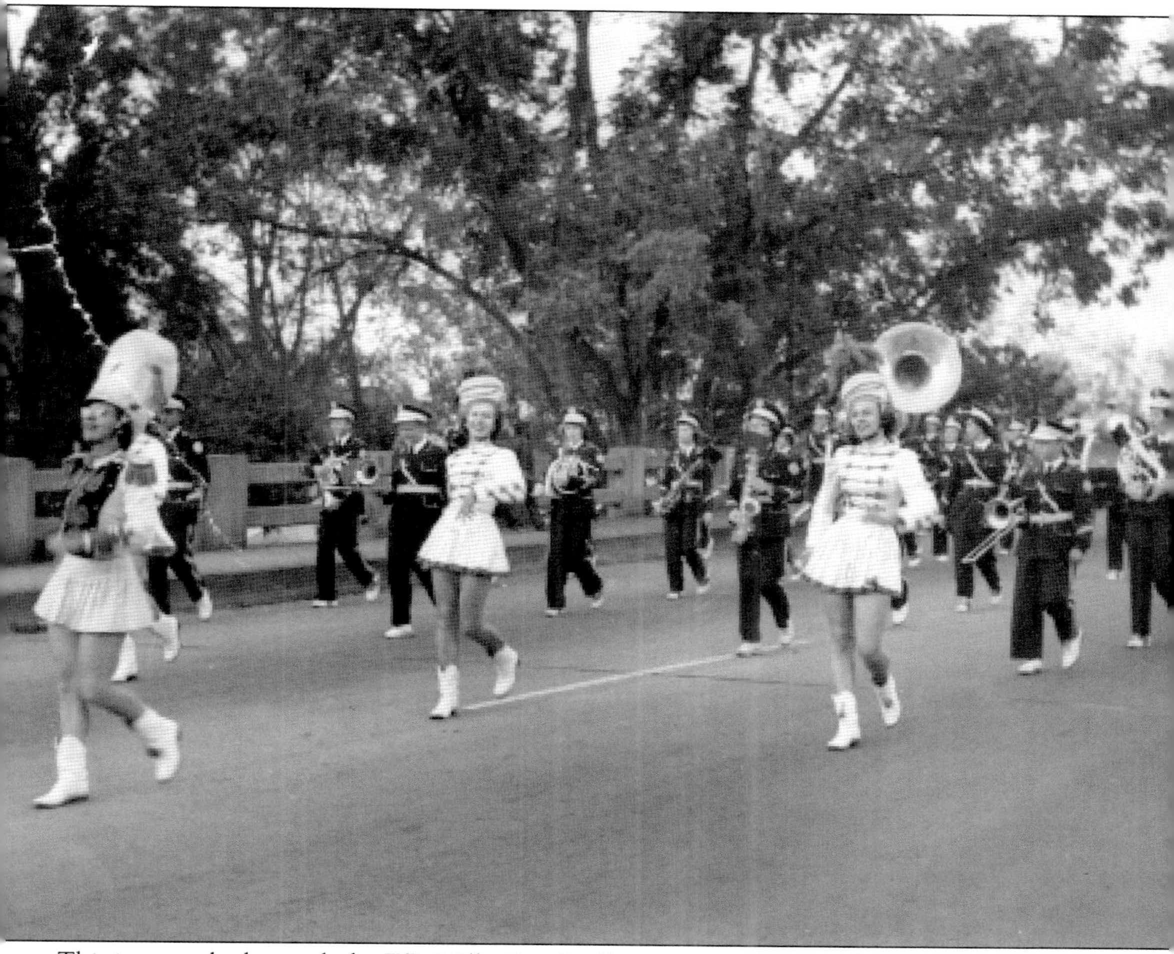

This is a parade that took the T.R. Miller Band to Evergreen in 1952. Leading the majorettes is Barbara Strain Carden. Other majorettes were Sara Byrd and Martha Ann Rogers. (Courtesy of Barbara Carden).

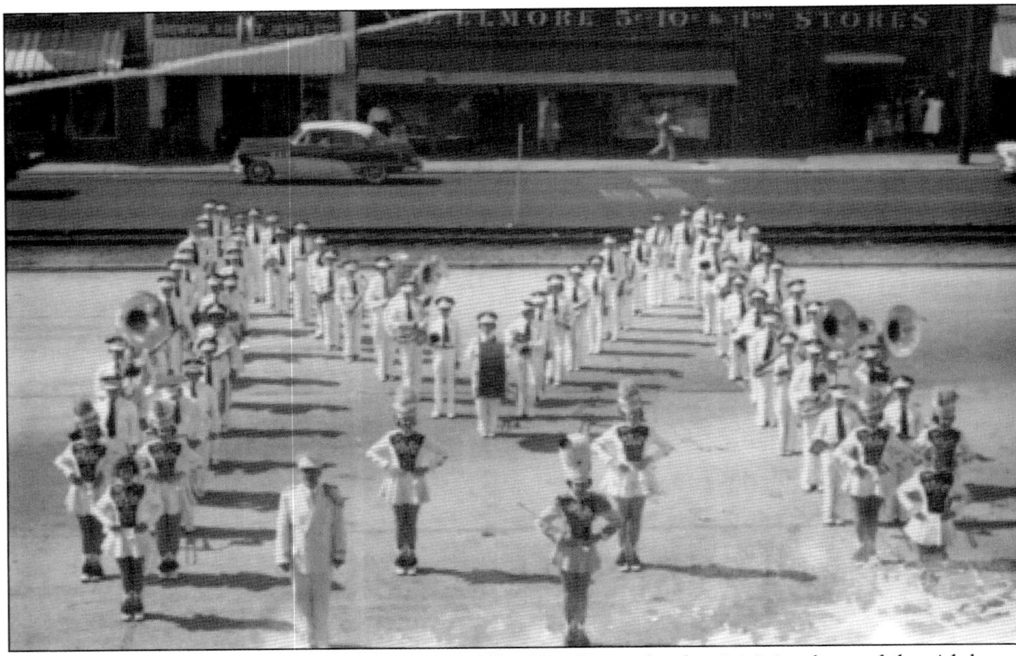

One of the popular formations of the T.R. Miller Band was this big M. Members of the Alabama National Guard said they remember this formation being used in 1951 when the band came to see them off on the train during the Korean War. (Courtesy of Barbara Carden.)

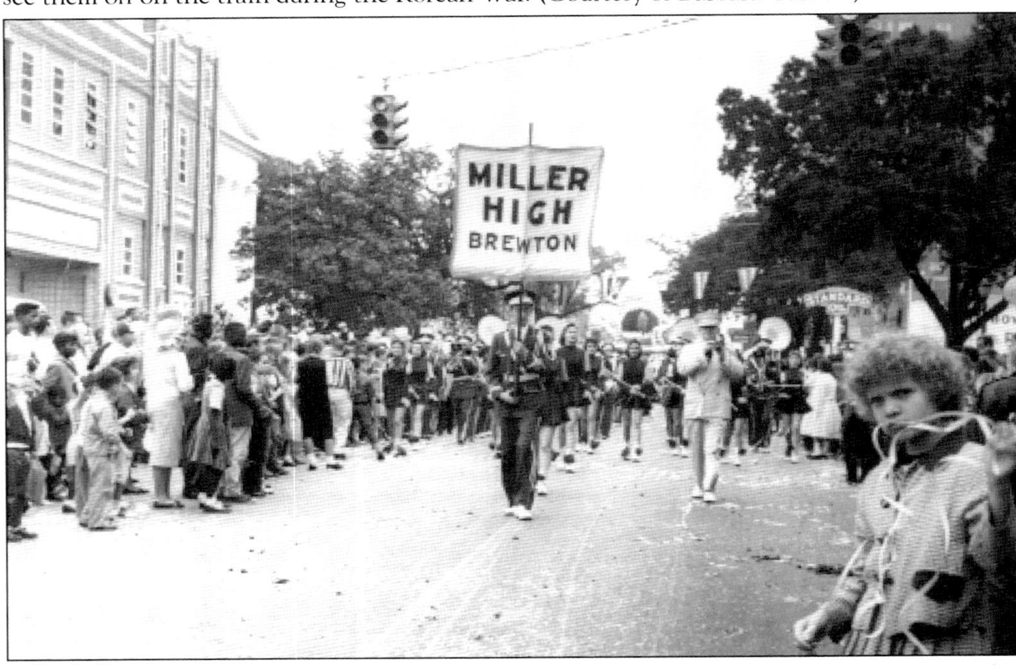

The T.R. Miller band participates in what is believed to be a Mardi Gras parade. This is another one of the trips to show their talent as a band. They have always been popular at band contests around the state, and many students can say they were chosen to attend special programs. Several students have gone on to play in college bands. (Courtesy of Robert Crenshaw.)

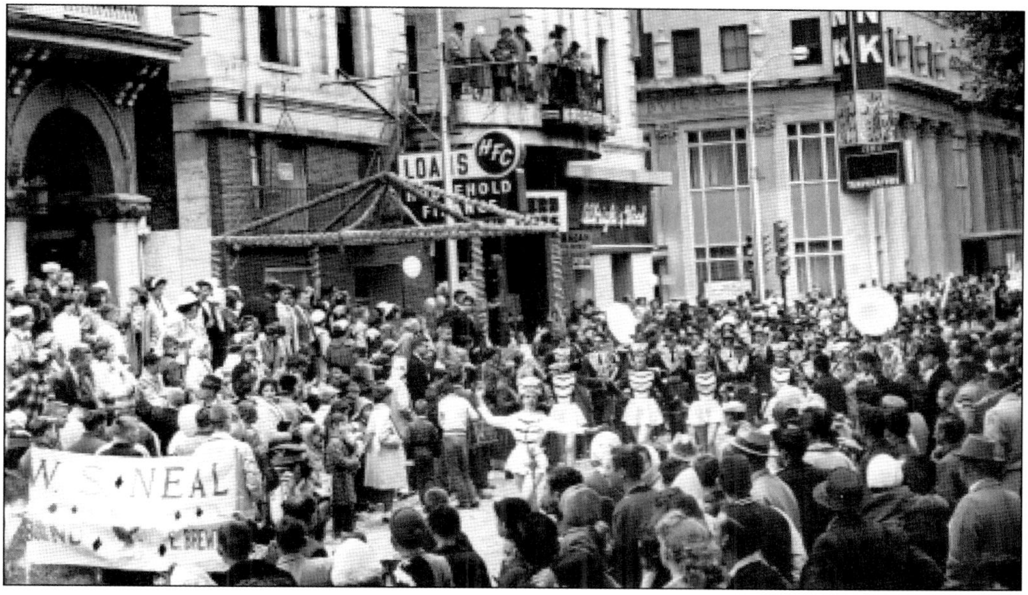

W.S. Neal High School has always fielded a good band. In fact, it has been invited to attend many parades and contests over the years. This is believed to be a parade during Mardi Gras. (Courtesy of Robert Crenshaw.)

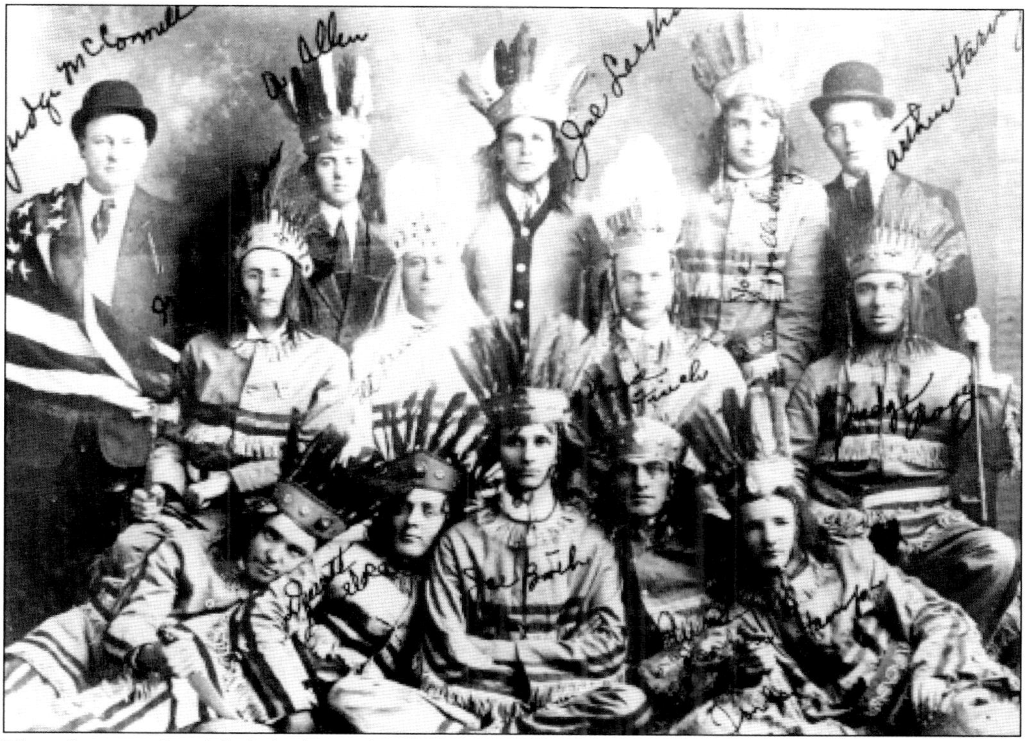
This photograph is labeled "the Red Men." It must have been some type of club. The members were popular young men in 1907. It must have taken a lot of nerve to wear these costumes. Evidently, it was a club of some distinction. (Courtesy of Barbara Carden.)

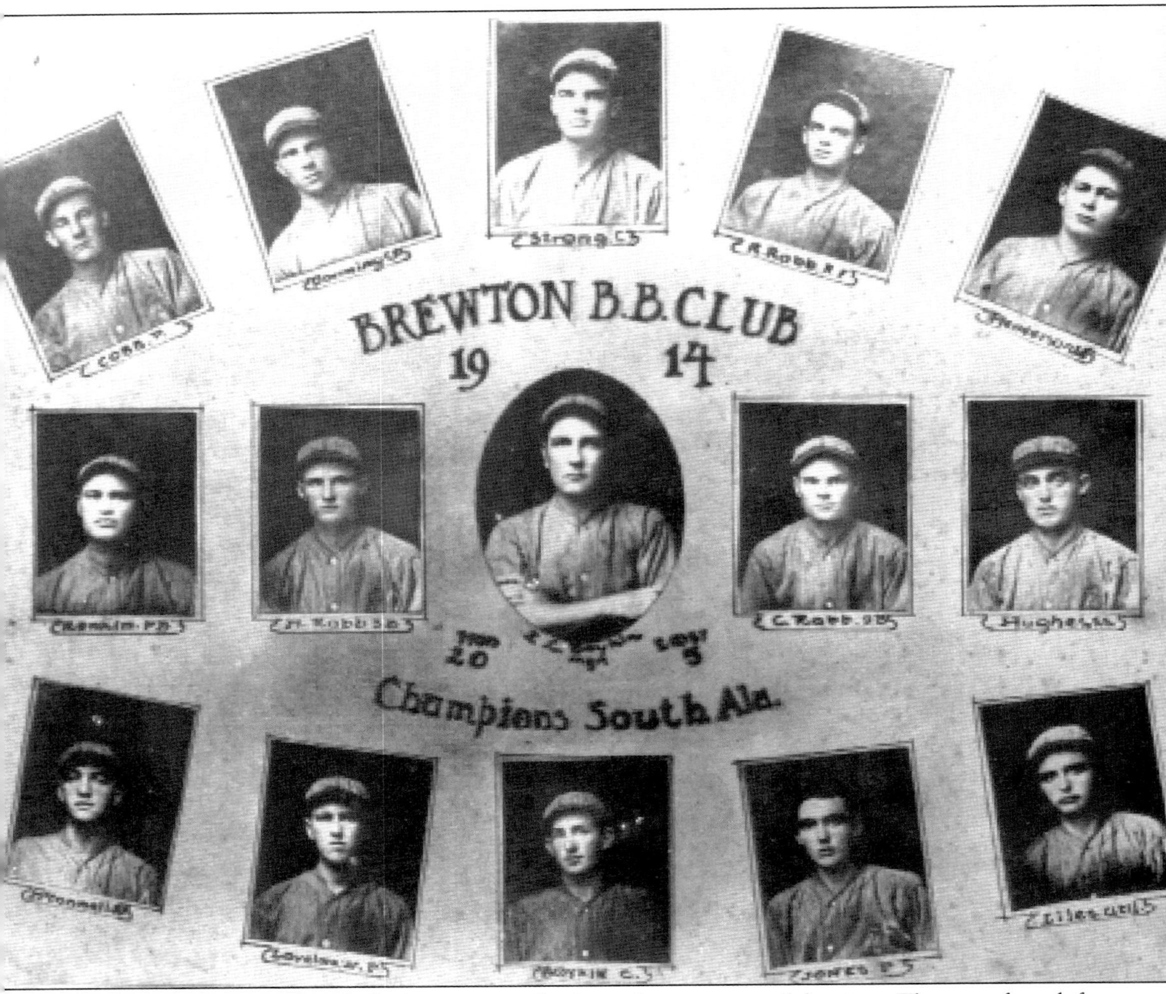

The 1914 Brewton baseball players were all talented young men of the time. They are, from left to right, (first row) Rankin; H. Rabb, third base; Boykin; C. Rabb, second base; Hughes, short stop; Lovelace; Boykin; Jones; and Liles; (second row) Cobb, pitcher; Downing, second base; Strong, catcher; R. Rabb, right field; and Henderson. (Courtesy of Tommy Liles.)

Ten

People of Brewton and East Brewton

Early settlers to the Brewton–East Brewton area were hard working and brave to enter into a world that was not only unknown but dangerous as well. Fort Crawford was erected on the bluff in East Brewton overlooking Murder Creek to protect settlers and soldiers from the Indians who still roamed the area. The ones that made it in the new country were only the strongest and bravest. They saw many hardships come their way. There were floods from two creeks nearby, (Murder Creek and Burnt Corn Creek); the Civil War touched so many, either in the war or during Reconstruction; and several major hurricanes did extensive damage on different occasions.

Those whose names are familiar from Brewton and East Brewton include Katherine Crosby, Miss Alabama; country music star Hank Locklin; and William Lee Golden, who sings with the Oak Ridge Boys. Others who have lived in the area may not be so familiar, but they, in their own ways, have made this area stay alive and well since Fort Crawford was built in East Brewton.

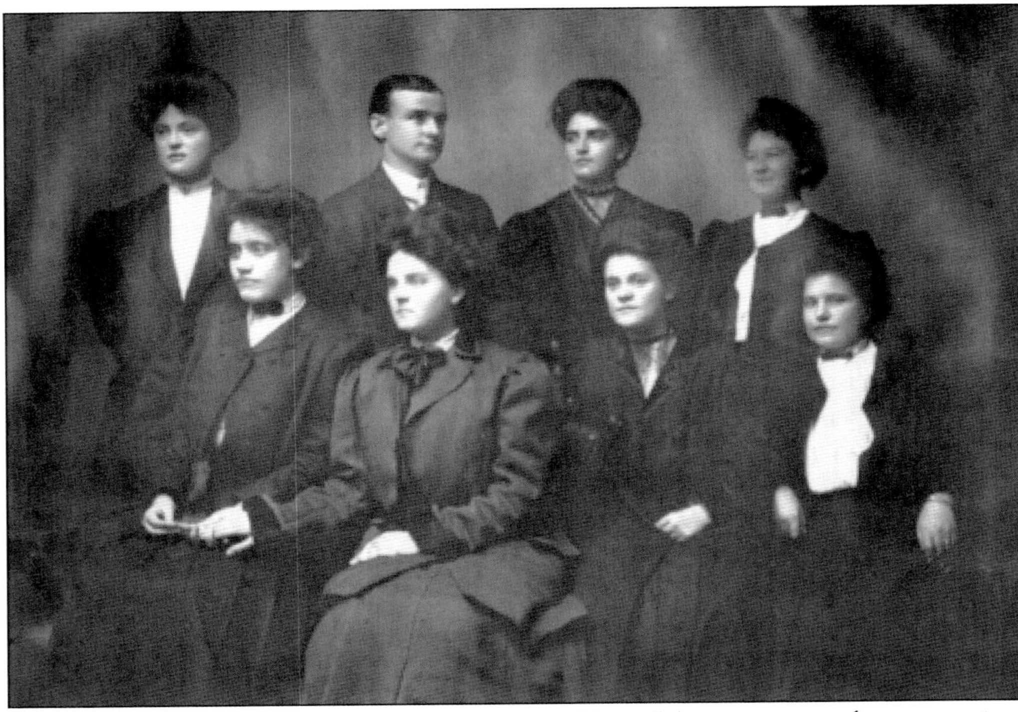

Most of these young people were cousins. They are, from left to right, (first row) Mary (Mamie) McLellan, Sarah (Sallie) Davison, Mary Douglas Lovett, and Sally McLellan Lyon; (second row) Lily Bell Rankin Sawyer, Erasmus Manford Blacksher, Ella Mae Penn Downing Foshee, and Sadie Padgett Liles. Mamie and Sally McLellan were twins. Mary Douglas and Manford Blacksher were first cousins of each other and the McLellan sisters. Erasmus Manford Blacksher was born in 1878, the son of James Uriah Blacksher; Mary Douglas was born in 1886, the daughter of Martha Emeline Blacksher; and Sally and Mamie McLellan were born in 1890, the daughters of Palestine Melinda Blacksher.

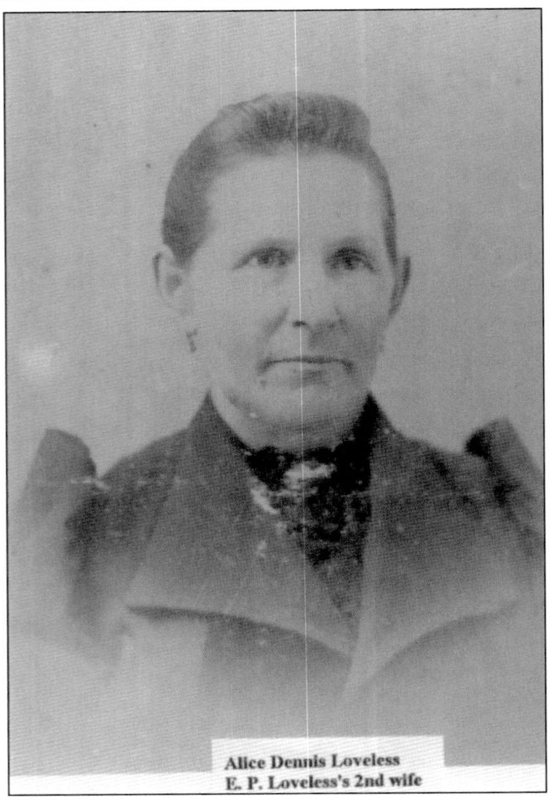

Alice Dennis Lovelace was the second wife of Edwin Marshall Lovelace. He served as president of the Lovelace Lumber Mill that was located between St. Nicholas Avenue and the banks of Burnt Corn Creek. (Courtesy of Yancey Lovelace.)

Edward Sylvester McMillan was the father of Ed Leigh McMillan I. He was the Escambia County sheriff during the early 1890s. At the time, there was a notorious railroad bandit on the loose in this area. Over several years, Sheriff McMillan and his posse chased Railroad Bill all over south Alabama, but he was always one step ahead of them. Things came to a head on July 3, 1895, when the sheriff and his posse slipped up to a cabin where they believed Railroad Bill was hiding. Someone got off a few shots, but one shot coming from the vicinity of the bandit struck the sheriff to the ground. Railroad Bill then escaped while the sheriff's men were busy trying to save the dying man. They were unsuccessful, and word went to Brewton and his wife telling of the terrible news. The next day was the Fourth of July, and a big celebration had been planned for Brewton, but with the news, the whole town went into mourning, and the celebration was forgotten. (Courtesy of the Escambia County Historical Society.)

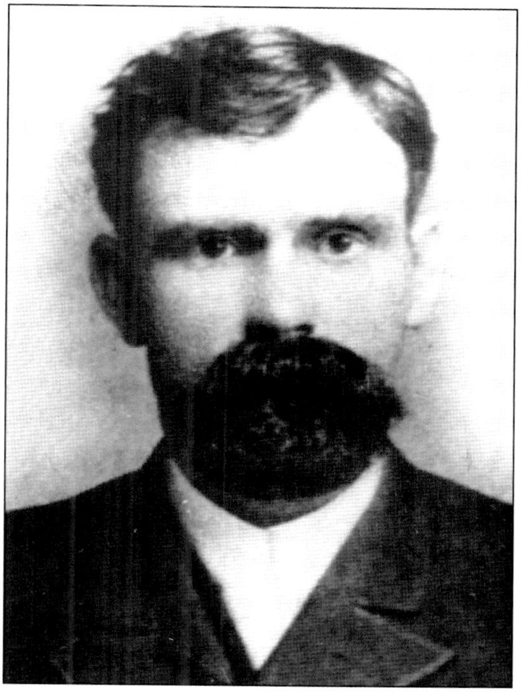

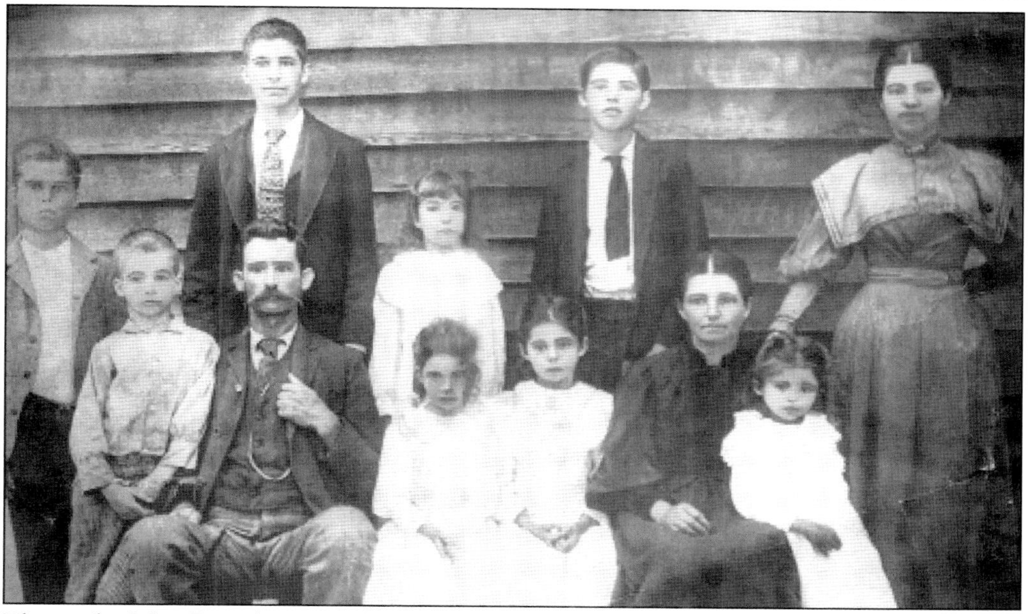

This is the John Daniel Weaver family taken about 1897. There were several Weaver families in the Brewton–East Brewton area. Pictured are, front row, left to right, Allen Thomas Weaver (1888–1979), John Daniel Weaver (1851–1943), Jessie Aline Weaver (1890–1085), Ellen Winifred Weaver (1886–1982), Nancy Ellen Holland Weaver (1853–1930), and Mary Pauline Weaver (1892–1979); back row, from left, William Atticus Weaver (1882–1903), John Boland Weaver (1879–1945), Amy Corinne Weaver (1885–1926), Martin Luther Weaver (1880–1956), and Elizabeth Matilda Weaver (1877–1957). (Courtesy of W.T. Baggett.)

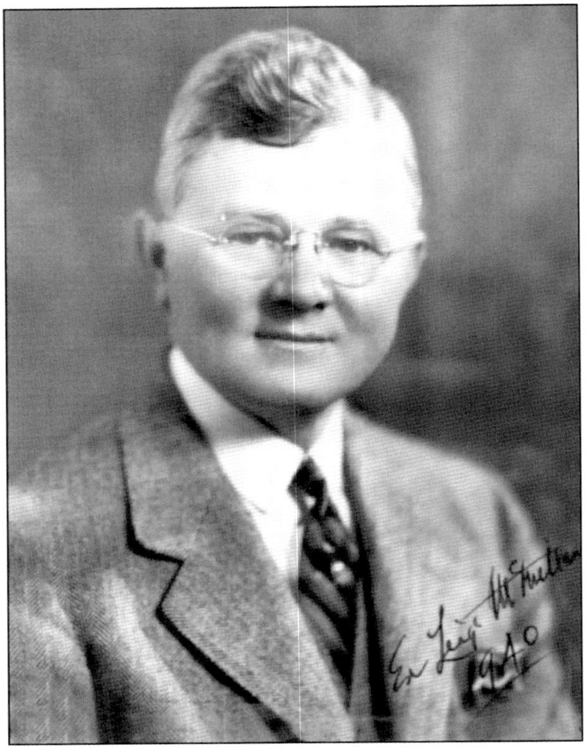

Ed Leigh McMillan I and his wife, Iva Lee Miller McMillan, were both very interested in their family genealogy and the times in which they lived, drawing from their past and present and planning for the future. They had many notebooks, scrapbooks, photographs, and notes, including correspondence from many other people. Much has been preserved in their files at McMillan Trust on Belleville Avenue. (Courtesy of McMillan Trust.)

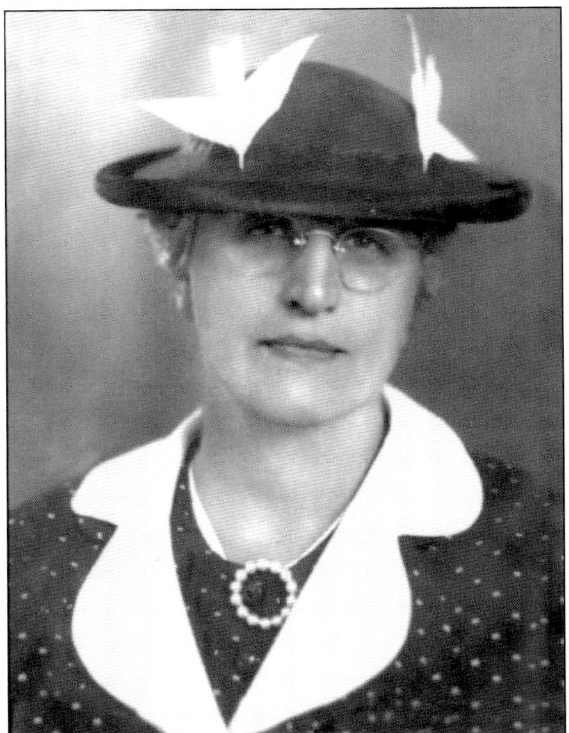

Iva Lee Miller McMillan joined her husband, Ed Leigh McMillan I, to collect and store materials throughout their lives. They had an employee whose job was to take care of and catalog the collection. This collection is one of the best-kept secrets in Brewton. It is not open to the public, but the trust is always willing to make exceptions. (Courtesy of McMillan Trust.)

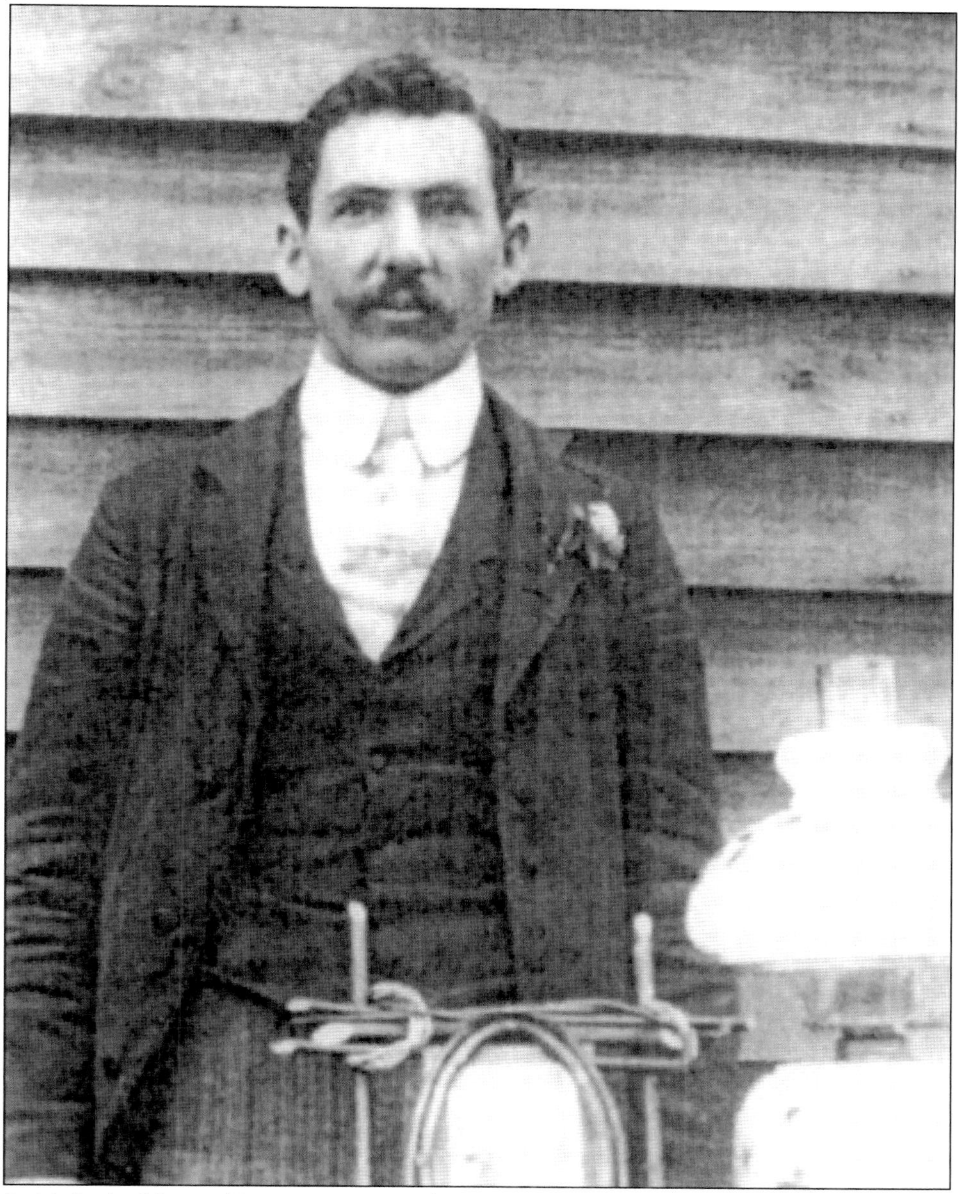

Frederick Leslie Hancock's story was not a happy one. He was upset with a young man named Troutman because of the attention Troutman was giving to Hancock's sister-in-law. He invited Troutman to a discussion of the situation, and when Troutman arrived, he came alone. That was a bad mistake. Hancock shot Troutman to death and was arrested and incarcerated in the jail in Brewton. Hancock never believed that he would be found guilty and did not seem to worry too much about his trial. He and many of his relatives believed he was just defending the reputation of the young lady and that the jury would never punish him for it. But to his surprise, he was found guilty. He later escaped and disappeared, but the authorities watched his wife. Sure enough, she led them to where Hancock was hiding out in another state. Hancock was brought back to Escambia County, but before his fate could be decided, he took matters into his own hands and committed suicide. (Courtesy of W.T. Baggett.)

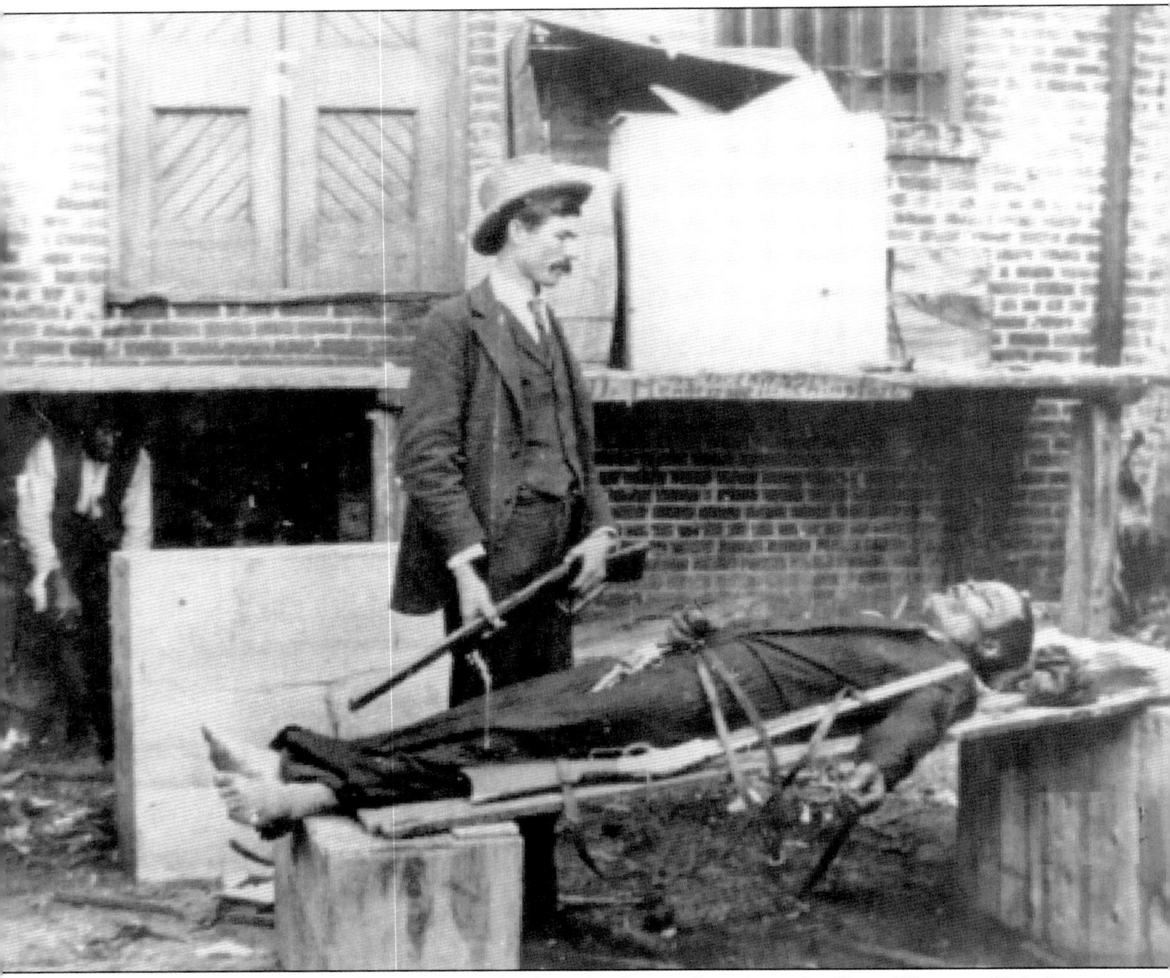

The body of Railroad Bill was put on display after being shot down by Sheriff Leonard McGowin. People paid to see him. The newspapers at the time said the money would be sent to McMillan's family. The family stoutly denies that they took any money that was raised for that purpose. The life and times of Railroad Bill had come to an end, but he is still remembered in this part of Alabama.

These young ladies strike a pose. They are, from left to right, Voncile Strong, Rosa Douglas, and Nava Lou Martin. Their style of dress looks as if the photograph was made in the 1920s or 1930s.

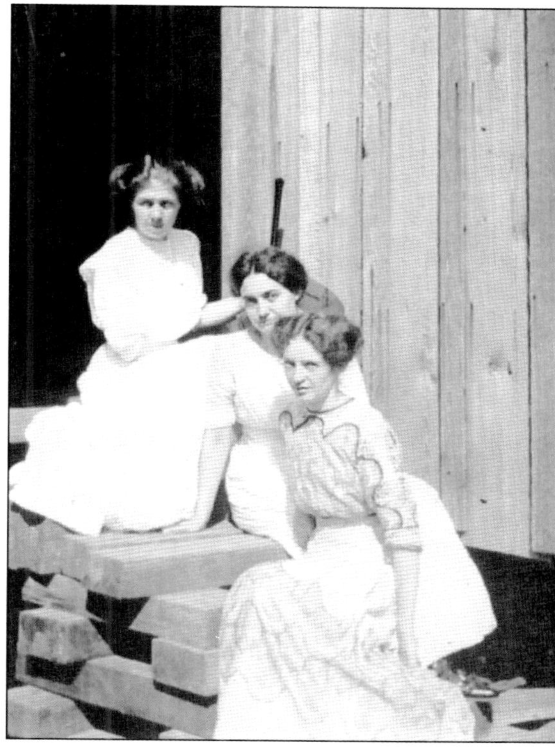

The Baggett family members are Cater Lee Baggett (sitting in front) and, from left to right, (first row) Alonzo Baggett, Ruth Baggett, Minnie Lee Baggett, and Lonnie Baggett; (second row) Bertha Baggett, Linnie Horton (sister to Minnie Lee), and Esther Baggett. Ruby Jean Long Wheeler is a descendant of this family. (Courtesy of Ruby Jean Long Wheeler.)

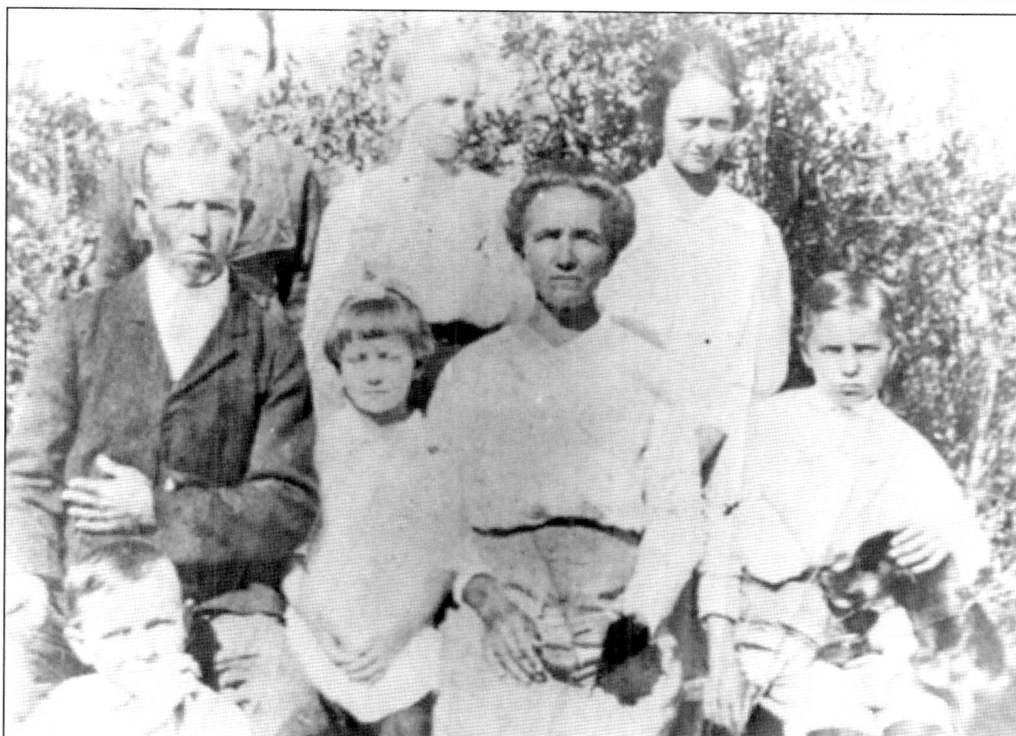

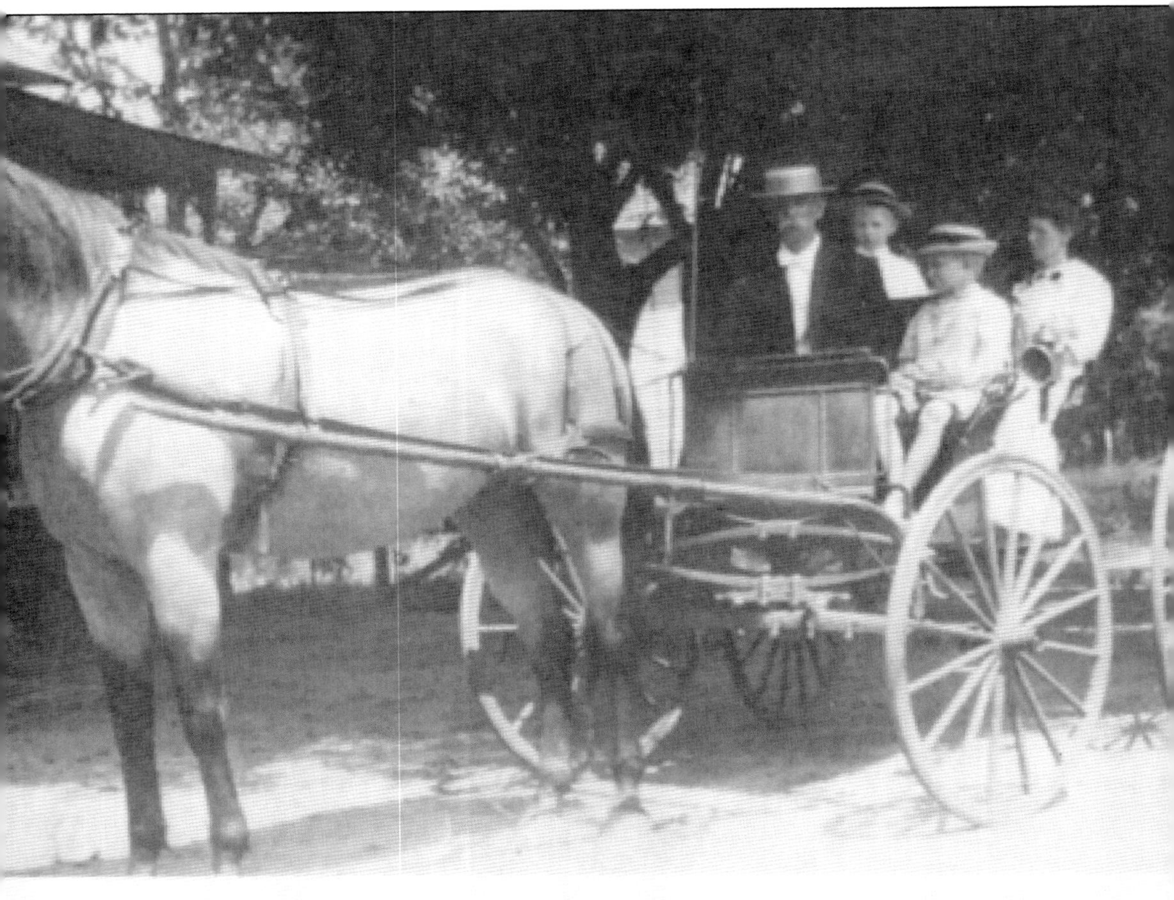

The W.Y. Jernigan Family out for a Sunday ride.

William Yancey Jernigan and his family are pictured on an outing. His family was in the grocery business, operating a successful store on the corner of Deer Street and the east side of St. Joseph Avenue (or St. Irenette, as it was originally named). There is a bicycle in the Thomas E. McMillan Museum that was used to deliver groceries from this store.

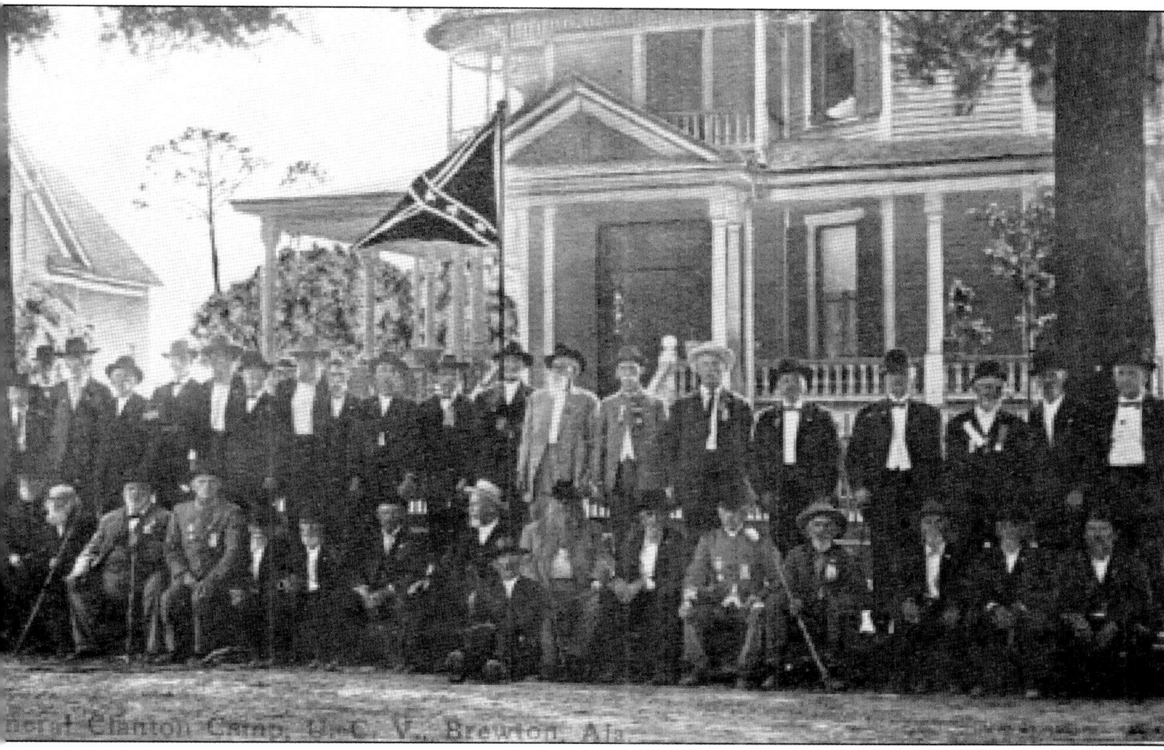

The members of General Clanton Camp near Pollard meet for a reunion in 1910. The Confederate camp was on a site where the soldiers were to protect south Alabama from the Union soldiers in Pensacola. At that time, Pollard was a major railroad junction, and as bad as the North wanted to do away with the railroad, the South wanted to protect it. (Courtesy of Yancey Lovelace.)

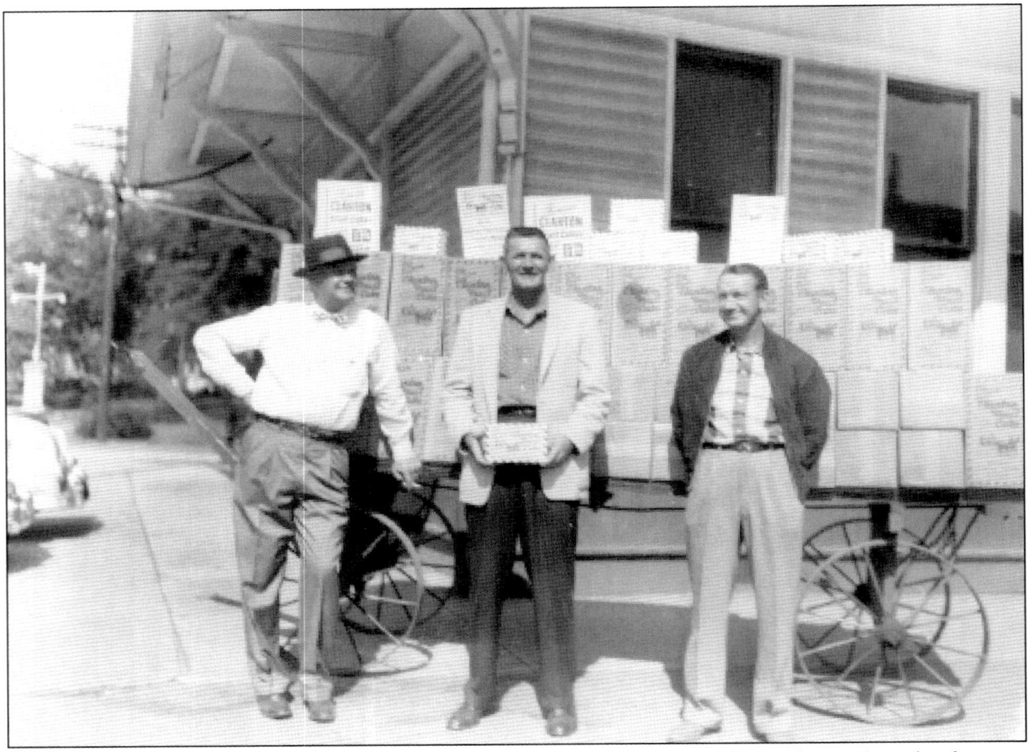

Brewton no longer has a depot, but the first one sat between the Robbins McGowin building and the railroad track. The depot was later moved to the corner of Deer Street and the east side of St. Joseph Avenue (formerly St. Irenette). Many items were shipped into and out of Brewton. Lumber went out and merchandise came to Brewton. In this photograph, Claxton Cakes come in for a fundraiser. The men, from left to right, are Slim Horton, Steve Dunaway, and A.R. Glass. (Courtesy of Robert Crenshaw.)

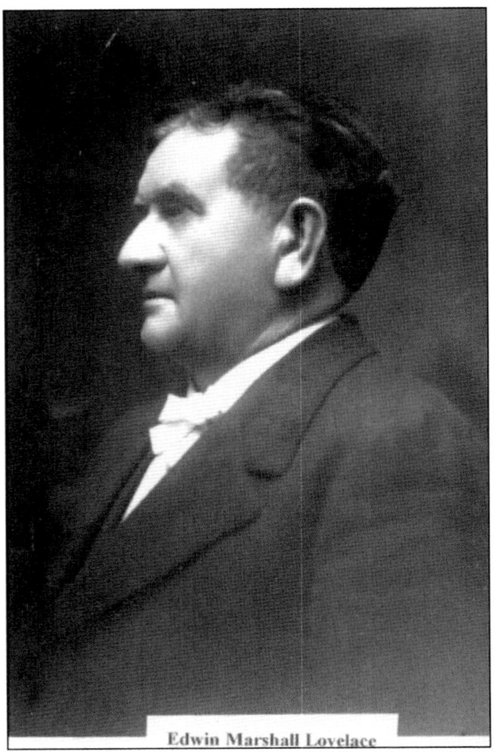

Edwin Marshall Lovelace was the president of Lovelace Lumber Company. He and his family have been a part of the community for a long time. (Courtesy of Yancey Lovelace.)

Leonard McGowin took over as sheriff after the death of Sheriff McMillan. It was McGowin who finally shot Railroad Bill, bringing an end to the terrors of the bandit.

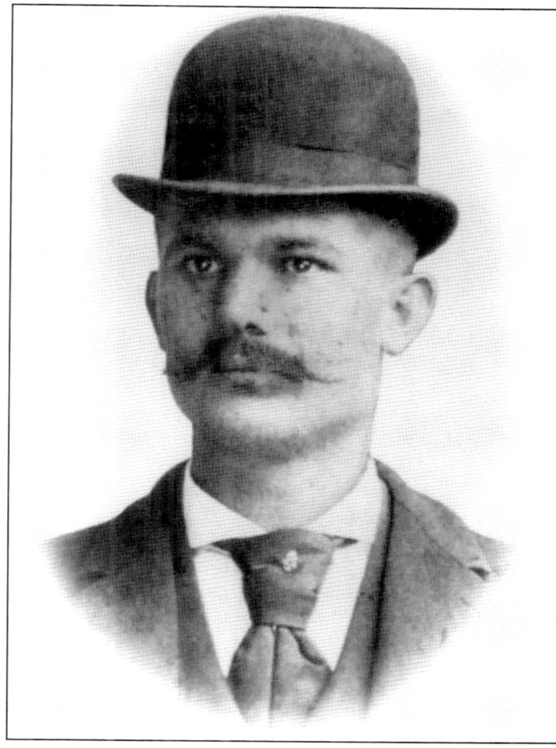

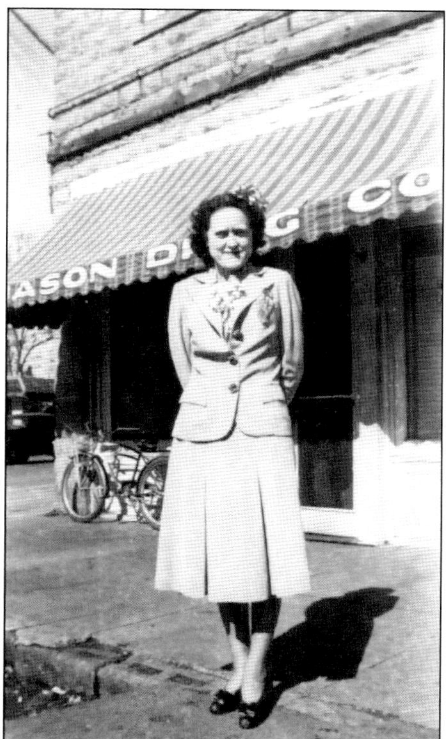

This is a photograph of Ima Lee Smith in front of Mason Drug Store. Her daughter Cathy McCurdy shared this photograph for this book. (Courtesy of Cathy McCurdy.)